THE REAL

DEATH IN
PARADISE

THE REAL DEATH IN PARADISE

Mystery, Murder and Mayhem –
A true story of a British detective
fighting crime in the Caribbean

By
Richard Preston

First published in the UK in 2025 by John Blake Publishing
An imprint of Bonnier Books UK
5th Floor, HYLO, 103–105 Bunhill Row,
London, EC1Y 8LZ

Owned by Bonnier Books
Sveavägen 56, Stockholm, Sweden

www.facebook.com/johnblakebooks
twitter.com/jblakebooks

First published in paperback in 2024

Paperback ISBN: 978 1 7894 6853 3
Ebook ISBN: 978 1 7894 6854 0
Audio ISBN: 978 1 7894 6875 5

British Library Cataloguing-in-Publication Data:

A catalogue record for this book is available from the British Library.

Design by www.envydesign.co.uk

Printed and bound in Great Britain by Clays Ltd, Elcograf S.p.A.

1 3 5 7 9 10 8 6 4 2

www.bonnierbooks.co.uk

CONTENTS

PART III: BUCCANEERS AND PIRATES

PART IV: MURDER AND ESCAPE

PART V: SAILING CLOSE TO THE WIND

Applications are invited from experienced UK police constables for a two-year secondment in the Royal Cayman Islands Police. Applicants must be male, under 30, single and physically fit to be considered for the 12 vacancies that will consist primarily of uniformed patrol duties. The salary will be paid tax free and includes an accommodation allowance.

GRAND CAYMAN

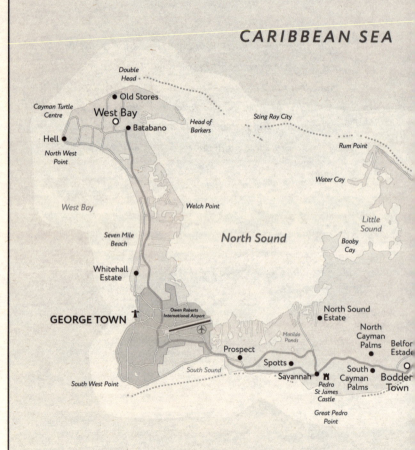

CARIBBEAN SEA

Double Head

● Old Stores

Cayman Turtle Centre

West Bay
○
● Batabano

Head of Barkers

Sting Ray City

Rum Point

Hell ●

North West Point

Water Cay

West Bay

Welch Point

North Sound

Little Sound

Booby Cay

Seven Mile Beach

Whitehall Estate ●

GEORGE TOWN ✝

Owen Roberts International Airport ✈

North Sound Estate ●

North Cayman Palms

Belfor Estade

Matilda Ponds

Prospect ●

Spotts ●

Savannah ●

South Cayman Palms

○
Bodder Town

South Sound

South West Point

Pedro St James Castle

Great Pedro Point

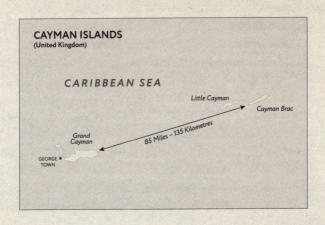

CAYMAN ISLANDS
(United Kingdom)

CARIBBEAN SEA

Little Cayman

Cayman Brac

Grand
Cayman

85 Miles – 135 Kilometres

GEORGE
TOWN

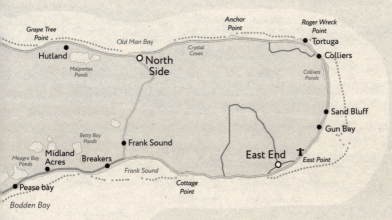

Grape Tree
Point

Old Man Bay

Anchor
Point

Roger Wreck
Point

Tortuga

Hutland

Crystal
Caves

Colliers

Malportas
Ponds

North
Side

Colliers
Ponds

Sand Bluff

Betty Bay
Ponds

Gun Bay

Meagre Bay
Ponds

Midland
Acres

Frank Sound

East End

East Point

Breakers

Frank Sound

Pease bay

Cottage
Point

Bodden Bay

PART I

THE JOURNEY TO TREASURE ISLAND

CHAPTER 1

A CARIBBEAN WELCOME

It was a lovely surprise when Bob Marley welcomed me to Grand Cayman – I didn't think my arrival warranted such an honour, but I treasured it just the same, especially when the High School Steel Band sprang into action, subjecting us to their cheerfully off-key version of 'Three Little Birds'. The rainbow-coloured bunting festooned around the airport arrivals hall flapped in time to the beat while the sliding doors clattered forwards and back, attempting to keep the cooled air in and the searing heat out. I soon realised that the more worthy recipients of this accolade were the all-conquering school basketball team fresh from their recent success in the US, who were roundly cheered before being ushered towards the VIP reception area. The remaining passengers from the Cayman Airways jet were herded towards the immigration officers who somehow managed to be even grumpier than those I had just encountered in Miami.

None of this bothered me in the slightest – I had been offered the once-in-a-lifetime opportunity to live and work on a tropical island in the Caribbean and this was just the start. I still felt like I was in a dream and I was willing to wait all day to get through if necessary. The next two years would doubtless fly by, so I relaxed in line, swayed along to the infectious rhythm, trying my best to remember the song's lyrics. *Don't worry…dum dee dum, dum… about a thing…dum dee dum, dum…cause every little thing's, gonna be alright…*

With the steel band still ringing in my ears I emerged from the terminal weighed down like a pack-mule to be greeted by Chief Superintendent Jones with his warm smile and firm handshake. Twelve UK police officers had been recruited for this unique adventure, and I for one intended to make the most of it. I had seen the job advertisement in the classified section at the back of the *Police Review* magazine that answered my dreams perfectly. I had longed to work abroad, the timing was almost perfect, and being just 29 it was far too early for me to settle down to a humdrum existence in the north of England.

Emerging from the airport on that April afternoon, I shaded my eyes and squinted towards the tall palms surrounding the shimmering runway, single-storey buildings and hangars. A police driver unceremoniously tossed the luggage into the back of a pickup truck and we were taken to the Cayman Islander hotel where we were to live for the next seven days. It was clean, basic but in a wonderful location just across the road from the beach, within a short stroll of the bustling Cayman Islands capital, George Town.

The first evening enabled us to catch breath at a restaurant we'd discovered overlooking the main harbour, listening to the metallic clang of the cords against masts as the yachts bobbed gently at their moorings. We relaxed into our new world, where at six o'clock my first Caribbean sunset disappeared in a semi-circular burst of turquoise and green. The next morning, after treating myself to an invigorating pre-breakfast swim in the calm, warm, clear blue sea off the gently shelving Seven Mile Beach, I sat drying in the sunshine, taking stock of my wonderful good fortune. The next two years were to be the most fun, the most intriguing and the most exciting of times, living and policing in Paradise. What could possibly go wrong? I asked myself.

CHAPTER 2

MOSSLEY POLICE STATION (FIVE MONTHS EARLIER)

The small but concise job advertisement that caught my eye was tucked away towards the back of the classified section in the *Police Review* magazine. For the previous couple of hours, I had been desperately digging a midwife out of a snowdrift to take her to an isolated farmhouse and attend to the mum-to-be. The tiny gas fire in the kitchen at Mossley police station had begun to thaw my numbed and ghostly grey fingers just enough to hold a mug of scalding tea, then smooth the curled pages of the magazine. It had been heavily snowing all morning and big clumps were sticking around the Victorian gritstone police station high in the western part of the Pennines. Our cleaner/cook/agony aunt Mrs H was busying herself in the kitchen preparing the breakfast fry-up so that I could relax just a little prior to my next interruption. It wasn't long before I roared off again, with the exhaust of the police Land Rover echoing along the terraced streets as the powdered snow billowed from the roof like too much castor sugar tumbling off a Victoria sponge. I was immediately consumed by the blizzard, the single blue roof light flashing through the mist as I hummed along to the urgent beat of Charles Williams's 'Devil's Galop'.

Despite how it sounds, I really enjoyed this part of policing too. It was all great fun but I knew I craved a new challenge. I had passed all my police exams and wanted to see the world before being promoted. As a detective constable working undercover for six months around all the dodgy dives, fleshpots and eye-watering spectacles of Manchester's seedy underbelly, I had seen all manner of society, many of whom I hoped never to see again. I knew I needed a break from it before deciding on my future career path, to let myself come up for air to properly evaluate what was right for me, and I knew it had to be somewhere different (and preferably warm). The classified advertisements in the now defunct *Police Review* regularly displayed interesting jobs around the globe for experienced British police officers. So when I was back in the warmth and safety of the station that afternoon, I opened the magazine to see if I could find just what I needed – the opportunity to work somewhere overseas, somewhere exciting but not too dangerous, and definitely somewhere warm.

It was time for a change. I had been working in a busy British police force for 10 years, gaining huge amounts of practical policing experience and generally having a good time. I was also in a relationship but I didn't yet have any inclination to settle down, so this was really my last opportunity to scratch that itch I had. So I began to research my options to carry on policing abroad.

- Bermuda looked nice with its pink fringed beaches and colourful coves but it was in the middle of the Atlantic and seemingly miles from anywhere. I would also have to resign and reapply if I wanted to come back to the UK.
- The option of joining the police in Hong Kong as an

inspector was the least attractive option, with myriad complications including having to master Cantonese, which would be of limited use back in the snowy Pennines.

- Papua New Guinea was recruiting directly into super-intendents roles on very high wages, which seemed a dramatic move but still well within my capabilities. There had to be a catch and as it turned out there was a huge one. A little research and a phone call to their government office in London revealed that the main policing problems were somewhat different to my experiences in the north of England. Policing in PNG focused on dealing with violent arguments between indigenous tribes who had been known to use ancient methods of defence, including firing poisonous darts from blow pipes. So, I decided not to apply after enduring several nightmares of me being darted and captured.

With all these things considered the options appeared limited and not ideal, so mainly out of frustration I applied for Bermuda and attended an interview. My girlfriend was with me when I opened the letter with the result.

Before revealing its contents to her, I said. 'Do you want the good news or the bad news?'

She looked me straight in the eye. 'That depends who it's good or bad news for.'

'Well, I've had the "knock-back" for the Bermuda job but… I'm thinking of applying for another job overseas.'

'Where to this time?'

'The Cayman Islands.'

'You bastard,' was her only reply as she slammed the door.

*

I had never heard of the Cayman Islands, so hadn't a clue where on earth they were. A bit of research in the local library helped me discover that they were a Crown Colony with a strong allegiance to Queen Elizabeth. The three islands that make up the Cayman Islands are in the Caribbean about 150 miles south of Cuba and 180 miles northwest of Jamaica. The reference book showed the weather to be tropically warm with winter averaging 24°C and summer around 30°C with cooling off-shore breezes. It all looked and sounded very, very pleasant indeed.

It is believed that King James the 'Forgetful' had mistakenly given the islands its tax-free status as pirates and buccaneers never tended to pay much tax. The king then omitted to rescind this benefit as no one in his kingdom actually knew where the Cayman Islands were. In fact, the story goes that one of King James's hard-of-hearing courtiers felt obliged to wear a cap made from a fox pelt after inadvisably asking the King about the tax situation in the Cayman Islands. The King replied with a shrug. 'The Cayman Islands? The Cayman Islands? Wear the fox hat.'

As a result of this status the islands have since developed into an extremely popular tourism and financial centre where residents and businesses pay no taxes whatsoever. Unsurprisingly, world banks and corporations flocked to George Town like gulls circling an open bag of chips. Financial corporations happily pay exorbitant fees to operate there, siphoning billions of dollars into bank accounts around the globe. In my fanciful state, it looked absolutely perfect, so I applied and was offered the post.

It all happened extremely quickly. There was a whirlwind of activity arranging my will, contracts and insurance, in addition to the leaving parties and visiting family, friends and colleagues. I had had long conversations with my girlfriend over the preceding weeks; my mind was made up and I wanted to work abroad but she also wanted to continue with her career in the UK. We agreed to keep in touch, stay committed, and I invited her to come over for a holiday later in the year when we could reassess our relationship.

I had to visit Police HQ to obtain documents from my service record and spoke to the Inspector in charge of the department, who enthusiastically greeted me with the usual refrain, 'I'd be there myself if I was a bit younger…'

Police officers feel emotionally attached to the collar numbers that they are issued with when they first join the police and these remain with them until they retire. Why is it called a collar number when nowadays it is displayed on the shoulder or attached to a stab-proof vest? Historically, Victorian police officers displayed these numbers on their tunics and cape collars to identify each one. (Interestingly, each member of Greater Manchester Police with the surname Bond was always issued with a collar number ending in 007.) The Inspector promised I could retain mine when, or indeed if, I returned, which was a great comfort. He escorted me to the inner sanctum within the basement where all the personnel records were stored. It was just like a scene from a John Le Carre Cold War spy movie where massive document lockers moved along creaking steel tracks operated by huge hand wheels, large enough to steer a battleship. He tracked down my cardboard storage box, extracted the paper file and asked me to guess what the first item in my personnel folder would be. I guessed wrong. It turned out that it was a letter I had written asking for information on a police career when I was 15 years old. I think it was written in red crayon and preserved on vellum. I'd forgotten I'd even written it but, all these years later, it reminded me that I had always wanted to join the police from a very early age. Working abroad would be the icing on the cake.

CHAPTER 3

INTRODUCTION TO GRAND CAYMAN

The recruitment of British constables had been a huge political gamble – with significant opposition from some elements on the islands – but it was essential to increase the numbers of police officers. Historically, the local Caymanians were reluctant to join as they could get better paid careers working in the thriving tourism industry, financial services or even through nefarious means. The public perception towards the police was very poor, and most people did not want to endure the elements of danger that the job required nor the unsociable hours.

We were recruited to be independent, supportive and provide training to the existing patrol officers and if this initiative went wrong, the Commissioner of Police and the UK appointed Governor would be loudly blamed. The islands had remained a Crown Colony after Jamaica became independent in the 1960s and the population was generally pro-British. Unsurprisingly there were several influential individuals vociferously opposed to the recruitment of British constables, including several Caymanian politicians, a number of local lawyers…and my girlfriend.

There was no direct flight to the Cayman Islands, so the 12 recruits gathered at Heathrow for the flight to Miami and the onward connection. Our eclectic group consisted of an interesting mix of experience and personalities from different forces around England, all relishing this one-off opportunity.

In Miami, we boarded the Cayman Airways plane that was emblazoned with the Sir Turtle logo. This cheerful image of a piratical turtle with a wooden leg had a vivid red scarf billowing from his neck that was a good introduction to two important aspects of how the islands came into being. Discovered by Christopher Columbus in 1503, they were named 'The Tortugas' after the large number of turtles found there. These were a useful source of food for the early settlers and still feature widely in the culture of the islands, together with a successful protection and environmental programme to save this charismatic and endangered species. Historically the islands were part of the Spanish Main and were used as a staging post for pirates, privateers and traders as they criss-crossed the Caribbean Sea either laden with or seeking gold, jewels and other valuable goodies.

The other passengers on the jet taking us to the islands gave me a snapshot of the occupants of the islands. They comprised a complete melting pot that included obvious holidaymakers from the US and Canada wearing garish shirts, pasty-faced expats like ourselves, and local Caymanians, some with naturally bright ginger hair and freckles mixed with West Indian features.

The flight took less than an hour to arrive at the main island of Grand Cayman after passing over the smaller islands of Little Cayman and Cayman Brac that are about 90 miles away to the north. We circled to prepare for landing on the single runway that spans the island between the sea and the adjacent mangrove swamps. All eyes on board looked across at the sandy-coloured jewel in the sparkling azure Caribbean Sea where we were due to spend the next couple of years.

The main island of Grand Cayman is in the shape of an inverted letter L and measures about 22 miles in length by 9 miles wide. From the plane it was easy to pick out the capital of George Town and the famous Seven Mile Beach that is a golden crescent shape on the western part of the island – which, it turns out, is only five miles long. The surrounding sea was a myriad of blues and greens, with the darker shades showing the locations of the coral reefs protecting the island and identifying the different depths of sea bordering on the neighbouring, and reputedly bottomless, Cayman Trench.

We were to be operational patrol officers and for the first 12 months we would be based in George Town until we became more established and moved elsewhere on the islands as required. The role was very much what we had experienced in our younger days in the UK, patrolling on foot and in patrol cars, issuing tickets for breaches of road traffic law and responding to reports of crime or disorder. The Governor and his home at Governor's House (GH) overlooking the beautiful Seven Mile Beach also needed protecting. This was a bit of a step back for most of us as we had all progressed on to more specialist roles back in the UK, but we all thought it was a sacrifice worth making.

Our Cayman work education started quickly after a couple of days of rest following the long flight. On our first day we toured the Central police station where we received an overwhelmingly positive welcome from officers and support staff who seemed genuinely happy to see us. That initial fortnight on the main island of Grand Cayman was an intensive period of absorbing the local laws and procedures that we were to enforce and adhere to.

The introduction period helped us acclimatise to the new environment, with inputs from all the units and departments within the police and criminal justice service. We were told that we had the use of a small minibus for a couple of weeks whilst we bought cars or bikes, as public transport around the island was non-existent. We actually managed to keep hold of it for about three months by hiding it well away from Police HQ and no one seemed to miss it.

Detective Chief Inspector (DCI) Timms could either be described as conservative in his outlook on the world or with the back-handed compliment of being 'old school'. His Drugs Squad office resembled an opium den, with shards of light slicing through wooden shutters closed tight against the oppressive midday sun, while the smoke from his smouldering ash tray was gently dispersed by the groaning a/c unit jutting out from the window frame. When we first visited, someone grabbed the only two chairs in his office so the rest of us had no choice but to sit cross-legged on the floor like six-year-olds ready to sing along to a nursery rhyme. 'If You're Happy and You Know It' was the one that sprung immediately to my mind.

The DCI seemed very happy to see us through the smog, addressing us in his crackling tenor's timbre. 'Right lads, you've got a bloody great opportunity to make a big impression on the drug problem here by disrupting the supply of ganga and cocaine on the islands. The judges are superb and usually sentence the druggies to six months for straight possession and five years for supplying.' And with that we were told to get on our way, it really was that direct.

We were sent to collect our police uniforms, which ended up being a slight disappointment as I thought khaki cotton shirts and shorts and tall black socks would suit my knees well. Unfortunately, that uniform was only for senior officers who tended never to leave their air-conditioned offices. We were directed to the vehicle testing officer who also doubled-up as the tailor and were issued with scratchy white polyester shirts that somehow smelt of fish and dark blue trousers with a broad red stripe down each leg. A white tunic and pith helmet with a spike on top were issued for ceremonial duties.

Next stop was the cell complex, which was a complete revelation, and for some unknown reason the local officers knew it as the gaol but pronounced it 'the goal'. It was in the rear cark park of the Central police station and on first inspection appeared to be a condemned, dilapidated concrete toilet block. There was a steel barred gate that led to an inner corridor with a chair, a desk with a slowly spinning electric fan, complete with a dull reading lamp perched on it. The inner door led to an internal courtyard that was open to the sky but covered with a metal grille, to prevent any escape. There were five cells leading off the central courtyard with doors made of steel bars and all were open to the air. Each cell had a raised concrete bed with a plastic-covered mattress, and at the end of the corridor there was a single toilet without a seat for use by the prisoners. There was no air-conditioning, indeed there was no air, just heat and humidity and small scuttling cockroaches. The insects and unpleasant smells of sweaty bodies were overwhelming, reminding me of an unsettling, creepy mediaeval dungeon, except this place had more bugs and frogs. It certainly was an eye-opening experience and was one of the first moments that I thought everything might not be as plain sailing as I'd initially believed.

I have always been a great believer in the overall effectiveness of a well-trained police dog controlled by an enthusiastic handler. On many occasions during my career, I have been thankful for the timely appearance of a dog van hurtling to my assistance, having the same impact as 10 officers arriving – except with much sharper teeth. We were introduced to the Cayman police dog handler in the rear yard of the police station, who told us his dog Blitz lived in the back of an air-conditioned Jeep Cherokee with its engine permanently running. Having a natural affinity for dogs, I asked if I could give him a stroke.

'No man, he'll rip your bloody arm off.'

'Well, can you just let him out then?' I said.

'I won't be held responsible if he kills one of you.'

We all stood well back as he went to the car, and slightly regretting my request I sheltered behind my much bigger colleague, Alec. The rear door of the Jeep was dramatically raised to reveal what appeared to be an extremely chubby grizzly bear hibernating in a very comfy cave. It looked quite dead.

The handler then shouted at Blitz, 'RAUS, RAUS', but nothing happened. The UK officers looked at each other with suitably raised eyebrows and equal amounts of confusion as to why the dog handler was speaking in German.

'RAUS, RAUS.'

Still nothing happened.

My other colleague, Cocky, whispered, 'I've seen more life in a tramp's vest.'

I was standing close to Chief Superintendent Jones and leant across to ask him what was going on, but at that point all eyes flicked back to Blitz. The handler reached into the back of the Jeep and produced two wooden planks with a hook on one side. He slotted the hooks into the top of the rear bumper and built a ramp to the ground. Slowly Blitz stood up, had a huge yawn accompanied by a full body stretch before strolling carefully down the planks accompanied by a further chorus of 'RAUS, RAUS.'

'SITZEN UND BLEIBEN.'

Blitz completely ignored the order to sit and stay and instead wandered to the rear tyre panting vigorously, cocked his leg, then had a long wee before flopping down in a cloud of dust. Mr Jones looked towards me, shook his head and mouthed, 'Later.'

When we returned to the classroom Mr Jones opened with a wonderful understatement. 'You may be wondering about Blitz? It all happened before I arrived here but there's never been a police dog on the island before, so someone asked the Miami Police what breed would be most suitable. Unfortunately, they took the advice all too literally…'

Mr Jones glanced out into the corridor before firmly closing the classroom door.

'Of course, we usually call our police dogs Alsatians but regrettably Miami recommended that the best candidate would have to be a well-trained German Shepherd. Yes, I think you're all following it, so far.' He waited for a dramatic pause before continuing. 'They went to Germany, bought a fully trained, long-haired Alsatian that can't stand the heat and only reacts to commands bellowed in German. I suppose we should count our lucky stars they didn't bring back Blitz's German Shepherd, Otto von Flock.'

CHAPTER 4

POLICE TRAINING

The formal training continued with numerous lectures outlining the local laws and procedures that were generally in line with UK laws but admittedly felt many years behind them. The Cayman Islands Penal Code included laws laid down during buccaneering times, some of which had never been repealed. The death penalty was still available for murder, piracy on the high seas and damage in Her Majesty's Dockyard, although it was the other less serious offences which caught my attention. Whilst on patrol I would definitely keep my eyes peeled for anyone insulting the modesty of a woman, taking part in a duel, depositing night soil on the Queen's Highway or discharging a cannon within the capital, George Town.

Initially we scoffed at the offences involving voodoo, or obeah as it is more correctly known locally, but the instructor stopped us mid-guffaw with a solemn shake of the head and wave of his hand.

'Please don't mock, gentlemen. The power of the unknown spirits is very strong here, obeah is endemic all over these islands.'

I saw my colleague Nobby grinning inanely, fashioning some blue tack into a tubby balding stickman. He then stabbed a sharpened pencil into its buttocks. Instantly, Alec jumped up from his chair with a yelp. He was sitting three seats away.

'Sorry, I think something's just bitten me.' Alec examined his seat very carefully before he sat back down. Nobby's face was ashen. Quickly rolling the figure back into a ball he put it carefully out of harm's way.

At that stage I did not understand the raw power that obeah had over some people, but I was soon to experience its impact, first-hand.

The Radio Room Inspector outlined the way the communications worked. It was a modern digital system integrated with the other emergency services that could enable contact in serious situations such as the constant threat from hurricanes. An unfortunate element of policing means that officers often experience unruly or violent behaviour. UK police forces all operate different radio communications protocols that provide either code words or numbers to indicate the nature of the incident that you are tasked to deal with. They also enable you to inform the radio operator if you are in a tricky situation. My own force used the most likely recognisable phrase 'Backup' if you needed an additional patrol to help you deal with anything complicated. The words 'Assistance required' meant that you needed every available patrol to attend, as some baddies were likely kicking your head in.

I asked the Inspector what the local protocol would be if a similar situation happened on the island. He raised his eyebrows, furrowed his forehead, then sucked on his pencil for a moment before offering a golden nugget of advice: 'I've never known it to be needed here on the island, but I suppose you could press the radio button then whisper… "HOTEL…ECHO…LIMA…PAPA."'

*

The Royal Cayman Islands Police is not permanently armed but did need access to firearms on a regular basis to conduct armed arrests or protect high-value consignments. Sergeant Benjamin was the Force Armourer, Drill Instructor and Firearms Instructor who appeared to live in the armoury. He was tall and slim and had served in the Jamaican Defence Force before arriving in the Cayman Islands. As part of the training, he took us to an area of the mangrove swamps away from civilisation that had been cut back and named the Rifle Range. We all struggled into the minibus or sat in the back of the police pickup truck for the bumpy drive along an unmarked, dusty marl track.

The Rifle Range consisted of six empty oil drums in a line about 30 feet away. Sgt Benjamin stuck a large paper target to each drum and issued the first group of us with ear defenders.

He walked up to me holding a plastic bucket full of bullets. 'Take 12 bullets if you can count that high without taking your boots off.'

Most of us managed this before he gave each of us a Police Service Colt .38 Revolver, which was terrifying as none of us had received any firearms training back in the UK. It was great though, just like the movies. He showed us the basics of loading and aiming at the target before lining us up for some practice.

'Now remember,' Benjamin said, '*squeeeeeze* the trigger like she's a beautiful lady. Don't pull it like you're playing with your plonker.'

Our eyes went wide at that statement but we followed this sound advice, practising first without any bullets until half of us were allowed to load, then stood shoulder to shoulder until he gave the command to 'aim and fire!' It was deafening as we fired our first six bullets at the target. After the dust, smoke and sound subsided, he quickly removed the guns from our quivering hands, then walked over to review the results.

My target was first. 'Well boy,' he said. 'You certainly hit the target and even if you didn't kill him, he'd have sure bled to death. You've passed.'

Cocky was next. The instructor went over to his target and looked closely at it, dropped to his knees, then ran his fingers all over it.

'You stupid bastard, you ain't put one bullet in it. You'd a done better with a truncheon. Go back and sit in the truck, you're never getting a gun off me.'

Cocky trudged off holding his head in shame.

It was now Alec's turn as Sgt Benjamin walked over and closely examined his target, then looked around in the direction of Cocky who was slowly climbing into the back of the pickup truck. He said to Alec, 'You've passed.'

'That's great Sergeant, how many times did I hit it?'

Benjamin grinned widely. 'You did real well, son. You hit it twelve times with six bullets, you should go 'n call the Guinness Book of Records.'

The induction course continued and I received my new uniform, which ended up needing a lot of effort to make it presentable. We had the use of the clapped-out minibus but had to sit on the floor as we were bounced around going from place to place. On the day we were due to have our class photograph taken – which was to be published locally and also back in the UK – we arrived at the training office with oily hands, dirty marks and scuffs after it broke down and we managed a running repair.

We began to organise ourselves for the class photo when one of my colleagues – Carlos – informed us that he could not have his picture published back in the UK as he had worked deep undercover and international terrorists had a contract out to kill him. This was the first we had heard of it and I was a little bemused – I'd only been focused on my own desires to up and leave the UK, now I was so intrigued at finding out who my 'band of brothers' really were. The police photographer took pictures both with and without Carlos to satisfy his concerns.

Afterwards, I reported the breakdown to the 'motor pool' Sergeant who was spooning mountainous amounts of powered coconut milk into his black coffee. He offered me a similar brew, which I declined even after he promised it would put plenty of lead in my pencil. I pressed him about the poor state of the minibus and asked when it could be repaired.

'You should take a leaf outa Bobby's book.'

'Bobby? Bobby who?'

The Sergeant leant over to his cassette player and pressed play.

'Bobby McFerrin, he's got the right idea.'

The Sergeant leant back in his creaky chair and joined in whistling the opening bars to, *Don't worry. Be happy.*

I knew I'd have to quickly re-assess things if I was to get by in the Cayman Islands.

The next day began with a Swearing In ceremony in the presence of the Chief Resident Magistrate. We professed allegiance to Her Majesty the Queen and to carry out the office of Constable 'without fear or affection, malice or ill will; and that I will to the best of my power cause the peace to be kept and preserved.'

The Magistrate was an impressive character. His Honour Judge Rudyard was a senior barrister originally from Jamaica where he had excelled in law leading to his appointment as a Queen's Councillor (QC). He was well over six feet tall, solidly built, with an appealing flash of humour in his eyes and later I found him to be a formidable tennis player. He possessed a cutting wit which combined with attention to detail made him a commanding presence in the court room. He entered our room prior to the official ceremony and greeted each of us to the islands warmly with a firm handshake and encouraging words. I was fascinated by his barrister's wig, which had mellowed with age to a shade of chalky grey.

At the conclusion of the ceremony, I was asked to assist him by carrying his belongings out to his car. He removed his formal judge's gowns and I expected him to do the same with his head gear. I took up his well-worn leather satchel and waited until he'd finished.

'I'm ready when you are, constable.'

'Yes, sir, I was just waiting for you to hand me your wig,' I said.

'Wig, what wig?' A beaming smile flicked across his face at the same time as mine went bright red.

It was a beautiful warm sunny day, so for lunch we walked out wearing full uniform, into George Town and sat in the Jamaican Pattie Shop overlooking the harbour. It had many attractions, including air-conditioning, cheap and tasty patties, deep-filled sandwiches made with locally caught tuna, freshly ground coffee – it was picture postcard perfect. It also had a huge picture window looking out over the fishing boats tied up at the dock and further out to a massive cruise ship disgorging its passengers into launches and bringing them onto shore to spend money.

In the Pattie Shop, the main topic of conversation was with Carlos who we enthusiastically encouraged to discuss the reasons for being threatened by international terrorists. He began to open up about the undercover work that had remained confidential up to that point. He waxed lyrical about previous roles in the Drugs Squad and explained that he had been called upon to be deep undercover in Europe, the Middle East and the Indian subcontinent. The stories kept coming, the details were distinctly embellished and he wasn't even drunk.

One of his 'taller' stories was reaching its exciting crescendo as he described how his cover was devastatingly blown by the terrorist group, resulting in a nail-biting chase through the red-light district of Amsterdam until he commandeered a speed boat to escape along a canal... At this point the rest of us stood up and moved quickly to another table at the rear of the Pattie Shop. Carlos was left open mouthed and alone in the shop window.

'Where are you lot going?'

'We're keeping out of the way in case a black sedan pulls up outside and riddles you with a bloody Tommy gun.'

The following day we decided that as our pristine uniforms were being slowly ruined by the oil, dirt and grime from the inside of the minibus, we would all attend the classroom in civvies. Not shorts, flip-flops or T-shirts but smart casual, in cotton chinos, shirts and the like. The mantra of 'better to ask forgiveness than permission' was in the forefront of our minds as it was a sensible group decision and we did not need to ask permission from anyone because we were all adults, weren't we? No, apparently not. Unfortunately, this was the day that the Commissioner left his office to come and give us a pep talk and was absolutely horrified at what he saw. He stood at the front of the classroom with his mouth open, surveying the 12 of us, from side to side, until he could contain himself no longer.

'Never in the history of the Royal Cayman Islands Police has there been such behaviour. It's mutiny, Mr Jones, mutiny I tell you!'

I began to explain, 'Well, sir, we're in smart civvies because of...' but I was swiftly told to shut up, so I did.

The Commissioner's tirade continued unabated, with his voice going higher and higher as he pointed his extended finger at us like a loaded gun.

'Minions like you shouldn't take decisions without written

authority from your superior officers. The next thing I know you'll take industrial action, work to rule, go out on strike and create civil unrest on the streets. If that happens I will…I will call on the Royal Navy to send a gunboat, get the Royal Marines to arrest you and have you all publicly flogged – but that would be far too good for you…'

He continued in the same vein – indeed the one in his neck seemed ready to pop – so sensibly I decided not to interject further. After he ran out of blood curdling threats he stomped out, slamming the classroom door, and headed back to his air-conditioned office at the government building, presumably to enjoy a much-needed lie-down and an appropriate 'sundowner' to help him relax.

'I think the Commissioner is quite tired and emotional,' Mr Jones explained after he left. 'And did not mean *most* of what he said. But go and get your uniforms back on and enjoy your lunch, gentlemen. It wasn't a good idea to wear civvies, so now I'll have to go and cancel the Royal Navy gunboat arriving with the cat o' nine tails.'

It had been a whirlwind of a week and as it was drawing to a close, it gave me the opportunity to reflect on what had been happening during the quickest seven days that I could ever remember. Every morning started with a swim in the sea, a lovely breakfast outdoors and hugely entertaining banter during the boring but essential local familiarisation lessons. Each evening, we went for a barefoot run along the beautiful Seven Mile Beach then enjoyed a delicious meal at the hotel. Then we'd head out to the various bars and clubs, experiencing what the night life on the island could offer like kiddies in a sweet shop – and why not? There were few thoughts about our colleagues back in the UK. We'd put all this effort into our careers to date, and it really felt that now we were just beginning to reap the rewards.

*

As our first week and our complimentary stay in the Cayman Islander hotel was coming to an end, we all needed to find proper lodgings. Accommodation was going to be a key factor for our stay on the islands as the cost of property was exorbitant and we could never afford to purchase anything, so we would have to rent. We were only receiving the local pay for constables, so were advised to double up with a UK colleague to make shared accommodation more affordable.

Covertly, some of the team had already arranged for their girlfriends to come over after the first few weeks so they were arranging work for them and suitable places to stay. I felt a slight pang because of my own relationship situation, but I was so busy in these first days and weeks on the island that I didn't feel too homesick, and I tried to distract myself with knowing that my girlfriend and a lot of my friends and family were hoping to come and see me during my two-year secondment – funny what moving to a Caribbean island will do! But it still left the quandary of where I was going to live. Those of us without partners on the island were encouraged to conduct a virtual 'speed dating' to identify a suitable flat mate and share the costs. In reality, my unconscious decision amounted to the question of who I could not share with, so I paired up with a colleague named Rupert. The most attractive element of Rupert's personality was the fact that he had already arranged to buy a car.

We moved into a modern complex of two/three bedroom villas and condominiums named the Blue Oyster Club that somehow brought the *Police Academy* film to mind. It overlooked the southern and more rugged coast of the island, which did not have sandy beaches; rather its coast was framed by grey 'iron-shore' rocks. The condominium was new, smart and clean and we had access to a couple of pools, tennis courts and BBQ cabanas overlooking the seashore. We had to budget for the rent and the expensive utilities which were affordable if we were careful, so agreed not to use the expensive air-conditioning and tossed a coin for the main bedroom fitted with a ceiling fan. I lost but we arranged to change over after three months. It felt like luxury.

CHAPTER 5

SUNDAY AT RUM POINT

Sunday was our first day off since we'd arrived on the beautiful island of Grand Cayman and I intended to use it well. I had rented a pristine white Jeep Wrangler and carefully folded back the fawn fabric roof to get the full impact of the tropical sunshine and sea breezes. Three of the boys jumped into the Jeep and the rest crammed into the minibus we had 'borrowed' from the rear of the police station. We hurtled across the island with the four-litre engine burbling cheerfully beneath the bonnet, bringing huge smiles to our faces. I raced off-road, along unmade marl tracks, then back to the tarmac, creating circular plumes of dust devils dancing behind as the wind whistled past my sunglasses. It was great fun and I promised to buy myself a Jeep to enjoy on the island during the next two years.

It was a lovely, warm, sunny Caribbean morning at the start of spring. The onshore breeze was fresh, the sun just warming up a little and a few fluffy clouds appeared above. We headed towards Rum Point, a place that I had been reliably informed was the most beautiful spot on the island and possibly the entire world. We sang loudly and enthusiastically to the chorus of UB40's, 'Red, Red Wine' as the Jeep's speakers boomed rhythmically to its reggae beat. We sped past a couple of locals sitting by the roadside, grasping tins of Red Stripe in their sun-scorched hands, just catching their friendly waving of fists – or at least I think they were friendly…

I enjoyed the 45-minute drive from the capital George Town as we headed towards the northernmost tip of the island. It was close to the glamorous yachting marina of Cayman Kai, where billionaire's yachts moored, admiring each other's net worth. I drove on to seek our idyllic beach of gently sloping white sand, picturesquely framed by palm trees and sea-grape bushes with a small, neat pier jutting out from the shore.

The only one missing out on the trip was my flatmate Rupert, who had complained bitterly of 'awkward tummy troubles'. He blamed the water, the food, the heat, the sandflies, the locals and even the total lack of decent avocado pears in the supermarket. So, it was a much happier bunch of buccaneers that finally arrived at Rum Point, which historically – and unsurprisingly, given its name – had been the spot on the island for landing contraband, well away from the prying eyes of the revenue men. The Jeep's tyres crunched to a halt beneath the palm trees and as the engine cut out, I heard a reggae band just perceptible above the sound of the sea lapping along the sand and the gentle brush of the palm tree fronds in the warm breeze. This was indeed paradise – paradise found.

I had pulled in close by the beach bar with its roof of coconut palm leaves stretched over the weatherbeaten, sun-bleached wooden frame. It was topped with a rough hand-painted sign that simply announced it as 'The Bar at Rum Point'. We stopped to take in the most awe-inspiring view I had ever seen.

Everything I had been told about Rum Point was true, the white sand, the clear turquoise sea, the gentle lapping of the waves.

It was all a dream that had become reality – and I was being paid to be there!

I dropped the boys off at the bar and they made their way over to chat-up the staff working behind it. The Jeep fuel gauge was winking orange at me in its own, worrying sort of way. I was now running on petrol fumes, so I was pointed in the direction of the single pump at the neighbouring Cayman Kai yachting marina.

A handwritten cardboard sign instructed me to give the attendant a dollar or fill up myself and pay at the nearby harbour bar currently serving thirsty mariners. Realising I now needed to be careful with my hard-earned cash, I also found it an alien concept to pay for something that I was quite capable of doing myself. The wish to save money ultimately won through as I decided not to disturb the scruffy, heavily tanned man stretched out on his blue, shabby sun lounger, slumbering noisily beneath a palm tree. A little bell tinkled nearby as I took the petrol nozzle from the pump. I looked on one side of the Jeep, then walked around to the other, but there was no fuel cap to be seen anywhere. I smiled cheerfully and nodded towards the now semi-comatose attendant who sat up and pushed his sunglasses onto his grubby LA Lakers baseball cap. I got the impression he did not want to miss anything of the behaviour of this poor, stupid tourist messing about with the Jeep and his precious petrol pump.

The little bell rang once more as I returned the nozzle into the pump and reviewed my ridiculous situation. Not wishing to be seen as a complete novice or an ignorant tourist I resisted the temptation to ask for help. As some bright spark had once pointed out to me that stupid and stubborn are very close in the dictionary, I was now even more determined to save face and, ultimately, that single dollar bill. Walking back to the Jeep I noticed another couple of locals had wandered up to watch my antics, so having run out of sensible ideas, I decided to look under the bonnet at the V6 engine. I will never ever know why I expected to find the fuel filler cap inside the engine compartment where a loose drip of petrol would have gone up like a roman candle, but it had rapidly become a question of pride and not losing face.

Then like a thunderbolt from the heavens, a brilliant idea came to me. My dad used to drive Jeeps in Normandy during the war and he told me that the petrol tank was beneath the driver's seat. That seemed to me to be a pretty dangerous place to sit, but I suppose it was designed by some army officer who was unlikely to drive. Needless to say, all I found was an empty crisp packet and some tumbleweed. At the height of my discomfort and embarrassment I now had to do the 'walk of shame' towards the ever-increasing audience of onlookers.

'Well, go on then, where do I fill it up?' I asked, now red with embarrassment.

The explosive laugh from him and his cronies caused a squadron of parrots to starburst from their perches in a nearby palm tree before resettling briskly in a series of screeches, squawks and a rainbow of bright reds, greens and yellows. Between his over-energetic guffaws his pot belly rippled as he pointed a knobbly finger at the back of the Jeep.

'Try behind the license plate, bud.'

Damn, of course it was. I swallowed my pride, smiled then laughed uncomfortably along with them, filled the tank and obligingly paid up. The audience were still giggling, pointing and commenting loudly as I left the marina.

Back at the beach the boys had set up the BBQ and bought drinks from the bar. The weather was stunningly beautiful, 25°C, clear blue skies with a couple of light, puffy cotton-wool clouds over the horizon and a gentle onshore breeze. With a welcoming bottle of beer, I walked out into the sea and let the sunshine and waves wash over me as I absorbed the ambiance and reflected on all the activities we had enjoyed during our first week on the Cayman Islands. The white sandy beach shelved imperceptibly so that even 50 metres from the palm trees, the warm Caribbean was only up to my knees as I strolled out to enjoy the panoramic view. Looking further out, probably a mile away into the North Sound, a small group of tourist dive-boats were gathered, gently bobbing around Sting Ray City, a sand bar barely five feet below where they were experiencing close encounters with these marvellous, friendly creatures. My bucket list was increasing steadily by the day.

Eventually the tourist boats took the sting-ray snorkellers back to harbour and as dusk descended, we relocated to the beach bar to sit and watch as our first day off-duty came to a stunning end with a rainbow-tinted sunset disappearing slowly over the far horizon.

Monday morning dawned and reality hit us with a bump. Sgt Benjamin had arranged for us to attend in overalls and subjected us to a period of drill and marching for an hour and a half. None of us had been in the military, so being issued with .303 Lee Enfield rifles was a complete novelty. We went through the rudiments of handling the heavy gun, taking care not to drop it on our feet, then he decided to make it really dangerous by issuing us with bayonets.

Mine was stamped with a War Department arrowhead dated 1942 and was still wrapped in grease and covered in waxed paper. I was instructed to, 'Take it home and polish it till you can see your ugly mug in it.' The drill practice had now just gone up a gear in terms of becoming a really dangerous pastime. Those bayonets were sharp and the drill movements were now concentrating the mind as we marched up and down the main roads greeted by various cat-calling and derisive hooting from passing car horns. After work we needed to replenish pints of lost fluid from hours marching in the sun so ended up at the Police Social Club, which was the cheapest watering hole on the island. Where, in spite of (or perhaps because of?) the heat and humidity I ended up doing a karaoke/dance-along to the very appropriate song, 'Happy Hour' by the Housemartins. After catching my breath Rupert, Carlos and I were told that we had been allocated to Inspector McDougal's shift based in George Town.

Later in the evening, a strange little man came up to me and tapped me on the arm. I don't think he could have reached my shoulder as he was just about five feet tall; he was chubby and quite difficult to understand, dressed in shorts and a string vest with tufts of body hair sprouting through the material. 'Do you like traffi ticki?'

I asked him to repeat his question.

'Traffi ticki, traffi ticki.'

'No, I don't think so... I haven't tried much of the local food or drink yet.'

He seemed to become a bit more agitated until Mr Jones sidled up to assist.

'Inspector McDougal is wondering if you are interested in issuing traffic tickets to offending motorists.'

'No I'm not, but thank him for asking.' I wandered back to the bar. My supervisor or not, I had not travelled four thousand miles to be issuing traffic tickets to unsuspecting motorists guilty of minor misdemeanours – a word of advice usually worked. My first priority was targeting criminals and drug dealers who made the lives of decent people difficult or unpleasant. The inspector walked away shaking his head, mumbling to himself, 'Must issue traffi ticki to evybody, evybody.'

CHAPTER 6

A VERY CLOSE SHAVE

I was not drunk, merely tipsy and full of the joys of spring, which goes a little way to explain my ridiculous behaviour that afternoon. After another greatly improved session of drill with those sharp, freshly polished bayonets, Benjamin informed us that we had to get our hair cut 'as he was scared of hurting us if he accidently stepped on it', so I took the not-so-subtle hint. After work I called into the Police Social Club and then found a barber in a dusty back alley behind the harbour in George Town. The rough, hand-painted driftwood sign read: TOD SWEENEY THE DIAMOND BARBER. EACH CUT – $7. Below this, in less distinct sun-bleached lettering, an A4 sheet encased in a plastic flimsy announced: BACK, SACK AND CRACK – NEGOTIABLE.

This appeared to be a bargain on this very expensive island, although the description as a barber's shop did not do it justice as it was a rickety wooden shed with an ancient, rusty galvanised roof above a small veranda. The barber's chair was occupied by a male that I took to be Tod, dressed in scruffy cut-down jean shorts, pink plastic flip-flops and a dirty T-shirt stretched over his beer belly that read: 'IT STARTED WITH A KISS'. He stood, stretched his back and waved me towards the chair that had seen better days – several decades earlier. Yellow foam leaked from a cracked seam, like lava from Vesuvius, with liberal strands of black tape stretched to stem the flow.

'I Don't Wanna Dance' was booming from a ghetto blaster perched precariously in the branches of a neighbouring poinciana tree. To the front of the shed four elderly men sat around a square picnic table playing dominoes in the shade. They each had dark grizzled features suggesting many hours spent on open boats. A bottle bearing a green and yellow label, half filled with clear liquid, was being passed around the players, who each took a swig swiftly followed by a gulp of enormous satisfaction. They were friendly types and offered me a slug from the bottle that I graciously accepted so as not to upset them more than anything. I really was just trying to be friendly and didn't intend to swallow any, but as the powerful liquor hit my lips it felt like a blow torch had been ignited and applied to my mouth. It caused me to cough as some liquid passed onto my tongue and down towards my lungs. My mouth and lips felt they were on fire but I couldn't spit it out as all their eyes were focused upon me. I coughed violently as my nose and eyes began to run and tried to focus on the label of the bottle I was clinging onto. It seemed to read, 'Ovenproof Rum' but as my vision returned, it actually read, 'Over proof Rum 63%'.

My tongue, mouth and lips were now numb and I found it impossible to speak properly as I returned the bottle of poison back to the players, declining more with a shake of my head and a couple of high-pitched coughs. I slipped into the barber's chair as Tod put a sheet over me. It had unpleasant looking stains that would have kept forensic scientists busy for months. Tod was soon 'up close and personal', smelling of a mixture of B.O., hair gel and rum leaking from his bushy armpits. All I could say was, 'A thwim and thwidy, pwlease.' He gave me a very strange double-take and with a raised eyebrow started with his scissors.

The chair was in the warm afternoon sunshine and my previous beers and the 63% anaesthetic began to take effect as I closed my eyes and relaxed, thinking about how much money I was saving. As is seemingly usual for hairdressers the world over, Tod began by grumbling about the weather, politicians and then asked what my job was. Being naturally cagey and never willingly admitting to being in the police, I said I was a newly arrived civil servant. One of the domino players shouted across, interrupting my slumbers.

'No boss, he's one of them new police officers come over from England.'

A crash beside me sounded like a gun going off and I opened my eyes to see Tod coming at me with an ivory-handle cut-throat razor, shouting, 'I've something special for all police officers.'

I jumped up from the chair clad in what I thought had become my shroud and grabbed his hand as it came towards my throat. I struggled with him for a few seconds before pushing him into the post supporting the roof, making it collapse around us with a bang, a clatter and a cloud of ancient dust and rust.

'What you doin', man?' Tod pulled away from my grasp. 'I'm only trying to give you a free shave.'

I turned to see the domino players howling with laughter with tears rolling down their gnarled cheeks at the silly spectacle. I gradually released my vice-like grip on his wrist and sat down totally embarrassed. As the dust settled and the final piece of roofing clattered to the floor, Tod smiled, showing his gold, diamond-encrusted canine tooth. 'Don't worry about the shed,' he said. 'It's always falling over an' you have given the ole boys the best laugh for days – no charge.'

The old boys continued slamming dominoes on the table, shouting oaths, sounding like a pitched battle. They were only in it for winning matchsticks – honest, as gambling was totally banned on the islands.

Tod wielded the razor like an expert giving me the smoothest skin since being born. My heart rate gradually got back to normal as I counted my blessings that the razor and the smash and crash of the dominoes had not coincided or it would have been a very close shave indeed.

The Royal Cayman Islands Police had a fleet of elderly patrol cars. The Ford Crown Victoria Police Interceptors were left-hand drive US imports with a 4.6 litre V8 engine. If you think along the lines of the clapped-out police car driven by Jake and Elwood in *The Blues Brothers*, you won't be far off. I was given a check drive by a Traffic Patrol Sergeant to test my ability to drive these behemoths around the island's small roads and adapt to the steering column gear selector, although the oddest aspect was the wailing siren operated by a foot pedal. Trying to coordinate hands, eyes and feet during any car chase caused disconcerting hokey-cokey moments. Other than that, I took to it quickly, those days on the windy roads in the Pennines coming in very handy in the similarly remote roads of the Cayman Islands.

Governor's House occupied an acre of Seven Mile Beach. The compound was surrounded by a tall concrete wall and entered by double gates from West Bay Road where a sweeping drive ended with a lawn pierced by a flagpole. We went on a visit to familiarise ourselves with the site before we formally started our duties as it had to be protected on a 24-hour basis to ensure the safety and security of the UK-appointed Governor and his wife. We pulled up at the beautifully polished mahogany doors as they were opened by the butler, who ushered us inside to the coolness of the front lobby.

The Governor welcomed us and showed us into the formal dining room where a light lunch awaited. He was a pleasant individual and enthusiastically explained the contents of his trophy cabinet that he had accumulated during his time travelling around the world. One interesting item caught my eye and I asked about it. He opened the case and withdrew an ornately carved wooden stick about two feet long, then waved it around his head causing me to duck.

'It's a knobkerrie,' he said with a grin. 'I got it in Kenya when the previous owner tried to bash my brains in. It could do some damage you know!' I did, it nearly had and would do so in the near future. His wife gently returned it to the cabinet.

We looked out at the gorgeous view across the beach fringed with palm trees to the crystal blue waves gently lapping up the sand and the colourful sailing craft beyond. A thick red rope lying on the sand was the only demarcation barrier separating Governor's House from the public areas.

'Whilst you're here, gentlemen,' the Governor said. 'If you look out of these French windows onto the beach, you'll see that there's nothing to block the wonderful view. Unfortunately, that means that occasionally sunbathers use my beach. I'd appreciate it when you're on patrol if you could move them along, and this especially applies to anyone having, well, intimate moments on the sand. I know, it happens more than you think. Could you tell them to get lost as it's quite off-putting, especially at tea-time?'

It was certainly a bit different from the activity on the moors back home!

The final day of the induction course dawned and we showed off our marching and drill to the Commissioner. We sweated for an hour and produced a display good enough to bring tears of joy to the moist and rheumy eye of a Chelsea Pensioner. We awaited the Commissioner's response, who considered it for a moment.

'It'll do.' He turned to leave, then stopped. 'Oh, I nearly forgot, you're getting a 23 per cent pay rise. I'll do anything to improve the quality of the police here.' This really was great news – I was realising with impending dread that the cost of living was astronomical on the islands, even with the tax breaks. It was a wonder how the locals survived – even with what I was realising were rather more modest lodgings than we were lucky to live in – and it explained some of the endemic issues at the heart of the police work we were tasked with.

On the final evening of the course, we arranged a sunset cruise aboard a catamaran which included food and unlimited rum punch. I got a lift with Alec in his recently purchased tiny Japanese car with a two-cylinder engine that sounded like an un-tuned lawn mower. As we drove off along West Bay Road I noticed a couple of gaping rusty holes in the floor. He explained, 'the bloke that sold it said they were to allow the flood water to drain away.'

Turned out Alec had paid $1,000 for it, which seemed a lot for a car on the island, especially after he pointed out that his seat was held up by a large piece of coral rock tied with wire.

'Did the car showroom have glass doors?' I asked.

'No, I got it from a bloke in the police pound.'

'But, what about when it needs an MOT test?'

'It's guaranteed to pass; he's the government vehicle tester…'

Maybe he was not so daft after all.

The trip marked the end of the first two weeks of our adventure on the island with another glorious sunset, hearty banter and a real sense of achievement. It was a fantastic way to prepare for whatever was in store for us in the next two years in Paradise.

We had a great night celebrating the end of the course, but I knew the hard work was just around the corner. I'd kept hold of the Jeep that I'd rented and did as many jobs and errands as possible in George Town before returning it that weekend. I arrived at the rental office apologising for the delay.

'No problem, I was just coming to pick it up,' the manager said.

'But you didn't know where I was.'

'Yeah man, you were in the insurance office, I was going to save you the trouble of dropping it off.'

It began to dawn on me just how small the island really was.

I really wanted a car and knew I needed one soon, so I asked if he would sell me one of the rental Jeeps. He took me on a tour of the yard where the servicing and repairs took place.

'You can have that one if you want.' He pointed at a Jeep that had its entire front caved in and appeared to have come to a sudden halt around a tree. The airbags were blowing gently in the breeze covering the steering wheel and front passenger seat. I said it wasn't a project I would take on and asked if anyone was hurt.

'Go and look at the back of the front windscreen, the rear passenger won't forget in a hurry – if she can remember anything at all.' I pulled back the airbag and my heart jumped as I saw a clump of long strawberry blond hair trailing in the wind, still embedded in the centre of the screen.

I decided to try my luck elsewhere…

You wouldn't have thought that opening a bank account in the Cayman Islands would have been much of a problem, would you? George Town is about the size of a small English town, say Stratford-upon-Avon, but that is where the comparison ends. The Cayman capital is the base for about 500 banks and financial institutions that funnel trillions of dollars around the world and in terms of the volume of money transferred on a daily basis is only slightly behind London and New York.

I approached an internationally recognised bank and asked to open a current account producing my police ID card, letter from the Commissioner, proof of address, passport etc. I was then asked to complete an application which seemed to require all sorts of ridiculous and irrelevant questions such as my inside leg measurement, colour and style of underwear and whether my grandma used to ride a bike. Whilst waiting in the queue I had to prove my coordination and fitness to possess an account by tapping my head and rubbing my abdomen clockwise whilst hopping on alternate legs. No, I'm not joking. As I waited for the decision, I glanced across the vestibule and noticed that in an adjacent VIP area there was a suite of gaudy designer furniture provided with a well-equipped drinks cabinet surrounded by tall bar stools. This area was bursting at the seams with people resembling an assortment of Russian oligarchs, Colombian drug cartels and terrorist groups. Looking through a lightly frosted glass panel I could just make out Long John Silver dragging an over-flowing treasure chest along the marble floor. He was discussing his latest episode of buccaneering with Cap'n Flint perched precariously on his shoulder, before depositing his ill-gotten plunder.

Some of the more suspect banks continued to hide and invest billions of dollars of suspicious transactions around the world, but, if you can believe it, I was declared a poor risk and wasn't approved.

Eventually, I managed to open a bank account, but was not granted an overdraft facility, though I got the distinct impression that if I'd have given them a 'tip' they'd have no problem granting it to me. It really did feel lawless but I was too relieved to really care at the time. So, to celebrate, I went to the Jamaican Pattie Café for lunch where Beryl was serving. You did not mess with Beryl, who looked and sounded like the housekeeper from a Tom and Jerry cartoon. I sat down to enjoy the view out to the cruise ships at anchor beyond the harbour and noticed that Willy Bishop had walked in and asked for a free pattie. Willy was a local 'rumhead' that bummed about the harbour area either drinking or looking for a drink. He was a bit of a nuisance, begging from the tourists, and made a bit of noise when drunken fights broke out amongst his pals. This was usually no more serious than a few shouts and mild threats if the shared bottle of Captain Morgan was not passed around in the right order or if someone had glugged too much. Willy had to earn his lunch, so Beryl gave him a large broom and sent him out to sweep the sand and litter away from the front door and rear yard of the café.

He returned a couple of minutes later after leaning on the broom and using it to sing out of tune calypso songs for the benefit of cruise ship passengers strolling back towards the harbour. Beryl let him have a spicy pattie (the *very* hot one with a red dot) and pointed to the door. He turned to leave, then with a surprising turn of speed grabbed a conveniently placed loaf of bread and ran in slow motion for freedom. Beryl was far too quick for him and in a split second she swung the business end of the broom right between his shoulder blades with a thud so solid it reverberated through my feet. Brandishing her broom at him like a lance, she shouted, 'I ain't goin' to tell you agin, now git, git, GIT!' He shot out as quickly as his knackered sandals would carry him. It was the most dramatic incident of Walloping Willy or Bashing the Bishop that I had ever encountered and just the start of some very surreal encounters during my Caribbean experience.

CHAPTER 7

DON'T SHOOT, IT'S THE BLOODY DEA

Now a fully-fledged member of the police department, I got stuck into my duties under the watch of Inspector McDougal. In policing you always seem to start on night shift and this time was no exception as I paraded on duty at 11pm. The Inspector seemed delighted to see me and put a pile of traffic ticket booklets on the desk. I asked if they were all for me. 'Yes, many, many traffi ticki. You can have new one next week.' I thanked him and put them out of harm's way.

I was assigned to front desk duty where I had to record all matters of importance in a huge lined ledger. At 2am I was informed to go and have a refreshment break and so I drove into the town, which was only a few minutes' drive away. It was a lovely warm night as I parked up to admire the gorgeous view of the full moon illuminating a few small craft rotating gently at anchor in the romantically named Hog Sty Bay. Yes, I may have been stuck on night shift but it was a pretty wonderful place to be.

That first week started well, but one day I went into the station and there was a distinct change in the normally calm atmosphere.

There was an obvious panic in the air and the usual *manana* had disappeared in the intense afternoon heat. Normally relaxed and experienced officers were running about the corridors knocking into people and shouting incoherent orders at no one in particular. I approached the much more chilled Sergeant Benjamin as he emerged from the armoury laden with weaponry.

Shouting above the ruckus he threw a revolver and belt at me. 'Grab yourself a handful of dum-dum bullets from that bucket and follow me.' I did and as I climbed into his red pickup truck he shouted above the roar of the engine, 'Load that thing, we've a job on at the airport.'

We left the police car park in plumes of dust and the stench of burning rubber as I struggled to load my Smith & Wesson .357 Magnum revolver with the specially adapted ammunition that the Sergeant kept for 'serious' incidents. I once found him working in the armoury converting bullets into dum-dums using a vice, metal file and hacksaw and asked what he was doing. His response was refreshingly clear and straight to the point.

'The Geneva Convention don't apply to me boy. If some badass needs shooting, you gotta have an edge. *Comprendi?*'

We hurtled through the airport gates, straight at a queue of passengers waiting to board the plane parked at the front of the terminal.

'Get out of my way,' he shouted as we threaded through the tourists who starburst like a lively Labrador launching into a full hen house. We hurtled towards the far side of the airport where a twin-engine executive jet taxied to a halt as DCI Timms and his Drugs Squad drove up in two cars and blocked the plane from moving. We came to a screeching halt beside the plane and I saw the two pilots' look of horror as we sheltered behind the pickup and aimed our weapons right at them.

The airplane engines were silenced with a diminishing drone as members of the Drugs Squad grabbed the larger and much noisier firearms from the back of the pickup and trained them on the plane. Detective Sgt Mac of the Drugs Squad approached the aircraft door and called on them in Spanish. The door opened and two pilots came out with their hands held high, soon followed by four other males in casual clothing who were searched, handcuffed and made to sit cross-legged on the ground. Six large identical grey suitcases were removed from the plane where Sgt Mac asked for the key but the men just glared at the tarmac. Suddenly, I saw the Sergeant pull a commando knife from his cowboy boot and run towards them. Their eyes widened horribly as he turned and stabbed his knife straight into the lock of the nearest suitcase, ripping it apart to reveal dozens of plastic-covered pouches. A little cheer went up as each suitcase was opened to reveal similar quantities of what turned out to be 100 million dollars' worth of pure cocaine destined for the US. I'd never seen anything like it. It certainly beat issuing traffic tickets!

We were loading the drugs into the pickup and the prisoners into the police cars when I heard the piercing roar of another aircraft coming into land. I shaded my eyes against the searing blue sky as a grey executive jet approached the runway, far too fast, then raced across the runway, stopping violently just yards away. Everyone with a gun aimed at this plane and I pointed my revolver at the aircraft door, my heart racing as I prepared to squeeze the trigger. The aircraft door was flung open and a number of heavily armed men wearing aviator sunglasses and combat fatigues energetically stepped out into the sunshine. My finger was tightening on the trigger until I heard DCI Timms above the slowing engines, 'Don't shoot. It's the bloody DEA!'

Members of the US Drug Enforcement Administration began

to vigorously shake hands with Mr Timms, celebrating the sting operation that they had arranged to stop this massive consignment of drugs reaching the USA. The very subdued prisoners were transported to the cells, so I returned my pistol with its illegal ammunition to the armoury and went home to prepare for the night shift.

I went back into work, this time in uniform and not my shorts, polo shirt and flip-flops of my earlier adventure and was informed that my first job was guarding the pilots and drug cartel gang we had detained earlier. Inspector McDougal sought to quell any nerves that I may have had, as the rumours had already begun to circulate that a rescue attempt would be made to release them.

'I presume you won't let me take a gun into the cells?' I asked.

'No, the prisoners may overpower you. If you hear any suspicious noises ring me and the Sergeant will come down to the cells with his revolver.'

Sgt Bodden swivelled round in his seat. 'Me? What are *you* going to do if I get shot?'

'I'll call for assistance.'

'Who from?' the Sergeant asked.

'Well, I'll bring my revolver as well.'

'Not much bloody good against a bazooka or helicopter gun-ship, is it?' The Sergeant turned his back on the Inspector.

I went to my fate unarmed and didn't hear anything suspicious other than the crickets, scuttling bugs and bodily noises emanating from the slumbering prisoners in the sleep-inducing heat and humidity. I had counted the prisoners a dozen times, so made myself comfortable awaiting the feared attack by the Drug Cartel rescue party. I must have nodded off when what felt like a violent blow struck me on the back of the head. I shouted, jumped up and grabbed my truncheon ready to fight. A set of heavy boots came across the car park as Sgt Bodden appeared at the outer steel gate brandishing his revolver. 'What's happening, boy?'

I had glanced around and seen nothing was amiss but didn't want to admit my startled cry. 'I heard a shout as well, I think it came from over there.' I pointed towards the town centre and the Sergeant made his way in that general direction as I tried to work out what had actually happened. The prisoners were asleep and everything appeared calm and undisturbed as the desk top fan whirred gently away until something hit the desk with a pulse-raising thud. It was a frog about three inches long that jumped from the desk top to the wall then clambered back up, and across the ceiling where it was trying to make its way to a tasty and unsuspecting nest of bugs up in the eaves. I did not even try to explain that one to the Sergeant.

Carlos and his girlfriend Suzy were staying in the same complex as myself and Rupert at the Blue Oyster Club but were hoping to move closer to the town, so they had only unpacked the essentials. They were great company and one evening Rupert and I were relaxing with them enjoying a cooling bottle of beer. Amongst the half-opened packing cases I saw a couple of commemorative Interpol and Europol wooden plaques wrapped in protective tissue paper. I examined the unmarked plaques and as Carlos was busy upstairs, asked Suzy where they had come from.

'Carlos bought them when he went over to The Hague on a day trip last year,' she said.

A few days later Rupert and I were on patrol around George Town. We had been told that our ceremonial pith helmets would need to be bleached brilliant white before we used them, so we called in to a shopping mall where I had seen a small sports equipment shop.

'Hello gents, how you doing?'

'Just fine, thanks,' I said. 'Do you have any shoe whitener?'

'There's a rack of it over there. I thought for a moment that you were Carlos coming to pick up his plaques – I've just finished engraving them, they look great.'

'Carlos's plaques?' Both Rupert and I repeated the words and looked at each other with a growing smile. 'Can we have a quick look?'

'No problem.' He picked up a couple of slim cardboard boxes and placed them carefully on the glass counter. The first bore the legend: *To Carlos. In appreciation for all your work fighting crime around the world. Best wishes from Interpol.*

The second plaque read: *To Carlos. With grateful thanks from all your colleagues in Europol.*

'Do you want to take them now?'

'Oh no,' I said. 'I imagine Carlos would prefer to pick them up himself.'

Both plaques were later displayed in pride of place on the wall at Carlos and Suzy's beautiful new apartment. I smiled every time I saw them.

CHAPTER 8

THE SINGLE LIFE

It must be the warm sunshine, holiday atmosphere and reggae music that contributes significantly to the topic of sex being a staple day-to-day conversation on the island. Moving to a new shift or unit back in the UK would initiate small talk involving a brief introduction regarding where you lived, worked, school you attended etc. In Cayman, members of my new shift cut straight to the chase. 'How many children do you have?'

This was greeted with total incredulity when the only answer was, 'None that I'm aware of.'

'What about wives?' This was the next question and received a similar response. One female Cayman officer on the shift was WPC 'Martini Henry'. Martini was actually her nickname, which she felt was quite upper class and happy to answer to. Unbeknown to her it was actually as a result of her constant string of boyfriends and related to the old theme tune for the alcoholic drink of the same name. *'Any time, any place, anywhere…'*

Martini had taken it upon herself to make herself available to all the new UK arrivals, and I don't mean as a tour guide. Rupert was sitting behind the front enquiry desk reading a very heavy book when she sidled up to him. 'Why is there no pictures in the big book?' He ignored this novel chat-up line so she tried a different tack. 'Don't you want to have a bit of fun with Martini?'

'No, I'd sooner stick pins in my eyes.' Rupert slammed the book closed and walked off.

This response to her hidden charms was met by her most considered opinion. 'He must be gay.'

I shook my head. 'He just doesn't fancy you – difficult to believe, eh?' Martini shrugged her diminutive shoulders, which caused her generous backside to wobble as she wandered off along the corridor in search of further prey.

The Cayman Island Tourist Board are an imaginative bunch and came up with all sorts of ways of creating more and more reasons to visit the islands. The innovative ideas included extending the Queen's Birthday bank holiday into a week of celebrations exploring the history of the relationship with the UK. Another example focused on remembering part of the buccaneering past of the islands' occupants during Pirate's Week every October, when the tourist numbers were dwindling due to the threat from approaching hurricanes. Other events included Million Dollar Month in June when this massive cash prize attracted expensive and luxurious boats from the entire region including the USA, intent on catching the largest trophy fish possible such as marlin and sailfish.

Spring Break week encouraged wealthy students to visit the island in the sunshine after enduring a bitter winter in the US and Canada. The islands' bars and clubs were teeming with students intending to have a good time and often throwing caution and certain items of clothing to the four winds. It was all great fun and lots of parties were enjoyed around the hotels and apartments along Seven Mile Beach.

Constable Benbow was one of the younger local officers out on beach patrol at midnight when he came upon the sound of high jinks and subdued laughter emanating from a pool area within a select beachfront condominium. He decided it was his duty to investigate and after peering through a thick hedge, discovered around a dozen young female students skinny-dipping in the pool. He then climbed through the prickly hedge to surprise them and began to take down their particulars – not that anybody had them readily available. Benbow stood them in a line along the poolside and began to report them for public nudity. You couldn't make it up, could you?

Meanwhile, my life in the Blue Oyster Club with Rupert was beginning to wear a little thin, especially when trying to sleep without a/c during the day following night duty. There was a new hotel complex approaching completion along Seven Mile Beach, so during my next shift I parked the squad car near to the reception area where there was a large sign welcoming me to Caribbean Suites. The gardener was tending to an attractive series of blue and pink bougainvillea box hedges framing the driveway and in answer to my enquiry pointed me through to the front atrium. Stepping out into the gorgeous inner courtyard I found the owner balancing uncomfortably on a rickety step ladder trying to tie a string of brightly coloured lights around the thatched roof above the cabana pool bar. I secured a couple of strands, helped him down and he introduced himself as Horatio, the rotund owner, developer and manager of this beautiful hotel suites complex.

He was happy to show me around and we went inside one of the suites. It was aimed at very discerning American tourists who were willing to spend a lot of dollars to get luxurious holiday accommodation, and the quality showed. The suite had an emperor-sized bedroom, bathroom, kitchen, dining/living room overlooking the pool. It even had a pull-out sofa bed for the stream of visitors who were threatening to visit.

'Have you got many bookings yet?' I asked.

'Not yet, but the busy time will be Christmas and New Year when it'll be full,' Horatio said.

'In the meantime, would you consider renting a suite to me?'

Horatio pursed his lips. 'If I agree, you'll have to leave for the month over Christmas and New Year, okay?'

'That won't be a problem, I was intending to go back to the UK anyway to spend it with my family. How much would you charge?'

'If I include a/c, satellite TV, cleaning twice a week, towels, bedding and all utilities, how much can you afford?'

I was trying to work out how much I could live on when he interrupted. 'Well let's put it this way, how much do you earn a month?'

'Two thousand dollars,' I said.

'That's not bloody much, is it? Can you live on half?'

After some quick mental arithmetic, 'Yes, I think so.'

Horatio shook my hand firmly. 'That's a deal for a thousand bucks a month and you can have free breakfast at the weekend, okay? Oh, by the way, you'll have some company here. I've already agreed to rent one to another of you English guys.'

'What's his name?'

'It's that pompous guy, Rupert – you'll know him.'

Crestfallen, my shoulders must have dropped to the bottom of the pool. I admitted to sharing a villa together.

'You poor bastard,' he said. 'But don't worry, he was so desperate to move in, I'm charging him an extra two hundred bucks a month. Don't let on now…'

Horatio smiled and tapped the side of his nose conspiratorially.

*

There were a number of high-quality jewellers shops dotted around George Town, selling expensive watches, bracelets and other valuable goodies of interest to the tourists. Mr Brown was a delightful man who owned a smaller establishment on one of the side streets with an attractive window where all types of treasures were displayed. Being nosy is a great attribute for any police officer and I always used it to its full potential. I was allowed through the bulletproof door which was buzzed open on sight of my uniform. The owner introduced himself and his sales assistant who also happened to be his daughter. A glass of chilled water was provided as he showed me the contents of various display cabinets filled with carefully selected treasure. There were doubloons, pieces of eight, sovereigns, lumps of silver and strings of pearls sensitively arranged with price tags clearly displayed. It was all well above my limited means but intriguing none the less.

'Hardly any treasure has been discovered on the island but there are rumours,' Mr Brown said as my ears pricked up.

'Think of what this island was used for, it was a stopping-off point along the Spanish Main and not very strategic. Do you want to see some real treasure?' He took me through to an inner room that was secured behind us. Working his magic on a further combination lock released a huge vault door that swung open without a sound. He slid open a felt-lined drawer and removed a heavy blue velvet drawstring bag which he placed on a table in the centre of the vault. Mr Brown opened the cord and using both hands brought out an item wrapped in cloth and began to unfold it. It was about the size of a slim paperback book and glistened beneath the bright lights of the vault.

'It is solid gold, would you like to hold it?'

I gingerly picked it up as it was surprisingly heavy for its size, weighing five and a half pounds. The ingot was roughly crafted and not like the smooth bars pictured in the vaults of the Bank of England with regular distinctive hallmarks. It was heavily marked with deep dents and gouges around its surface but had a rich, lustrous glow.

'Where's it from?'

'I got it from an auction of treasure recovered from a Spanish galleon shipwrecked near the Bahamas. This is a single ingot from a shipload of treasure ships making their way from the Spanish Main back to Spain. They were destroyed in a hurricane that hit the 1715 Plate Fleet after they tried to outrun the British Navy, privateers and buccaneers. Sensibly, the British took shelter before the hurricane hit, sending the entire Spanish fleet to the bottom of the ocean. Dozens of ships were lost each with a crew of 30 or 40 men with hundreds of bars of gold, silver and coins. It'd be impossible to calculate the value – probably billions in today's money.'

It was quite spooky to be holding this piece of history and of the hands it had passed through. Not merely because of the lives of the perished sailors but also those of the Mayans or indigenous peoples from Mexico. My mind went to those that had dug for the gold then crafted it into beautiful works of art before the conquistadors came, stole it from them and melted it down to this ugly, more transportable shape.

I asked the inevitable question: 'How much is it worth?'

'About 250 thousand dollars,' Mr Brown admitted in a whisper. 'It's part of my pension.'

Sadly, he never did get to reap the benefits of that as this pleasant, welcoming man was to die suddenly and senselessly a few short months later, but it's a memory that has long stayed with me, just as has the effects of the island.

I returned to the police station and took over the front desk duties where it was notable that an increasing number of callers were asking to speak to one of the new English officers. In the main it was a minor matter that was easily resolved but often members of the public preferred an independent listener – not a local officer that knew them and the background to the issue. A bit like telling your sins to the parish priest in the confessional – you would prefer them not to recognise you.

Sgt Bodden was preparing a meal and offered me some of the 'World's Tastiest Fish'. He handed me a portion and mixed it with rice and peas. I munched away happily and asked what it was.

'It's barracuda – the World's Tastiest Fish.'

'Very nice and tasty,' I agreed with just a few morsels left.

'But you got to be careful with 'cuda,' he added. 'Normally we use ants.'

'Ants. What for?'

'It's often poisoned but there ain't no good way of telling?'

'Do you have to eat the ants or something?'

'No, man. Before you eat it, you sprinkle a bit on the ground and let the ants try it. If they don't eat it, neither do you.'

I took the plate outside the front of the station in search of a convenient ants' nest where I dropped the remainder of the meal. My heart sank as the insects went up to it, sniffed it and walked away in disgust. But luckily I lived to see another day.

When it rained it was always a torrential downpour and provided a beautiful sight when the thunderstorms happened at night. Often you would not hear the thunder but could see the forked lightning far out to sea stroking the horizon for hours at a time. It was always pleasant to sit in the dryness of the cabana, enjoying the warm air, watching nature's free firework display going on in the background – I was gradually getting into this lifestyle.

The afternoon shift was to the cells for a couple of hours looking after the inmates, of which our regular, George, was the most sensible in spite of him being totally barking mad. There was no permanent facility on the island to detain those with mental health issues of a dangerous nature, so Jamaica was called upon to hold those needing permanent secure treatment facilities. George was about 6 feet 8 inches tall, weighing over 20 stone, and subject to spasmodic episodes of poor mental health. His parents were local business owners who arranged for him to be held temporarily in the police cells until his medication kicked in. He was a complete gentleman, very respectful, and when I came on duty he saw me and called out from his cell.

'You from England, boss? Has the Queen sent you to look after us, man?'

'Yes, George, she certainly has and she asked me personally to send you her best wishes and hopes you feel better soon.'

'Thank her, boss, when you sees her again.'

George's parents called in to see him every day and brought him food and batteries for his only possession, a ginormous ghetto blaster. He was usually stark naked and stood at the cell gate for hours on end. That particular day he continued to play one particular song at full volume, over and over again. 'A Message to You Rudy' by the Specials, for the benefit of a neighbouring cellmate of that name who had told him to turn it off.

Neither George nor I knew it then but towards the end of my time in Grand Cayman he was to be instrumental in helping me uncover the identity of a key corrupt official.

PART II

UNHOLY SPIRITS

CHAPTER 9

THE ISLAND OF LOST SOULS

Monday evening between five and six was Happy Hour in the Police Club where the drinks were half price and all the UK boys turned up, but most were anything but happy. It was now midsummer and we had been on the island for about three months. The heat on the islands was at its most extreme at this time of the year and we were glad of the roaring, clanking a/c units sticking out of the window trying to cool the room. Some were cheesed off with the world, short of money, hot, sticky and unable to use any air-conditioning in their accommodation. Alec had a misty faraway look in his eyes and nursed a beer whilst he played the Blondie song, 'Island of Lost Souls', quietly on his Walkman.

It was one of those times when you could have wished for the cool breeze of the English countryside, but I intended to enjoy every moment I could where I could.

I was a bit homesick and missed the company of my girlfriend but we had kept in touch by very expensive phone calls and regular letters, so I was still very happy to stay and tough it out on the island. Anyway, she was booking flights to come over and visit and I was looking forward to seeing her and showing her the island. Some of my colleagues remained miserable, but the next day I got on with enjoying my adventure on the islands and went and bought a car ad magazine to source my own Jeep from Florida. I made a full English cooked breakfast and set about finding a car. You could not be depressed with a pot of tea, a spot of sunshine followed by toast and marmalade. I saw a couple of likely Jeeps at a reasonable price and rang the dealers in Miami and Fort Lauderdale where they regularly shipped cars to the island. All the other problems dissipated like the morning mist over the calm sea as the sun rose high in the sky.

The increasing heat of the summer had an unexpected effect on the flora and fauna of the island, which other than man-made cultivation, tended to be palm trees and mangrove swamps. To become more familiar with the unnamed roads and lanes, I drove around the area of Prospect and came upon a wonder of nature. Seemingly overnight a tunnel of scarlet foliage had erupted from Royal poinciana trees that lined the inner coast road. They were like Christmas poinsettia plants but towered above the road, touching in the middle. As the petals began to fall over the following days, they created a beautiful deep carpet of orangey-red blooms that seemed a crime to drive over.

One hot and humid day, after a heavy tropical downpour, I drove along West Bay Road where the cars in front slowed down and abruptly stopped. Very slowly the queue began to move forward, I presumed to avoid the flood water. Glancing past them the road surface appeared to be moving very slowly towards the beach and inexplicably pedestrians began to jump and dance, kicking out at some invisible being. I stopped the squad car and got out to investigate.

Here was another remarkable work of nature that would not

be stopped. Hundreds of thousands of female crabs had left the swamps and flowed like brown lava towards the beach to deposit their eggs in the sea. They kept on coming and coming; only death would prevent them reaching their destination. It went on for hours all the way up and down the road in spite of the man-made structures blocking their way. They clogged drains, drowned in swimming pools and cracked their claws into air-conditioning units that were preventing their progress along the historic route. It seemed cruel but cars and trucks began to crunch over them to continue their own essential journeys along West Bay Road and in a couple of hours the depleted numbers of empty, exhausted crabs sidled sideways back to the safety of the swamps.

The Queen's Birthday was the culmination of a week of celebrations including an air show and the visitation of numerous warships from around the region. The Royal Navy was represented together with US Navy, US Coastguard, US National Guard, French Navy and even a sail training ship from the Royal Netherlands Navy. The ships were brightly festooned with flags and pennants along the masts from stem to stern. There was even a suggestion that an Italian frigate had been sighted approaching the harbour, but after seeing all the other nations' warships it ran up its ensign of a white cross on a white background and quietly departed. We expected a bit of fuss from the drunken sailors but none surfaced over the weekend. The harbour and the entire bay was a beautiful sight especially at night with all the vessels and warships lit up and decorated more dramatically than the trams during the Blackpool Illuminations.

As Bank Holiday Monday dawned, I had prepared my uniform to a very high standard. My boots were polished, or bulled, to a mirror finish; my pith helmet whitened to reflect all the sun's rays;

my white tunic and trousers had been ironed to perfection. My bright red braces would allow the blue trousers with the red vertical stripe to be displayed to the best effect even though I felt it looked a little like a dashing Wild West cavalry officer.

The parade formed up outside the police station where we attached the gleaming sharp bayonets to the Lee Enfield .303 rifles, thus creating a very dangerous spectacle as, unsurprisingly, we began prodding each other with our new toys. We led the parade into the town centre following the police band and lined up beside groups from all the organisations on the island. The heat was intense as we waited and I glanced down at my boots to see that the bull was melting and the polish was no longer shining in the sunshine. The helmet shielded most of the heat but as we stood absolutely still, awaiting the VIPs' arrival, the beads of perspiration dripped uncomfortably down my face as I wasn't able to wipe them away.

The Governor was resplendent in white trousers, tunic and pith helmet adorned with a plume of ostrich feathers, to keep the flies off I presume. He wore a chest full of medals and his sword clanked up the podium to take the Royal Salute. We marched past to the strains of the band playing the Monty Python theme tune that drowned out the orders of the parade commander, but it seemed to pass off without any embarrassment. At the conclusion of the event we attended the 'Tea and Sticky Buns' Garden Party at Governor's House, resplendent in our formal tropical uniforms and had great fun enjoying the free drinks and sandwiches.

I was careful not to enjoy the party too much as I was back on guard duty at GH at 3pm and I imagined that it would pass off as a nice, quiet bank holiday afternoon, but how wrong could I have been?

CHAPTER 10

DUKE AND THE PALE HORSE

A new American member of staff had joined my shift after completing the initial training course. His nickname was 'Duke' as someone had told him he reminded them of Big John Wayne – I have no idea why. Duke was about 6 feet 2 inches tall and wide but he was around 20 stone of pure blubber and wore round steel-framed spectacle lenses glazed to NASA re-entry shield specification. He was just 19 years old and had just begun to shave and, in his quest to appear mature, was trying to cultivate his facial fluff into a luscious moustache. Hailing from the deep southern state of Mississippi, he had amazingly already been a deputy sheriff for a short while before deciding a change of law enforcement agency was called for. I asked why he had applied to come here.

'Well, boy, I was a deputy sheriff and decided to leave after a bad ass shot at me, missing my shoulder by six inches.'

'Wow,' Rupert interrupted, 'which bit of your head did he hit?'

I drove Duke up to GH where I showed him the duties and responsibilities of looking after the Governor and the compound. The Queen's Birthday festivities were still in full swing and the Governor's Garden Party was just coming to an end as Duke decided to salute everyone that left through the main gates – just in case they were important. The public holiday had encouraged huge numbers of visitors to the beach to enjoy the watersports, picnics and BBQs. We had just walked out on to the beach when a lady in floods of tears ran up to us. She was breathless, carrying a mask and snorkel, dripping from the sea. 'You've got to help me, I was snorkelling with my daughter and we were a long way out when a speed boat came between us. I can't find her, she's only 10!'

I used my radio to ask for the inshore police boat *Lima 1* to be sent to search the area. The reply from the control room was unsettling.

'He's gone home after having too much rum punch at the garden party.'

Lima 2, the larger police boat, had been damaged months ago when it had hit a reef and was lounging in the harbour, awaiting repair. The crew had been reassigned as police tailors so my options were limited, other than getting them to instantly sew a new boat for me, I suppose. Nearby, an off-duty sergeant came over to help. I told Duke to take the distressed mother into GH and calm her down. I decided to commandeer the nearest boat and search for the missing girl, so we ran along the beach and saw a beautiful blood-red speed boat tootling by. I shouted and waved at it and the driver jumped out and swam to shore, still wearing his sunglasses. It was Sgt Benjamin – the Force Armourer! I explained the situation and he brought the boat in close enough for me to scramble on board as we took off to seek the missing snorkeller.

The sea is a very large place, especially when you are looking for a very small object, and we combed the area for a long time fearing the worst and looking out for the girl. We criss-crossed the bay out as far as the reef protecting us from the bottomless Cayman Trench, stopping each craft we encountered to make them aware of our search. After a long drawn-out search of around an hour, it was not looking good. We did not want to hit the reef as it would slice through the hull of our boat and no one would be coming to rescue us, so our options were fading. Then we spotted something coloured red just beneath the surface, very close to the reef. Benjamin slowed the engines to a stop and we drifted up to it on a calm steady swell. It was motionless and drifting with only the movement of the waves as we came gently alongside. We looked at each other without any comment as we closed in on this lifeless shape and I felt an unpleasant tightening within my abdomen.

I shielded my eyes from the glare and saw it was a young girl in a bright red swimming costume with a snorkel breaking through the surface of the sea and my heart sunk. There was no sign of life.

I gently touched her long dark brown hair, rippling along her back, then suddenly her head popped up with a surprised look across her freckled face. She removed the snorkel and goggles to the top of her head.

'Hello' I said. 'Are you alright?'

'Yes, I'm fine, how are you?'

'Do you know how far out you are?'

She glanced back towards the distant beach, probably two miles away. 'Oh sorry, I didn't realise. I've been following that beautiful turtle.' She pointed down to a leatherback turtle about 20 feet below, swimming steadily away from the beach.

'Your mum's been worried about you. Let's take you back in.'

Much relieved, we helped her aboard and headed back to Governor's Beach where I could see the large outline of Duke standing beside her mum, the butler and his wife. As we approached the beach, the girl jumped into the water and swam up to her mum where they had a heart-warming embrace that gave me a large lump in my throat. The next problem was how to get me back on to shore without getting too wet. I offered to remove my boots and socks, roll up my trouser legs and jump in, but the two gallant sergeants decided against that. Sgt Benjamin placed the speed boat parallel to the beach then they both jumped in to the sea, and with my arms around their shoulders they carried me from the boat up the beach like a conquering hero. As we approached the shallows Benjamin whispered in my ear, 'Thank God it wasn't Duke, we'd have needed a bloody forklift truck.'

They plonked me on the sand to the rapturous applause of the reception committee that now included the Governor, his wife and dozens of onlookers. I gave a theatrical bow to my rescuers, thanked them enthusiastically and let them resume their normal relaxing public holiday on the beach. All in all, it had been a wonderful day.

The following week Rupert and I were due to move out of the Blue Oyster Club and into our new lodgings, but Rupert announced that evening, 'I think I'm going to resign and go home.'

'Any particular reason?'

'I'm going to go under the ill-health clause.'

'You seem healthy enough to me.'

'I'll just tell the Commissioner I'm sick of the place.'

I'll admit, I now felt far easier about the situation and I went out to enjoy a pleasant bottle of beer in the cabana and watch the thousands of stars uninterrupted by any ambient light. The roaring and crashing of the waves along the shore reinforced my intention to tough it out and get through the difficulties as it would get better once I got my Jeep, moved into Caribbean Suites and settled into the more relaxed way of working here.

Duke had one great endearing quality – he owned a pickup truck. He called it the 'Pale Horse' even though it was dark green, so I asked him to help move me out of the Blue Oyster Club to my hotel suite, with the promise of a meal and a couple of flagons of beer. Moving into the hotel was like switching on a light in a dingy cellar. I knew it would be the single most important way to enjoy the island with all of the attractions – and it certainly was. I took Duke to the Lord Nelson English Bar for a slap-up meal: steak and kidney pie, chips and peas washed down with two pints of foaming British ale. It was supposed to represent an inn providing sustenance to the British Fleet in Portsmouth in the 1800s. I had anticipated a plethora of amenable serving wenches with part-exposed bosoms calling me 'dearie' and singing raucous sea shanties. Unfortunately, the only person pulling the pints was a local chap wearing a bandana who when you ordered a drink muttered, 'Yo, ho, ho and a bottle of rum.'

'No thanks,' said Duke, 'just a beer.'

From then on, Duke and I became good friends – he meant well and continued to try hard so it was easy to help him, but he also provided much-needed entertainment. I was assigned to carry out beach patrol with him, which involved a walk up Seven Mile Beach starting at 11pm until around 3am. It was hot and sticky, so you had to dress in overalls to prevent the sandflies and mosquitoes eating you alive. I paraded for duty in the police issue dark blue overall with police signs stitched all over it. Duke turned up wearing facial camouflage paint and full 'Stormin' Norman' combat overalls (Tiger Stripe pattern) that looked like a huge onesie. Naturally, I asked why he was wearing such an article.

'Just in case, man, I've been shot at before.'

'Who by, a great white hunter?'

We went about our duty and checked all the possible sites of concern covering miles of sand, trudging along beaches during the evening before returning to the station. As we entered, Sgt Bodden sat back open-mouthed at the sight of Duke soaked in perspiration with his facial camouflage paint melting and running into an awful mess – i.e. his face.

Duke had been bragging and boasting ad nauseum about his wide policing experience and willing to take on 'any son of a bitch'. This was too good an opportunity to miss, so Carlos and I hatched a little plan as Duke replenished gallons of lost fluids before we continued duty.

It was a calm, misty night with a full moon hovering above the palm trees at 3am when we booked back on duty. The control room told us to attend a suspicious incident along Eastern Avenue in the vicinity of the cemetery. All the other squad cars were busy so Duke volunteered to take us in the Pale Horse. It was all quiet when we arrived, so I called the control room for some extra details of the incident. The reply was basic but concise.

'Some unknown person phoned to say they had heard strange noises coming from inside the graveyard. Can you investigate?'

Any call to a graveyard is a little unnerving but those around the Caribbean have an added layer of concern. The power of the undead is taken seriously, resulting in the distinct lack of local officers volunteering to attend as voodoo/obeah are real in the eyes of the more superstitious people in the West Indies. We pulled up outside the entrance where one of the gates was hanging off its hinges, squeaking in the gentle breeze and distinctly uninviting. The white concrete walls reflected the luminescence of the moon, looking even spookier than normal.

'Come on then Duke, let's see what's going on,' I said.

'No man, I don't see anything out there. Let's drive off and call up in a few minutes – search made – no trace.'

'You're not scared, are you?'

'You shouldn't mess with graveyards – they can be haunted! I didn't mess with them back in Mississippi.'

'That's just a load of nonsense, I don't want to be embarrassed if it's something criminal going on. Come on, off we go.'

I saw Duke rummaging in his glove box. 'What are you doing?' I went around to see.

'I'm taking this just in case.' He was holding a Colt .45 pistol.

Aghast, I said, 'Oh no, you can't take that. Put it back now – you might kill someone.'

A cold trickle of sweat rolled down my back as reluctantly he locked it away and armed only with Maglite torches we entered the silently spooky cemetery, gently stepping on the crushed luminescent marl along the path. The graves were concrete slabs with small headstones and due to the heat there was no grass or living plants separating each plot. A number of the older disfigured gravestones leant at drunken angles like a mouthful of decaying teeth. Previous hurricanes had disturbed the foundations, forcing open the tombs and slabs to reveal sharp, dark shadows in the moonlight. I heard Duke breathing shallowly and encouraged him to keep the torch switched off until we saw something or it might spook any intruder. 'I don't give a shit, man, I'm ready to piss my pants anyhow.'

Suddenly a metallic sound came from inside the graveyard and made us stop dead in our tracks, then we heard it again. Duke whispered, 'Shit man, I'm going back for my pistol...' I grabbed his arm.

'No chance,' I said even quieter. 'We're nearly there.'

I pushed him on as his breathing got louder and less regular. The metallic ting was repeated as we got closer. In the moonlight I saw something move ahead of us, close to a line of headstones, and pointed my arm towards it. I gave Duke a further nudge towards the headstones and the hairs on my nape were standing on edge. Even though I knew what Carlos and I had planned, just being there was still terrifying. The sound of the metallic tings was now being regularly repeated in sharp, urgent bursts of three or four as we closed in upon it...

We got to about 20 feet away from the noise when suddenly Duke turned on his torch to reveal a brightly clad figure glowing with phosphorescence, crouching close to a tall fresh headstone. It held a hammer and chisel in its hands up against the stone. The head slowly turned and we saw huge googly eyes peering straight at us, then a strange, strained, high-pitched despairing voice spoke.

'They spelt my name wrong.'

We both turned and raced back to the road as Duke began screaming, 'Oh shit, oh shit, oh shit man, I think I've crapped my pants!'

He dropped his keys trying to get back in the Pale Horse and as he bent over, I detected an awful smell and saw a tell-tale stain on his Tiger Striped derriere. I could hardly speak as my heart was thumping inside my chest – it was very realistic.

'It's alright, Duke, it's only Carlos playing a little joke on you. Calm down, it's not real.'

At that precise moment a squad car pulled up next to us from the direction of the town centre. The window went down revealing Carlos in full uniform at the steering wheel. 'Sorry about being late boys, I was delayed having a brew with that gorgeous waitress at the Burger Bar.'

Duke and I glanced back to the graveyard, then jumped into the Pale Horse and got the hell out of there.

On this particular day, it was nice to see that there were a couple of naval ships out in the harbour, one from the US Navy and the other from the US Coast Guard. The island was an attractive and welcoming port for all friendly warships around the Caribbean and beyond. It was a safe and secure anchorage for the vessels, and the crew could relax in the bars and restaurants along Seven Mile Beach knowing that they would not be bothered or hassled.

I was the squad car driver on the evening shift and after it went dark at around 6pm, I got a call to attend at the back of the Holiday Inn hotel where a body had been found. On arrival, the security guard offered me a helpful clue: 'I think he's dead, boss.' He then directed me to the area beneath a neighbouring bush.

There was a male lying on his back and clothed in shorts and a garish floral design shirt. As I felt for a pulse, I noted that his knees were both badly scratched, with fresh blood trickling from the wounds that were already covered in ants. I quickly realised he was actually alive and when applying a quick twist to his ear I heard him give a grunt in confirmation. We dragged him out of his shelter as he kept hold of an empty bottle of rum. I went through his pockets and found a US Military ID badge in his empty wallet and deposited him in the squad car. The Sergeant suggested arresting him and putting him in the cells, but I convinced him that in this case discretion was the most sensible option. He wasn't fighting or being obnoxious – he was just fast asleep.

The next question was: 'What do we do with the drunken sailor?' Arresting him would only result in him missing his ship, receiving a fine and court martial, which to me seemed out of all proportion. So I deposited him with the US Shore Patrol who had based themselves down by the clock tower adjacent to the harbour.

'Is he one of yours?' I asked the officer in charge.

He gave a shake of the head. 'I don't recognise him but he can join us anyway.' They carried him up the gangplank and put him aboard the US Navy vessel.

As I watched the ships depart early the following morning I considered whether I had actually witnessed the modern 'press gang' in action.

*

Keeping fit on the island was reasonably straight forward as long as you kept out of the searing midday heat. Most days, having a game of tennis or squash or an energetic swim in the sea was a fantastic way of keeping fit, both physically and mentally. The more time I spent on the island, the more friends I made and now, having been there for a few months, I was really enjoying myself.

One acquaintance was Burt, who worked for the Mosquito Research Laboratory and flew the tiny but noisy plane that sprayed poison and diesel fuel on to the swamps to kill the insect larvae. He was a regular sight buzzing around at dusk as he flew at the height of the palm trees and sprayed the swamps. You can imagine the oppressing presence of mosquitoes on the island, which were a complete pest and appeared at dusk disturbing many happy-hour drinking events in the evenings. They lived in the mangrove swamps behind the main residential areas around the islands and a number of initiatives were used to try and bump off these non-malarial irritants. We used to meet up with Burt at the Lone Star Bar and Grill where he regaled us with tall tales of wrestling with lions and biting snakes to death during his previous life in Rhodesia (he refused to call it Zimbabwe).

One evening a little later than normal, I was out for a jog along one of the marl tracks that criss-crossed the swamps behind Captain Morgan's Harbour. Out of the blue the mosquito plane buzzed me at around 20 feet above my head. I gave Burt a friendly wave and he waggled his wings in recognition before he banked steeply in a sharp turn and came roaring back at me from the front. I heard his laugh over the roar of the engine as he deposited the entire contents of the spray tanks over me, bringing my run to an abrupt end in a series of coughs, sneezes and wheezes. For days afterwards I kept away from all candles and naked flames in case my diesel-filled lungs made me give a poor impression of a fire-breathing dragon. But I took it in good faith, all the while feeling more comfortable every day on the island I was coming to know more about.

I was becoming familiar with the more negative sides of the island too though. 'Toadface' was an unpleasant local hoodlum who I'd had a couple of interactions with in the short time I had been on the island. He lived in a shack in the down-at-heel area called Dog City and was a minor drug dealer with ideas above his station who was regularly arrested for minor matters. He had been detained for beating up an addict that had not paid for his drug supply, and Toadface himself was now feigning a medical ailment. Rupert, who was still weighing up whether he even wanted to stay on the force, was assigned to look after him at the hospital where he was examined by the medical staff. Prior to leaving the hospital clinic, Toadface politely asked to use the toilet and was allowed to do so.

A few minutes later Rupert entered the toilet to check and – surprise, surprise – Toadface had escaped through the small window and, as his name suggested, hopped off back to the swamps. A large-scale search was launched without finding him and Rupert wandered around looking at the floor in total embarrassment. The Drugs Squad was even more annoyed as they had been hoping to search various locations after an informer had reported that the escapee had access to a pistol which was hidden in the swamps. The rest of the day was spent scouring the island and various haunts for him without success.

There was no chance of Toadface leaving the island, so his escape must have been to move the gun and hide his stash of illicit drugs. There had not been any sightings of him until two days later when Rupert and I left the police station just after 3pm. A tall distinguished-looking man wearing a formal suit with a clerical collar approached us in the front car park and asked if either of us was Rupert.

With a nod from Rupert, the man identified himself as a local pastor who had been contacted by Toadface who wished to give himself up.

'Where is he now?' Rupert asked.

The pastor pointed over to a car with blacked-out windows. 'He's in there, but wants me to confirm that you won't beat him up for escaping.' We looked at each other incredulously at the sheer mention of that, nodded in agreement and the pastor went over to speak to him.

Rupert and I quickly agreed that he needed to enhance his 'street cred' and embellish the version of how he had traced and apprehended the escapee after much detective work. Toadface walked up to us with a smirk on his face and we took hold of him and returned him to the cells.

The following day I took Toadface to the courts where Justice Rudyard sentenced him to a 'seven-day lie down' whilst enquiries were ongoing relating to his alleged offences. His girlfriend was at the hearing and as I was taking him to the cells to wait for the escorting squad car, she stopped me and asked, 'Can I just speak to my lover, boss?' I locked him in the cell and allowed her to speak to him through the closed hatch to say their fond farewells. I made a point of noisily walking off telling her I would be back in a few minutes, then quietly returned to listen to their 'private' conversation – unseen. Stupidly they continued their conversation as if I was not there.

Toadface: 'Did ye' get the gun from the house?'

Girlfriend: 'Yeah.'

Toadface: 'Well, what about the other one?'

Girlfriend: 'Susan say she take it and put it so nobody find it!'

Earwigging constable: 'Right, so you're locked up as well.'

Toadface: 'Shit man, why didn't you check, you stupid bitch.'

I put her in another cell and arranged for them to be arrested and collected independently, and conveyed to the police cells to let the CID investigate further. I mean, I had done all the investigating so far – it was only fair to let them do something.

At that time I certainly had no inkling that Toadface was to feature in further incidents during my time on the island, one of which resulted in the brutal death of one of my friends.

I continued to make much of life on the tropical paradise and scraped the money together for a diving course. The PADI scuba course was run from Parrots Landing over a couple of weekends, which I passed with flying colours. It was great fun to be able to dive down to 30 feet exploring the boats that had been purposefully sunk for this reason. The clarity of the warm water enabled me to see up to 100 feet away, providing freedom to explore with a dive buddy a vivid array of colourful fish and coral around the reefs protecting the island. It was a wonderful experience and I could remember the sight and sound of an old television programme featuring Jacques Cousteau on board his dive boat *Calypso* on his various adventures exploring the undersea world. I doubt that the clarity of the sea here could be matched anywhere else on earth.

A few weeks later I went back to the UK for a family function and my return flight was delayed by four hours by the time I arrived at Miami but it actually suited me as I had always intended to stay over and scour Florida to find a suitable Jeep to buy. On the plane over the Atlantic, I had struck up a pleasant conversation with a couple of Danish language students – Inga and Torhild – who were destined to study Spanish in the mountains of Mexico. As they had also missed their connecting flight, Pan Am booked us into the same hotel, so I rented a car and all three of us enjoyed an excellent meal paid for by the airline and a trip around the eclectic nightlife of Miami Beach. They were really pleasant company and I thoroughly enjoyed the evening. The following morning, I dropped them off at the airport and we exchanged addresses with an invitation to meet up if we ever got the chance.

On my return to the islands and work, Inspector McDougal reduced the level of morale by forcing the UK officers onto the streets of George Town. He told us we were not to return until we had reported someone for a minor infringement, and issued us with more books of 'traffi ticki.' Rupert, Carlos and I wandered into the town centre and sat in the Jamaican Pattie Shop until we sighted a likely customer. It was all quite pathetic really.

Rupert pounced on an unsuspecting cyclist with a deflated tyre: $25 – 'ker-ching.'

Carlos spied a driver who had stopped too close to a pedestrian crossing: $25– 'ker-ching.'

I stopped an ancient cyclist by the name of Appleton General. He was riding a tatty Raleigh 'sit up and beg' bicycle with a dark brown leather saddle that was as wrinkled and battered as his skin. He was a lovely old man originally from Jamaica who told me he had worked on ships around the world. His unusual name originated from his father's love of a particular brand of Jamaican rum and he told me all these facts with a glint in his heavily bloodshot eyes and a flash of bright white teeth. One ridiculous local law required all bikes to have a government issued 'tag' that had to be attached to the rear of the saddle.

'Have you got a tag?'

'No, sir, I haven't got the money to buy one.'

'You understand you should have bought one – it's only $10, you know.'

'Yes, sir, I understand, but I've only got $20 to last me 'til my war pension gets paid next month.'

'War pension?'

'Yes, sir, I served as a stoker in His Majesty's Royal Navy in the Atlantic convoys during the war.'

'Oh, I see.' I looked around, ready to use my discretion and send him off with a word of advice but saw the Inspector parked up in a squad car watching me intently.

'I'm sorry but I've got to give you a traffic ticket for not having a tag on the bike. You'll have to pay a $10 fine.' I felt absolutely awful. I began to write out the ticket and handed it to him. He was calm and accepted it in good grace.

'You've got to do your duty, sir.' Then took the ticket from my hand.

Out of the corner of my eye I noticed the Inspector drive away, presumably well satisfied that I had finally succumbed to his ridiculous orders. I couldn't let the old chap starve so I delved into my pocket where I had $10 for my lunch and handed it to him.

'Listen Mr General, please use this money to go and buy yourself a tag so I don't have to go through this again.' He took it carefully and folded it into his battered ancient wallet then thanked me and the 'Good Lord' and cycled off on his way.

Later that week, I was up at the rifle range having a reclassification and passed with a score of 180, which seemed pretty good to me. Duke was next and achieved over 200. 'It's all the practice shooting the black out of the Ace of Spades, boy!'

Sgt Benjamin's radio burst into life. 'You're needed at the airport – the US Navy is chasing suspected armed drug dealers in a plane heading towards the island.'

He pointed at Duke and I. 'You two are coming with me for some real action!'

We got to the airport fully tooled up to be told that the plane had landed two hours previously with a couple of tourists and a broken radio. 'Operation Damp Squib' came to a premature end.

I drove home and saw Rupert slowly walking along the road towards Governor's Harbour with his shoulders hunched. I pulled up and saw a sad-faced young man with red-rimmed eyes. 'It's all finished,' he said. 'I've been sending her letters and phoning her and she's just rung me. She wants us to finish.'

His girlfriend had continued to live in his house back in the UK and didn't even want to visit him. I couldn't blame her but I pretended to be sympathetic. 'Look on the bright side,' I said. 'Why don't you kick her out of your house and get some rent from it.' He started blubbing a little bit more.

'She's denying it but I know she's seeing someone else!'

'Oh, I see, that's not good is it, but I suppose it could be worse?'

'No, it couldn't be worse – he's a traffic officer!'

I suddenly developed the greatest sympathy for him; it was just typical of a traffic officer to be so devious and underhanded – the absolute rotter. Rupert went to see Mr Jones and explained his predicament, which resulted in permission being granted for him to take leave and then return to the island within a fortnight.

I knew Rupert wasn't happy, so I had a feeling he would leave the island soon, and therefore I'd have no access to his car. It spurred me on to fly to Miami and buy that Jeep – it sounds like a hassle but it was a commonplace journey with daily flights to and from the island. I settled on one in my price bracket and arranged for it to be shipped down to the island. The rest of the day in Florida was used to buy all the difficult-to-purchase or expensive items unavailable on the island. I even managed to drive down to the Florida Keys after hearing that catchy tune and tried to find the world famous Key Largo, but unfortunately I blinked and missed it.

CHAPTER 11

OBEAH / VOODOO

The Cayman Islands Penal Code was jam-packed with laws and legislation that had been handed over to them when they were part of Jamaica, and many had not been removed from the statute books since they'd parted ways. Many of the laws were quaintly endearing, such as 'insulting the modesty of a woman' for which you could go to prison for three years. Whereas others harked back to earlier buccaneering days and included substantial fines or prison terms for:

- Duelling
- Emptying 'night soil' (poo) onto the road between 4am and 10pm
- Discharging a cannon in George Town

The practices of witchcraft, casting a spell or paying someone to catch a guppy (spirit) were also outlawed, although still practised and indeed revered by the more superstitious residents in the island.

Obeah was an altogether more serious matter. Outside the Caribbean it is called voodoo and has been the subject of many hours of film, TV and horror stories, but the actual belief and practice of it in the Cayman Islands took me by surprise, especially when I experienced its power, first-hand. In modern Jamaica, the practice of obeah has morphed into one where criminals, policemen and other members of society from all economic classes tend to visit the practitioners for protection from evil spirits and to keep them free from harm in their daily lives. In this modern day and age, a centuries-old tradition is still surrounded by mystique and is highly feared and misunderstood by most.

It was one of those hot and sticky summer mornings when tempers are easily frayed. I was driving the ancient patrol car Zulu 1, which had an inefficient air-conditioning unit, and I was accompanied by an inefficient colleague. Benbow was a young Caymanian officer and inexperienced, but his 'get-up-and-go' had already got up and gone. He was content to tell me all about the adventures he'd had during his 18-year life and the extraordinary number of girlfriends he had. At 10am the radio grumbled into life and told us that a fight was taking place outside Marmaduke's Bar on the south side of George Town. There was not much happening when we pulled up outside but leaning against the doorpost was a fat, dark-skinned man of middle-age who wore a trilby decorated with myriad rainbow-coloured feathers. I opened the conversation.

'Morning, has there been a bit of a fight here?'

'I don't know nothing, white man.'

Not exactly helpful. I was suddenly regretting my decision to skip breakfast.

'Let's try again,' I said. 'What's been going on here, then?'

'White man, why don't you go back to England?'

'What's your name, then?'

He pointed át the sign above the door.

'Well, Mr Marmaduke…'

'It's Professor Marmaduke, white boy, an' don't you forget it.'

Oh dear, I thought. It must have been approaching the full moon, so I'd better humour him.

'What are you a professor of…?'

'A Professor of Spirits, white boy, a Professor of Spirits, an' don't you forget it…'

I wasn't likely to. The engine of Zulu 1 suddenly started up and Benbow was in the driving seat, so I tapped on the window. He put it down an inch and when I asked him what he was doing, he glanced back towards Marmaduke.

'You shouldn't mess with him, he's an obeahman. He's bad news…let's go.'

'Officer, officer don't go…' I turned and saw a youth running out of the alleyway beside the bar waving at me.

'What's up?' I called across to him as Professor Marmaduke moved from his doorway and stepped in his direction.

A look of terror filled the youth's face that was bleeding from fresh scratches and had a red swelling around his eye. 'Don't go, for god's sake…'

I walked up to the youth, who gave his name as Rob, guided him to the police car then turned to face Marmaduke.

'What do you know about this, then? What's happened?' He just smiled and strolled back to his doorpost. I sat the youth in the back of Zulu 1 and asked him the same question.

'He beat me bad for not paying enough for one of his spells, but I won't give any statement – just take me away – I sort it myself.'

I explained the need to give me a written statement and I could take some action against Marmaduke but Rob only agreed to sign my pocket notebook confirming what he had said and no more.

Marmaduke suddenly appeared by the car. 'You boy will suffer much pain for talking to the white policeman – you jus' wait…'

'I suggest you clear off or I'll lock you up for interfering with witnesses.'

Marmaduke totally ignored my nugget of sound advice and banged viciously on the car window. I got out and pushed him away as he swung a punch at my head. Before very long he was lying in the dust having his wrists handcuffed behind his back.

Marmaduke was foaming at the mouth as he raged at me, 'I curse you with all the spirits of obeah…'

The squad car door sprung open as Rob ran like a whippet towards the swamps. I held the professor in the rear of the squad car as Benbow drove us to the police station continuing to mutter, 'Oh dear, oh dear, oh dear,' several hundred times during the journey. I booked Marmaduke in with the custody sergeant and formally charged him with various breaches of public order offences, attempting to assault a police officer and threatening me with obeah. Then I went for breakfast.

On my return, Inspector McDougal was waiting with a sickly grin across his face. 'You in the sheet, go see Inspector Rowe.'

Inspector Rowe was a local officer who had made a point of welcoming us to the island. He seemed quiet but friendly and as expected usually used the chain of command without needing to deal with lower ranks. As back in the UK, we tended to keep out of their way and gratefully they did the same, but this was very different and I felt uncomfortable in my bones that something dramatic was about to unfold. I knocked on his door and walked in to find him constructing a daisy chain out of unused paperclips.

'You are a disgrace to the Cayman police. You has viciously beat up Professor Marmaduke an' I want all charges dropped, damn quick.'

'Well sir, he tried to assault me and a young—'

'You shut your mouth. I don't need to hear you. I've known

him for years since we played football at school. He done nothing wrong, so go drop the charges and release him, NOW.'

'Well sir, there may be a problem with that as I've already charged him and he's at court at the moment.'

His eyes blazed as his fingers grabbed at the blotter on his desk, clenching and unclenching his fists in temper.

'I think I'll leave then.' I turned on my heel and heard him screaming at me as I walked away along the corridor. It was all very surprising and totally unexpected as no one else had shown such a nasty side to them or anything like the unnecessary tirade. I blamed the humidity and approaching full moon.

A few days later I was called as a witness to give evidence in the Professor Marmaduke case. The prosecution lawyer had told me that one of the islands' dodgiest lawyers, Mr Adamson, was representing him, a number of influential people had also voiced their support and Inspector Rowe had given him an unblemished character reference. PC Benbow's witness statement was as useful as a chocolate teapot, stating that he was in the squad car and neither heard nor saw any offences take place.

It was going to be a difficult day, I thought, as I walked towards the court building and saw that a crowd of staff and onlookers were standing at the public entrance. I wasn't sure why the doors were not opened until I made my way through the crowd who were in a semicircle about 15 feet away from the doors.

No one would approach the doors and I then saw why. The obeah witch doctor had arranged a message for me and anyone thinking of giving evidence against him. Tied securely around the stainless-steel door handles of the glass door was a massive cane toad – about two feet long and very dead. As I walked up to it the nauseating stench of decay caught the back of my throat. It chilled me to the bone and even in that extreme heat, sent a shiver tumbling down my spine. The toad had a huge padlock through its top and bottom lips, holding them tightly shut.

My temper was up, I'd now had enough. I approached the door accompanied only by a loud 'oooh' from the onlookers who physically recoiled. I grabbed the toad, ripped it from the handles and threw it into the nearest bush. The crowd screamed like a pack of banshees and starburst wildly away into George Town. I walked in alone, ready to give my evidence.

It was very pleasing to see that HH Judge Rudyard was presiding as I knew he would deal fairly with this case, so I spoke to the prosecutor and explained the issue at the entrance door. He passed a note to the Judge who nodded. Professor Marmaduke was called to the dock and was ready to swear on the Bible when the Judge interjected.

'Take that ridiculous hat off your head in my Court – looks like you lost a fight with a chicken…' I could sense a positive change in the air.

The case proceeded and all the evidence was heard with the Judge asking pertinent points of clarification on both sides. Neither Rob nor Benbow were called as witnesses and it was all down to my evidence. Marmaduke waxed lyrically and stressed the point blaming me for assaulting him, denying any offences. It was all stacked up against me when the Judge suddenly spoke to Marmaduke.

'Why did you curse the officer with all the spirits of obeah?' His lawyer stood to protest but was waved away by the Judge.

'Cos he assaulted me…'

'Therefore you admit using obeah?'

He did not reply but looked at his legal team, who stared down at their briefing paper as Judge Rudyard continued.

'The officer has no reason to lie – but you do. Unsurprisingly you have not denied dabbling with the spirits and using curses against the officer. It would not help your perceived standing as an obeahman if you denied it, would it? No, I thought not… I find you guilty of all charges and fine you five hundred dollars. Good riddance to you.'

Rupert returned from the UK after only a week. I collected him at the airport and his first sentence said it all. 'I'm resigning tomorrow'!

I counselled him that he should consider this earth-shattering decision before formally putting pen to paper. The Commissioner would not be pleased and Rupert may live to regret the decision but his mind was obviously made up.

'Is your girlfriend really worth it?'

'No, but I can use her as a bit of an excuse.'

Rupert submitted the report to return to the UK and it was signed up almost immediately by Mr Jones and the Commissioner. It appeared to be indecently swift and that seemed to bother Rupert even more. 'It's like they wanted me to go anyway.'

A pleasant leaving do was organised for Rupert and was well attended by the social circle that had grown steadily around the UK officers. We presented him with a Royal Cayman Islands Police Service (RCIPS) plaque and leaving gifts and Carlos gave an entertaining farewell speech. The following day I took Rupert to the airport and watched him depart. His girlfriend had phoned him late the previous night and told him that she was leaving him, leaving his house and moving in with the traffic man. After everything, it was still sad to watch him go – I felt he must have regretted returning to the UK, but it was far too late to change that and he was definitely leaving for all the wrong reasons. I just wanted to get on with life here, collect my Jeep and enjoy the experience in spite of the minor unappealing aspects of the job.

Work was a good distraction and continued to keep me very busy. I tended to be the squad car driver as I presume I was deemed to be better able to deal with the more complicated jobs. Or maybe not. I noticed a brand-new Chevrolet Corvette Stingray drive past me with a well-known drug dealer named Nicky at the wheel. I was happy to see that one of his rear lights was not working, so I turned the car around and went after the guy, to stop him, check out his car and generally give him a hard time. My colleague Benbow was with me and said, 'I wouldn't bother stopping him, he's my cousin.'

I had heard this phrase a million times from him and ignored it. I switched the siren and blue lights on as I came up behind, saw him glance in the mirror, and he floored the accelerator. A high-speed chase took place towards West Bay, but Nicky clearly did not want to be stopped and my elderly squad car was lagging behind. He came off the road and in a cloud of marl dust disappeared from sight near to the wonderfully named Hamlet of Hell. I followed him down the track but he had managed to turn and hide in a lane until I'd just gone past. I considered ramming into him, bringing the chase to an abrupt halt, but it seemed out of proportion if it was only because of his light not working. I tried to do a 'donut turn' as seen in the movies but stalled the car miserably. Damn and blast. He must have had a stash of drugs on board but I could never catch him now and he made a rude sign at me and left quickly. I would be a bit more creative next time I saw him or his car to exact my revenge, which as they say is a dish best served cold.

Carlos, meanwhile, had been taken on by DCI Timms at the Drugs Squad for a 'top secret' job. Our Inspector told us that he was working in 'Top, Top Secret' work and we must not tell anybody because it was too secret. I arranged to call and find out about the top, top secret mission.

I took the elderly Zulu 2 squad car for a brew with Carlos and Suzy at their current accommodation, a pretty and colourful single-storey cottage at the end of a cul-de-sac of similar quaint properties. The car was not equipped with anything as sophisticated as parking sensors but its solid chrome bumpers served a similar purpose. I did a three-point turn and misjudged it slightly, reversing into a white picket fence belonging to one of their neighbours. It fell over with a thud and I heard a muffled shout. I pulled away from the fence and glancing in my mirror saw an elderly man on the ground. He was holding his hands to his head.

Oh Lord, what had I done? I stopped the car, jumped out and ran to help. He was a slightly built, darkly tanned local man dressed in working dungarees who appeared to have been weeding the garden immediately behind the fence that was now lying on top of him. I dragged the picket fence off the unfortunate gardener and helped him to his feet, apologising profusely. He took his hands from his face and I was appalled to see that he was seriously cross-eyed and I recoiled at the shock. What on earth had I done?

'Would you like to sit down?' I asked.

'No officer, I'm fine, it didn't hit me much.'

'Can you see alright?'

'Just fine officer. Has the bang knocked my eyes straight?' He laughed out loud and his wife came out to see the commotion. I apologised to her as well as I leant the fence back roughly to where it had originally been. She confirmed that he had not suffered any undue effects of the bump and his eyes always looked like that. I moved Zulu 2 to a better parking place, returned to the scene of my crime and offered to pay for any damage to the fence. I was extremely embarrassed at my actions but his response proved that he was the coolest character I had encountered on the island.

'You ain't the first to hit my fence and you certainly won't be the last. Forget it and have a great day.'

Like a puppy with my tail between my legs, I scampered into Carlos's cottage to recover with a brew and find out all about the top, top secret mission that turned out to be no such thing. It was another of Carlos's tall tales where he had volunteered to convey some illegal drug samples to Miami where they would be analysed by the US Drug Enforcement Administration (DEA). In actual fact, he was doing a favour for the Inspector while also going shopping for clothes and shoes as they were very expensive in Grand Cayman.

CHAPTER 12

JAMAICA PROOF

I had kept in regular touch with my girlfriend back in the UK with letters, and long, expensive phone calls often filled with silence as we discussed our relationship and the future. Unsurprisingly, it was becoming difficult to maintain this long-distance contact and our lives were going in very different directions. By now, we'd both realised that we secretly wanted to move on. But, to find out one way or another, I invited her over on holiday and arranged for her to travel with a number of other people's girlfriends, other boys' parents, and, unintentionally, 24 hours prior to her own luggage. It was lovely to see her and surprisingly there were no obvious unsettling silences or embarrassed conversations. It was more like welcoming a good friend into my new world and I suspected she was cultivating a friendship back in the UK – probably with a traffic officer.

I had booked a trip for us to Jamaica but before then I was still working, so she enjoyed the hotel facilities in the daytime and we went out around the island sight-seeing just like real tourists and visited as many of the highlights as possible when I had my time off. We ended up at a suitable pizza restaurant overlooking the beach. The location was perfect and we watched as the sunset disappeared over the horizon, nursed a couple of bottles of beer and joked about the waiter that had shown us to our place who had very unusual rat-like features and not a tooth in his whole mouth. He introduced himself as Billy and served the meal impeccably. When he arrived with the bill, he asked me where we were from.

'Lancashire,' I replied.

'I thought so, whereabouts?'

'Burnley.'

'I'm from Royton near Oldham,' he admitted.

I pointed at my girlfriend. 'She's from Saddleworth.' It was barely two miles away. I couldn't believe it – halfway around the world and he lived barely two miles away from us back in the UK.

'We must all go out for a drink together,' Billy shouted after us. 'My night off is Tuesday, see you then.'

I made a mental note to return only on Tuesdays.

The next day my girlfriend and I left for a five-day trip to Jamaica and flew to Montego Bay. I had been advised by some of my Jamaican friends that it would be sensible to avoid the capital, Kingston, and stick to the more tourist-focused areas along the northern coast. Before it was consumed by an earthquake blamed on the wrath of God, one of Kingston's suburbs, Port Royal, was described as the 'The Wickedest Town in Christendom'. This told me all I needed to know. The friends said it was more dangerous to be in the capital due to the presence of armed drug gangs who had regular shoot-outs amongst themselves and/or the police.

Montego Bay it was, then. I booked the flights and my plan to save money was to book a car for the five days when I arrived at the airport and travel along the north coast of the island visiting the attractions and organising the trip ourselves. It seemed like a good plan and a better way to enjoy the island other than being herded around like cattle on a tourist bus.

The first problem presented itself when I found that the cost of renting a car was extortionate – apparently most visitors stayed in the resorts or joined organised tours, and we realised the car rental companies in the airport were all price matching at a much higher price than that quoted back in Grand Cayman. A rethink was called for. Secondly, I had not booked the first night accommodation as my Jamaican friends had advised me that there would be great bargains to be had if I just approached a B&B along my route. That was not much help as we did not have a car to travel along the route. A *major* rethink was now called for.

I like a challenge and tried to remain calm as we sipped a very welcome rum punch, reviewing all the options. We decided to approach the local tourist information desk and put our situation to a lovely helpful lady. She called across the taxi rank manager and outlined our plans, to which he replied with that wonderful West Indian phrase, 'No problem.'

We went with him to the taxi rank where he picked out Norbert, put our bags in the taxi and explained our requirements to him. He said he could rent a car to us and his wife ran a local B&B. Our prayers were answered as he took us to his beautiful, clean home where we slept soundly before a delightful breakfast of fresh fruit, pastries and coffee overlooking the sea. Norbert brought a modern car and left us to fill in the forms after we agreed the very reasonable price. I spoke to Norbert's wife to pay for the B&B. Her reply set the relaxed tone for the entire visit. 'You'll be back to drop the car off in a few days – pay me then.'

We planned to travel east along the north coast road, stay where seemed pleasant and visit what appeared interesting, making it into an adventure. The first port of call was a well-publicised plantation house built on a grand scale on the outskirts of Montego Bay, or 'MoBay' as the locals call it. Rose Hall still causes a shiver to trickle down my spine. This grand plantation house was an impressive mansion built in 1760 and is regarded as one of the finest in Jamaica, having fallen into ruin, then rescued from decay and rebuilt to its former glory.

Wishing to find somewhere to visit to keep out of the noonday sun, we were lulled into the driveway by the sun-bleached signs and I parked under a protective grove of trees. Hoping to find a snack we approached the entrance and found a slumbering attendant who jumped in surprise; we were the first and probably only visitors of the day. After a pittance was paid she gave us a tour of the mahogany panelled walls, furniture crafted in exotic woods and a magnificent carved staircase. There was a distinctly sombre feel to the place that darkened considerably when I discovered there was no tea room.

The guide gave us a comprehensive explanation of the buildings and gardens showing evidence of the rusting foliage-encrusted machinery of the sugar plantation that had created untold wealth for some and unbelievable misery for the slaves. She told us in graphic detail about a previous, infamous owner of the hall who went by the innocuous name of Annie Palmer and was regarded by all as a 'white witch', practised voodoo and mistreated her slaves appallingly. Described as a 'restless young woman', it was rumoured that she had numerous, miscellaneous lovers, including many slaves, and murdered at least three of her husbands for their money and property.

My girlfriend looked at me. 'Sounds like a great idea.'

The white witch came to a sticky end when one of the slaves murdered her, burnt down the building and headed for the Cockpit Hills to escape the authorities. These events had been made into a song by an American singer living in the adjacent plantation and I had visions of some talentless hippy crooning away to himself. 'You may have heard of him, he lives in Cinnamon Hill, over there.' The guide pointed towards some neighbouring trees. 'He's called Johnny Cash.'

The spooky atmosphere and lack of refreshments were now becoming too much for us. Some lunch and a cheering rum punch were needed to rejuvenate our own souls and we left in search of less frightening spirits.

Our next stop was Ocho Rios that means Eight Rivers, which basically describes the number flowing from the hills into the sea. After living on the flat Cayman Islands for a number of months during the heat of the summer, it was a pleasure to be driving around a more tropical island. Jamaica is a beautiful place with a lush mountainous interior and a coast blessed with innumerable sheltered sandy bays and beaches of golden sand. The mountains attract the rain clouds which fall on the forests and woods, ending up with streams and rivers cascading down to the coast. The hills and cooling breezes provided a respite from the much more oppressive humidity back in Cayman and travelling the coast road east of MoBay gave us the chance to enjoy the stunning views of this part of the Spanish Main.

On the outskirts of Ocho Rios, there is a place described as 'The loveliest, most refreshing spot in the Caribbean', a statement difficult to argue with. Dunn's River Falls is where the clear water from the rainforest cascades down over a varying set of limestone terraces and pools to a sandy beach, then out to sea. The edges of the falls are fringed by palms and other wood clinging to gaps in the stone. It is the epitome of a tropical scene and has attracted thousands of tourists since it featured in the first Bond movie, *Dr. No.*

We parked up at the falls and walked down to the shore to take in the magnificence of the area. Local guides offered to assist us to walk barefoot up the falls, which involved sitting in crystal clear pools and climbing through mini rainbows up to the next level. It was an adventure with the cheerful advisor telling tall tales of island life as he manoeuvred us to the river at the top, out of breath, soaked to the skin but exhilarated. Back at the car park we were sitting drying off in the sunshine when an elderly 'Rastaman' suddenly appeared out of a bush, brandishing a large shiny machete and a huge green coconut. 'Do you want some coconut water, missy?'

'How much is it?'

'No charge, missy, if I can just touch your golden hair.' She looked towards me and I shrugged. We had not seen any other tourists driving around the island and we were the youngest visitors by at least 40 years. After a smile and a nod from her, he put his machete and coconut on the ground and reached out to gently touch her damp hair with the back of his wrinkled hand.

'I can die happy now, boss,' the old romantic said. 'I never touched such softness, it's like liquid gold.' He took up the coconut in his left hand and with the machete whipped the top clean off, spinning it yards away. The cool contents were refreshing with a nondescript taste but it certainly slaked the thirst after our exertion up the falls. I gave him a dollar for the entertainment and went on our way.

On the lookout for a likely B&B I pulled into a gateway in the vicinity of Oracabessa to consult the guidebook. The gates were open and I saw a pleasant house in some grounds overlooking a small beach. There was no sign that it was a guest house and a gardener shook his head when asked. It was then I saw a paint-flaking sign GOLDEN EYE that stuck in my mind. It was only later when the name came back to me that I realised we had been parked in the driveway of Ian Fleming's Caribbean refuge where he created all his books including the most exciting, enduring and bloodthirsty of them all – *Chitty Chitty, Bang Bang*.

A little along the coast road we came across a panoramic view of the Bay of Port Maria where a scruffy B&B sign welcomed us into a dusty driveway up to 'Blue Harbour'. Thankfully they had vacancies – in fact, no one else was staying there at all. We unloaded the bags and booked in glancing at signed photographs adorning the walls. Here were more stars than the Milky Way, everyone from the 50s and 60s movie stars to the great and good, including one of the Queen Mother. We had walked into a time warp.

The chatty receptionist was happy to explain that Blue Harbour had been built by the multitalented British polymath, Sir Noël Coward, as his tropical island home. He was widely known as a great wit, writer, singer, playwright, raconteur and actor, starring in many and varied films that included classics such as *The Italian Job*. He also managed to compose and perform numerous songs including, on that day, the especially appropriate, 'Mad dogs and Englishmen.'

The accommodation was in one of three bungalows dotted around the small estate all enjoying sumptuous views over the coast. We really were sleeping in the shadow of all the major celebrities of the Golden Age of Hollywood that had flocked to the area during the postwar period. Coward had first visited the islands during the latter part of the Second World War when the apparent benefits of living in the Caribbean impressed him. This was a far cry from the restrictions of life in Britain of food and petrol rationing, the blackout, a constant danger from bombing when attacks from V1 and V2 rockets prevailed. After the hostilities finished, many of those fortunate enough to be able to relocate looked to the West Indies where the cost of living was very low, food and clothing good quality, and plentiful cheap land. The weather certainly helped.

One of the first to arrive was Ian Fleming who holidayed in Jamaica after his wartime role in Naval Intelligence and began working for the *Sunday Times*. He used his leave to stay in Jamaica for the winter to write his novels uninterrupted. His friend Coward visited and became enamoured with the climate and beauty of the island and found some land at £10 an acre at Blue Harbour. As I was to find out back in Cayman, once you offer an invitation to visit, no matter how tenuous, the hordes will come and eat you out of house and home. Coward had the right idea though: he eventually kept Blue Harbour for his hangers-on and moved half a mile away. He built a one-bedroom cottage with a wide picture window overlooking the Bay of Port Maria and called it Firefly Hill after the myriad of these tiny creatures which lit the night sky. He loved the place so much he is buried here beneath a simple marble slab.

We continued on our journey eastwards and at six in the evening, it was as dark as Blind Pew's spot. The roads were peppered with bottomless potholes, unlit cars and pedestrians seemingly tired of living. Eventually we came to the top of an incline and had to stop. Before us sat the picturesque fishing village of Port Antonio. Its position was like an amphitheatre with its harbour as the stage watched over by an audience of brightly lit rows of cottages strung along the hillside. At its centre Navy Island watched over the bay for pirates, enemies and celebrity visitors. My guidebook recommended the small hotel on Navy Island that was 500 yards offshore with no visible means of getting there. I parked on the harbour and accosted a local who pointed at a large wooden box with flaking blue paint attached to the harbour wall. I opened it up to reveal a telephone with a wind-up handle. I cranked and listened to the receiver last seen in a 1930s Will Hay comedy film. A similar, high-pitched voice answered and told us to wait. It was a warm night and dark as pitch around the harbour save for a few hurricane lanterns hanging outside the inns, swinging gently in the breeze and casting spooky shadows across the moorings as the iron signs above the doors of the hostelries creaked and squeaked. It would not have surprised me one jot had Captain Jack Sparrow been launched out through a swinging tavern door on to his backside, closely followed by his tri-cornered hat.

A few lights began to sparkle on the island as if the occupants had just woken. A faint put-put-put sound reached my ears, becoming louder, then more distinct, until a tiny launch suddenly appeared in front of us. It was an outboard motor with a canoe attached, lacking any navigation lights. We climbed aboard, sitting behind one another, clutching our bags between our knees as we pushed off and headed out to the twinkling lights hanging on the sea.

A few flaming torches on thick bamboo staves lit the path leading towards the plain concrete building where we were greeted by a smart-suited, smiling manager. 'Welcome to Navy Island, the Jamaican home of Errol Flynn!'

'Oh, I really like him,' my girlfriend said. 'He's my favourite singer, is Errol. '*It started with a kiss…I never thought it would come to this…*'

Even at this late stage in our relationship I hadn't appreciated, firstly, just how good a singer she was and secondly, how ignorant of movie stars of the silver screen. I didn't need to upset her as the helpful manager leapt to my assistance. 'Yes, he's another great son of Jamaica, too.'

The manager confided in me the history of the island that had been a navy fort as he gave us lanterns and led the way to our wooden cabin overlooking the sea. Flynn first encountered Port Antonio when a storm blew his 118-foot schooner *Zaca* off course to its shores; he described the town as 'The most beautiful woman I have ever laid eyes upon.' And he would know…

The island was used by the movie star of the 1930s and 40s to moor his yacht after winning it in a wager. His insatiable appetite for girlfriends meant he had to build a number of cabins dotted around the island for visitors, including Coward and Fleming. He welcomed the beautiful people of the 1950s and 60s and by all accounts had stupendously raucous parties on the island, resulting in the phrase, 'In like Flynn.' 'In like Brown' does not quite have the same ring to it.

Hurricane lanterns were dotted along the path to our cabin that had a hammock slung across the veranda and a large bedroom with basic facilities. We were absorbing the peaceful ambiance when a waiter gently tapped on the door offering complimentary rum punches. He presented a sheet of paper torn from a school exercise book with the menu in pencil:

Conch Fritters
Lobster
Jamaican Rum and Ginger Cake

The option was to take it or leave it, so happily we took it. The restaurant area was closer to the reception, looking towards Port Antonio, occupied by several diners ready for the sole sitting at 7pm. The weather was perfect, beautifully warm and we were not bothered by insects as they were frazzling themselves on the open lanterns illuminating the scene. I could easily understand why celebrities flocked to the area and we felt at ease.

The simple fare was delicious and it made our last night on the island very special. As I was cracking open my second lobster claw my girlfriend tapped me on the arm and pointed towards the beach where two figures moved furtively from behind a bush. Perhaps I should not have felt so relaxed.

The figures kept to the shadows but then were lit up as the kitchen door opened. They were wearing combat fatigues with one holding a pump-action shotgun and the other an automatic rifle. They moved off towards where our cabin was and I thought of the valuables we had left lying around. Damn. I stood up and my girlfriend stopped me with a sensible question.

'They're armed. What are you thinking of doing – hitting them over the head with a flip-flop?'

The waiter returned and I garbled out what had just happened. He laughed. 'No worries boss, they's our security guards. Relax and have another rum punch on the house to get your heart rate down.'

The following day we left Jamaica and my girlfriend left the Caribbean for home – and my life for good. We parted on the very best of terms. It was time to move on.

CHAPTER 13

MY WICKED, WICKED WAYS

It had been sad to see my girlfriend leave the island, and my life, but I think we both accepted that the time spent apart had convinced us that we weren't right for each other. I did not want to return to the UK yet and we agreed to move on and, if possible, still remain friends. It was the right thing to do for both of us. I didn't have much time to wallow either as the following day my next visitor arrived. Ged was my best pal and we had worked together for years, getting into and out of many scrapes, relatively unscathed. He was going through a divorce and had just scraped together enough money for a much-needed fortnight in the sunshine.

I collected him at the airport with the roof of the Jeep down to give him the full effects of vitamin D on his balding dome. My annual leave was minimal and had to be used wisely whilst still entertaining my visitors. He was going to use the pull-out bed in my hotel suite and arranged all his holiday essentials around the bed area. These included aviator sunglasses, enough sun lotion to float a battleship, aftershave for men on the prowl, and a well-thumbed copy of Errol Flynn's autobiography *My Wicked, Wicked*

Ways. He hoped to emulate the swashbuckler's life and go through all the island's entertainment and attractions during his stay. He nodded off gently and I left him to his dreams as I went to my night shift.

Another midnight beach patrol starting in George Town resulted in a much more interesting tour of duty as I was ready to finish and return to the station. I had been walking along the sand for a few hours giving a few words of advice to courting couples and calming a rowdy pool party. In the darkness I could just make out a shape lying on the sand close to where the sea was gently lapping up the beach. It did not appear to be moving and I assumed it was a drunk or a couple of romantics taking in the stars above. It was neither, it was far more remarkable and beautiful.

I got near enough to see and then had to stop myself from using my torch in case I disturbed this wonder of nature. It was a huge, green sea turtle crawling slowly up the beach. About four feet long and two feet tall, it had strong fins that pulled the ancient creature through the powder sand further up the beach. I had been told that they could grow up to 300 pounds and did not doubt that this specimen was in that bracket. It was totally absorbing to watch this wonderful creature as she strained every sinew to climb the sandy slope.

After about 15 minutes of struggle and strain she stopped and began to dig with her front fins, spraying the sand vigorously to the side. She dug and dug without a break until she had cleared a hole nearly two feet deep, then took a breath and laboriously began to turn clockwise until she faced back towards the sea. I was tired just watching her efforts. She then manoeuvred her vast bulk backwards over the hole and began to plop one egg after another, after another, on and on, down into the hole, gently filling it up. I lost count then noticed a small group of people had gathered to watch this wonder of nature, smiling and sitting or kneeling in total silence other than the slight grunting from the exhausted mother turtle.

With the last egg dispatched, the turtle rearranged herself and using only her rear fins began covering her nest with the sand. The mighty fins worked hard covering then flattening the sand until little would betray the site of the nest. With her exhausting task complete she gently heaved up on her fins and crawled back towards the sea. A couple of young tourists sat in the sand crying with the emotion of what they had just witnessed and I fully understood. I marked the nest by building a loose barrier of sunbeds then arranged for the hotel security to regularly check for the remainder of the night.

I finished work, woke early and arranged to meet the representatives of the Government Turtle Farm at the nesting site. The Turtle Farm was a research organisation as well as a tourist attraction, focused on saving endangered turtles around the Caribbean. I took Ged with me to witness this once-in-a-lifetime event and arrived at the beach to find my barricade still intact. The experts brought insulated boxes with them and set about digging for the little white oval pieces of treasure.

They told me that if they left the nest to its own devices, in the wild, then perhaps only 1 per cent of a nest would actually reach maturity and end up breeding. By collecting, hatching, nurturing and ultimately releasing the hatchlings into the wild, the numbers of adults could increase tenfold. A small crowd of onlookers gathered around and as each egg was lifted from the nest, they gave a little cheer and counted aloud. The numbering of the eggs got steadily more exciting – 95, 96, 97, 98 and finally 99 – all out! A ripple of applause accompanied the sealing of the insulated boxes as the staff carefully carried their precious cargo from the beach. It was a wonderful way to start the day and I still felt quite emotional, so Ged and I went to the Lord Nelson Inn for a full cooked breakfast to celebrate the safe delivery of my new babies.

Ged by now was as brown as a berry having put hundreds of miles in the Jeep with the top down soaking up the rays, mainly whilst I was working and he was having the time of his life, playing beach volleyball, tennis and squash, swimming and snorkelling. Over the two weeks we went to all the island bars and night clubs including Silvers, Island Rock and Radisson, usually ending up at Sunset House.

After a fortnight of constant partying I was exhausted and skint, then when I least expected it, a letter arrived and fate took a hand. It arrived with a postmark from the Chiapas region in Mexico. I was intrigued and immediately opened it without damaging the postage stamp – my Chief Inspector back in the UK wanted it.

It was from Inga and Torhild, the two Danish chums I met on the flight to Miami. The letter described their world in the Mexican mountains, speaking the real and unadulterated Spanish that was still used by the indigenous people. It included an invitation to visit them if I got the opportunity. I looked into the flights, which were expensive but possible. I replied thanking them for the welcome invitation, placated by Mexican daydreams, and then went back to the job at hand.

A Royal Navy frigate was tied up at the harbour and I was allocated the role of driver of the police minibus to transport the Shore Patrol. They were a decent team of lads and constantly took the mickey out of me during the evening when the clapped-out vehicle began to gently fall apart in front of me. Initially I could not open the driver's door, the lights refused to work and finally the gearstick came off in my hand. It earned me an invitation to a party in the Petty Officers Mess the following night. Nobby came along and we enjoyed the bangers and mash with a few snifters of Navy rum to wash it down. It was a great night until the alcohol got through to Nobby's brain cells and he decided to verbalise Winston Churchill's comments regarding the navy, specifically regarding rum, sodomy and the lash…

It is never a good move to insult your hosts especially when they were so hospitable and capable of inflicting untold injuries. I had to gag Nobby after he began an increasingly loud tirade of so-called jokes relating to:

- Being made to work the cabin boy's passage.
- And the fact that he had never seen such a large amount of seamen.

The black looks darkened perceptively as he started on his off-key rendition of the Captain Pugwash sea shanty with highly inappropriate verses referring to Master Bates, Seaman Stains and Roger the Cabin Boy. I thanked the Officer of the Watch for his hospitality as I dragged Nobby down the gangplank back to the relative safety of the dock.

Numerous games of tennis and squash kept me fit, sociable and more determined to continue to work hard and hope that a more interesting role would develop. I volunteered for anything different and one morning I was asked to collect a US Air Force crew from the airport. Expecting a bunch of fit and healthy individuals resembling Tom Cruise and his colleagues from *Top Gun*, I scanned the crowd until a tubby tourist waved to attract my attention. I ignored him and continued my search until he stood in front of me and identified himself as the Captain of his aircraft. I looked around at his crew – how disappointing, I thought. It was more like a group of overweight members of *Dad's Army* wearing Hawaiian shirts and sunglasses. The enforced visit was due to this group of USAF National Guard being deployed on manoeuvres to the area but their Hercules aircraft had collided with the passenger steps as they pulled up at the airport terminal. Looking at the amount of luggage the four of them put in the boot of my squad car, I was not convinced the impact was accidental. The ancient pilot in charge said that they would have to stay on the island pending the arrival of a USAF engineer to inspect the very minor dint on the body work – in fact I could not see a thing. I carried them off to the best hotel on the island and watched them heading straight for the pool bar. What a great jolly it was and I wished I had thought of it as the Hercules did not move an inch for the next four days.

Remember the drug sting operation during my first few days on the island? Well, the two Colombian pilots were on trial for the importation of the $100 million worth of cocaine and I was part of the daily armed escort going to and from the courts and Northward Prison. We were on high alert as we had received information that the Colombian Drug Cartel was planning an attack to spring them from custody. In addition to my trusty .357 Magnum Smith & Wesson revolver loaded with dum-dum bullets, I was also in possession of a pump-action Winchester shotgun loaded with rifled slugs each capable of destroying a car engine. It was quite a thrill. Sgt Benjamin made sure we retained an edge and we would offer overwhelming force if we were challenged. He was bristling with all kinds of weaponry, including a couple of hand grenades hanging from his belt. I was quite looking forward to any rescue attempt in a strange, apprehensive sort of way.

The trial ended with His Honour Rudyard sentencing both pilots to 12 years in prison and a $20,000 fine. We returned them to prison to begin their sentence and were starting to relax as we returned to Police HQ when a radio message stopped us all in our tracks. The prison governor had been passed information regarding two very suspicious people seen in the vicinity taking photographs and videos of the area behind the prison compound and the approach road.

We raced off back to the area on the lookout for a 'red-coloured rental car with a man and woman of Colombian type features' – whatever that might mean. We scoured the area for the suspect vehicle and then saw a possible match pulling into the car park of Pedro's Castle. Benjamin executed a perfect 'donut' turn and we pulled our car right up behind their car and pointed all our guns at them. The dusky-looking pair immediately put their hands up as high as humanly possible and after a bit of rough handling we had grabbed them, handcuffed and lay them prone on the dusty floor. I glanced up to see a number of tourists watching us from the viewing platform on the castle where they gave us a ripple of applause.

After seizing a camera and video camcorder from them we took them back to Police HQ where they were interrogated by Special Branch. Scenes of Crime officers developed the films and viewed the video. Feeling quite pleased with ourselves we had a well-earned lunch whilst we bathed in the afterglow of a job well done. Harry, the Special Branch Inspector, came out of the interview room with a quizzical look on his face. 'They say they're botanists researching rare banana tree sucker plants. What's on the film?'

I found a beautiful selection of flora and fauna on all the developed photographs, oh dear, oh dear. We apologised, dusted them down, drove them back to their car and handed them the gorgeous photos with a new roll of film for any trouble caused. I think they were too shocked to complain, especially after I gave them a bit of baloney about it being a training exercise, and they thanked us, apologising profusely for wasting our valuable time.

CHAPTER 14

THE FIRST MURDER IN PARADISE

The afternoon shift did not start well and all my plans and enquiries were turned upside down. The police radio told me to attend an address at the bottom end of Captain Trelawney's Harbour, which I knew to be expensive villas protected by high-walled compounds. A garbled phone call had been made by a distraught female. When I arrived I found two visibly upset females dressed in maids uniforms, crying uncontrollably by an open gate where their bicycles were propped up against the wall. One of the maids managed to say, 'It's terrible. He's dead.' She then burst into tears once more.

I stepped through the gate, then stopped as I smelt that unique and pervading smell of death. I walked up to a set of French windows and looked in to see four gaunt Alsatian dogs who hurled themselves barking and snarling at me against the glass, making me leap back. This was not going to be easy. I nipped around the back where I spotted a door slightly ajar that led into a kitchen. The dogs were still in the lounge and I saw a door that would secure them while I searched the house. I ran through and slammed it just in time as I felt them throwing their bodies against it trying to get at me. I walked through clouds of buzzing, swirling swarms of bluebottles and my heart sank. As I entered the open door of a large luxuriously appointed bedroom I stopped still. There on the bed were the remains of a body with shredded items of clothing still attached to the skeleton. It was like a scene from *Treasure Island* where bodies had been left to bleach under the Caribbean sun. Police training had instilled in me the phrase 'Preserve the scene'. I had seen enough and backed out of the room to allow the Scenes of Crime officers to conduct a forensic examination.

The body belonged to a well-known British expat businessman and he had been undiscovered for some time until his cleaners had arrived and made their gruesome discovery. A flurry of activity – and the extra attention the crime received in the press – had mobilised the CID to reroute as much resource as possible to begin the enquiry to trace the murderer. The post mortem revealed that he had been hit by a heavy object that had caved his head in.

The following day we were tasked to conduct a fingertip search of the grounds of the victim's compound, so I came prepared with my scruffy duty overalls, boots and stout stick to beat back the undergrowth in the search for clues and discarded weapons. Initial enquiries suggested that the dead businessman was wealthy with a string of girlfriends and received many visitors from the local criminal fraternity within the islands and beyond. Various valuable items had been stolen from the villa and this was a sensible line of enquiry for the CID to pursue.

The murder investigation was the priority for the entire force but our other police work continued. Rupert's nemesis, aka 'Toadface', had been released on a bail bond of $3,000 provided by his girlfriend, but he was now wanted for a further six offences and continued to evade capture in spite of numerous sightings. I was out on patrol when he ran across the road in front of my squad car and I was just too slow to run him down. The sergeant and I took off after him through the Almond Tree restaurant, scattering diners and linen-covered tables as he dived into the cemetery and disappeared from view. He was then seen by another patrol and vanished near to a school bus. I stopped it and went on board to check the passengers but he was not there.

We were standing around quite perplexed until I crawled on my hands and knees underneath the bus to find him cleverly wrapped around the prop shaft. How long he would have lasted there when it drove off I could only guess, but he came out without too much of a scrap and was securely returned to the cells. His life was becoming more and more chaotic because of his consumption and supply of cocaine and I knew that he would continue to spiral out of control and commit a more serious crime. At that stage I did not know just what terrible step it would take.

To keep costs down I had brought a toolkit with me from the UK, enabling me to service my Jeep. I bought the oil and filters and moved the Jeep out of sight of the manager to the rear of the hotel complex, managing not to spill a drop of oil on the pristinely laid tarmac. It gave me a real buzz – especially when my spanner touched the battery terminals and I ended up unconscious in a neighbouring hibiscus bush.

My Jeep was a provider of enormous fun but it had one un-endearing feature: the windscreen wipers had a mind of their own, indeed they seemed possessed. I had an idea that they were controlled by the lunar cycle or possibly the obeah curse from Professor Marmaduke. They often sprang into action at the most inconvenient moment including one occasion when it was parked up in the middle of the night – it was very character building to be disconnecting the Jeep battery at 3am. During certain times of the year the island experienced a lot of short, sharp rain showers and tropical downpours occurred frequently, often followed by brilliant sunshine. The lack of reliable wipers was not usually an issue on a sunny day but it could be a bit dicey at night when the visibility was poor and street lighting non-existent and they wouldn't work. I had tried to repair them on various occasions but they resisted strongly. In desperation I had even used a tried and trusted Second World War solution used for clearing windscreens, as suggested by my dad. He told me it was guaranteed to work as he had used it on his army Jeep that only had a hand-operated wiper whilst he was 'underfire' during the Normandy campaign in 1944.

'Cut a potato in half,' he said. 'Rub it up and down the screen, absolutely bound to work.'

It didn't and the muddy mess around the windscreen and bonnet always provoked searching questions from my various passengers. This was in addition to my explanation as to why I always had a bag of potatoes and a sharp knife in the back of the Jeep. On one particular evening I went for a meal at Carlos and Suzy's house that was along a dark and ill-lit heavily rutted track. As I left the party, the rain was hammering down, so I ran to the Jeep, waved my farewells and felt obliged to move off straight away. Normally without functioning wipers, I would wait for the shower to pass before setting off into the unknown, but you can't have hosts waving at you for an hour, can you?

The Jeep had doors fitted with plastic fold-down windows that kept most of the weather outside, but as the wipers would not move I drove off with my head sticking out of the window. I took extra care to avoid repeating the demolition of the white picket fence belonging to their cross-eyed neighbour, who I noticed, despite our previous good-natured exchange when I ran him over, was watching me intently from his veranda. The track was rough and undulating and the potholes were filling with rainwater as I splashed through them. I carried on regardless, trying to look through the torrential downpour, frequently wiping my eyes as I crawled on hoping to reach the well-lit main road, until I came to a shuddering and sudden halt. I got out to see what had happened, then everything went blank.

After an unknown amount of time, I heard someone say, 'Is you alright, boss?'

I opened my eyes to find I was lying in a puddle looking up at the same cross-eyed neighbour I had reversed over a few months earlier.

'Dat coconut hit you on da head, boss, when you hit dat tree.' He pointed to the offending item lying beside me. 'Do ya need a doctor?' I had a banging headache but it was mainly embarrassment – once more – so I declined.

I staggered to my feet with his help, thanking him profusely. The Jeep had suffered only minor damage to its front bumper and had had no apparent impact upon the tree other than the loss of the coconut that had already exacted its revenge upon my head. I got back in the Jeep, started the engine and – miracle of miracles – the wipers jumped to life. I bade my helper a fond farewell and raced off whilst they continued to clear the screen.

The murder investigation into the British businessman continued apace but nothing was going to stop the Annual Police Ball taking place. A very grand affair, dubbed the 'Social Event of the Year', it was held at the ballroom of the nicest hotel on West Bay Road. The raffle tickets were a bit expensive but we bought a few expecting to win a bottle of rum for our troubles. I went with Suzy because, yet again, Carlos had said that he been asked to liaise with the DEA in Miami for a potential drugs 'sting' in the near future.

Actually, it turns out he had just gone shopping…again. But it was a very enjoyable event with excellent food and live entertainment. The Commissioner provided us with his rendition of a drunk slurring and mumbling his words at a party by reading out the winning numbers for the raffle.

He mumbled into the microphone. 'Ticket 140!'

Suzy leapt up with the winning ticket and ran to get the prize off the Commissioner who tried to kiss her. She ducked under his outstretched arms and grabbed the envelope from him before returning to our table. It contained a voucher for return flights for two from Cayman to any location in the US – wow – it certainly beat the expected tin of biscuits.

DCI Timms and his wife were next to us and making the most of the free wine. He was leading the investigation into the murdered expat and between sips gave my arm a sharp poke.

'What the hell's she doing here?' He pointed to a tall, attractive raven-haired woman on the dance floor gyrating wildly to the live band, closely coupled with an inspector from another shift. I had seen her around the night clubs and various bars but said that I didn't know her name.

'I do,' he said. 'She lives in the same complex as the dead expat. She's the main bloody suspect!'

The woman was bumping and grinding along to the beat and grasping the inspector's buttocks, to his obvious delight.

'What's that clown doing?' the DCI said. 'He knows she's involved and I interviewed her for hours yesterday, but she denies having anything to do with it. All she did was tell me which of the police she'd been with.'

'Anyone we know?'

'About half the force, she reckons. She's had more prick than a second-hand dartboard.' The DCI pointed a thumb towards a

My journey begins! Here's my photo shoot for the *Police Review* article taken at the beautiful Smith's Cove.

Me and Zulu 2, the five-litre V8 patrol car, after enjoying lunch at Smith's Cove.

Armed to the teeth and ready to escort a gang of Colombian drug dealers to Northward Prison.

Taking part in the Queen's Birthday Parade in George Town with fixed bayonets.

My Jeep parked between the Royal poinciana trees at Governor's House.

Replenishing lost fluid at the Governor's Garden Party after the
Queen's Birthday celebrations.

Time to take it easy on Seven Mile Beach.

The prettier part of Hell from where you can expect to receive a postcard.

My Jeep parked at Public Beach, with a cruise ship preparing to depart before the sun sets.

Rum Point, the idyllic tropical beach looking out towards the sandbar named Sting Ray City.

One of the 99 turtles I rescued from Seven Mile Beach enjoying life at the Cayman Turtle Centre.

The prize-winning swordfish caught during Million Dollar Month at Cayman Kai.

My bungalow on Navy Island, Errol Flynn's hideaway in Port Antonio, Jamaica.

Sunset over Barry's Reef where I spent many happy hours snorkelling. After two wonderful years in the Cayman Islands, sadly it was time to return to reality.

senior officer sitting at a neighbouring table. 'She calls him "Peanut" and says he has a small willy, premature ejaculation problems and doesn't know what to do with it anyway.'

'I presume there's no forensic evidence tying her to the murder?'

'Nothing yet,' he admitted, 'but it doesn't stop her trying to find out. Only this afternoon I told her to get lost from the SOCO office – she's been offering sexual favours to anyone that'll let her know. You just bloody couldn't make it up, could you?'

Mr Timms got back to his interrupted glass and continued to stop the wine from going off whilst contemplating his next move in the murder investigation. The entertainment carried on as we watched the unfortunate 'Peanut' glower in misty-eyed envy at the raven-haired suspect pulling provocatively at the chest hair of her current squeeze on the dance floor.

The enquiries into the businessman's murder continued but the leads ground to a halt due to the lack of forensic evidence or any eyewitness able to testify with relevant evidence. We could prove the chief suspect had been a girlfriend of the murdered businessman, but she somehow managed to persuade a local supermarket owner to provide her with a cast iron alibi which we could not contradict. Such is the reality of policing, where frustrations abound when a suspect literally gets away with murder.

We had been on the island for eight months at this point and had relaxed into the work and social life available to us. Many of my colleagues had developed steady long-term relationships and the weather had cooled to a perfect climate of warm, temperate days without the humidity and fierce heat of the summer months and cooler evenings.

Muriel was an American working in 'Real Estate' on the island and had now moved in with my colleague, Nobby, and she was certainly ruling the roost. They had moved into a more expensive villa overlooking the sea where she was hosting a 'Tree Trimming Party' in time for the Christmas season. Cocky had misunderstood the event to be a risqué Bush Trimming party and attended wearing his smallest speedos, carrying his electric razor; he left quickly to get more appropriately clothed. We had been invited to bring our own beer and something to hang on the tree, which seemed a quaint colonial celebration.

I came bearing a delightful red box about two inches square and waited for it to be hung on a convenient branch. Others had made their own small decorations. I was quietly chuffed with mine as I had made a number of adjustments to it after purchasing a number of explosive party poppers and other electronic gizmos. In the meantime, we had to sample the drink concoction produced by Muriel, which was a sickly alcoholic cream affair in bright yellow. She called it egg nog and I think there was too much egg and not enough nog to make it palatable, but I politely sipped it until she was out of sight.

As I waited my turn, all the new attachments to the tree were greeted by polite applause and suitable oohs and aahs from Muriel and her chums. The pleasant snowman and winged woodland fairy were joined by rolls of tinsel, strings of lights and small golden nets of tasty chocolate coins. Next in line came my red box, which I had not associated myself with, and I watched with interest as it was attached to the tree. Muriel spied the exposed string dangling below and pulled it. She screamed as it exploded with a loud boom and copious amounts of smoke, flame and confetti shot out, closely followed by the ugliest miniature Captain Blackbeard I could find. The contents of the 'Jack in a Box' blew off most of the neighbouring tree decorations causing Muriel to burst into tears and lock herself in the cloakroom. I was mortified but hoped I'd managed to hide it well enough as we discussed who could possibly have done such a terrible thing to poor Muriel.

The weather in the run-up to Christmas was beautiful with warm sunshine, balmy breezes and cooler evenings. I managed to enjoy my lunch break on my favourite bench at Fort George overlooking the harbour packed with three huge cruise ships. I opened my Christmas cards and welcomed the greetings from pals and relatives – some of whom I would be seeing soon back in the UK, as I had arranged to vacate Caribbean Suites over the most lucrative season of goodwill and excessive profit for Horatio. A more enticing letter had arrived from my new friends in Mexico, having taken three weeks to arrive by donkey. It included an invitation to visit them, and with a bit of creativity I could curtail my UK trip, then fly to the Chiapas region of Mexico. I replied that day. It was going to be a very Merry Christmas after all.

CHAPTER 15

FRANK SINATRA AND THE LONDON DERRIERE

The 'Second Best Social Event of the Year' was organised by St Ignatius Catholic Church in the run-up to Christmas. The level of prizes could not compete with those at the Police Ball but the ceilidh band and dancing was a definite step in the right direction, with no murderers in sight. Duke had got a ticket and during the entertainment asked me the name of one of the more tuneful songs we were all singing along to. I answered him then went back to my meal, but later he collared me at the bar where something was troubling him.

'Why does that great tune have such a goddamn awful name? I mean to say, why call it after your capital city's asshole. Being from the Deep South, I speak a bit of French you know.'

More like double Dutch, I thought. As was normally the case with Duke, I did not have a clue what he was talking about and put it down to the amount of beer he was absorbing. Later on I found him still propping up the bar, spouting the same nonsense.

He shook his head mournfully, 'I honestly can't work it out, man... I mean... London Derriere...'

I moved swiftly on and did not put him out of his misery – it would have hurt his brain too much, but I haven't been able to think of the correct title since without a smile. 'Danny Boy' is a much more suitable title.

A large proportion of expats on the island came from Ireland to work in the hotel and hospitality sectors and some elements of the civil service. A pal of mine worked in Cayman during the winter months and returned to Killarney in time for the spring and summer when the Irish tourism season was at its height.

Now, this event was free! Not often you could say that about a church social, it was funded by the parishioners and was to raise funds for the parish and other poorer parts of the diocese, especially Jamaica. The Dutch auction was a great success and everyone was offering contributions for the prizes well above their actual value. Somehow I managed to bid for a box of those Irish biscuits with fluffy pink and white marshmallow coverings that I have never liked, but they were highly sought after by others at the meal. I swapped them for an original bar of Irish Cadbury's chocolate, which was delicious and reinforced with me just how much you could miss these delicacies when they are prohibitively expensive overseas.

The parish priest was the Master of Ceremonies and entertained us merrily with anecdotes of his life and times from studying in Oxford, to the army during the war, followed by teaching around the Caribbean until he arrived to entertain us at the dinner dance. It was an enormously entertaining evening and had passed far too quickly when the carriages were called at midnight. The priest's actual title was Monsignor and he had partially retired to the island from Jamaica but ran the Catholic school and church with a cheerful and positive demeanour. He was usually seen riding around the island on his small and very unreliable moped attending to his various duties and responsibilities. On a couple of occasions, I pulled up beside him as he was pushing his conked-out moped along a road and offered my assistance. One time he accepted my help and as we lifted his bike into the rear of my Jeep, his holy patience almost spent, he said, 'The Good Lord moves in mysterious ways – unlike this moped!'

One quaint tradition for the Royal Cayman Islands Police was to provide all the officers with some free Christmas food to feed their families. I went to collect my parcel on the Saturday morning before Christmas Day and carried it to the Jeep, before opening it to reveal…a huge fresh turkey, a side of ham and a case of fizzy pop. It was a nice thought but not much use to me as I was returning to the UK for a couple of weeks and had no means to either store, cook or consume them. I was sure that some worthy cause would soon become obvious to me as I drove off to my regular Saturday afternoon on the rifle range with Sgt Benjamin and his wide assortment of weapons.

I usually bought a couple of boxes of cartridges from him and merrily fired away at the targets. There were a few more young shooters present and he had given them the spare ear protectors to shield their sensitive ears. I finished off the session using one of his more powerful pistols – a Colt .45 automatic – and it was bloody loud. After the first round had nearly knocked me over as well as deafened me, he gave me a couple of empty cartridge cases and told me to put them in my ears to reduce the noise. They seemed to help and I emptied the magazine in a more relaxed manner. I left the range, headed back into town and as I drove past St Ignatius church remembered my unwanted gifts. I parked up at the presbytery and rang the bell. The Monsignor answered and invited me in. His chubby, jovial face beamed as he spoke, but I did not catch a word of what he said and asked him to repeat it, fearing the big Colt had dramatically affected my hearing.

He raised his voice and said close to my face, 'So you've been shooting at the range, I presume?'

I was very impressed and shouted back, 'You've the intuitive powers of Sherlock Holmes, Father.'

'No, it's elementary,' he bawled back, then leant towards me and with both hands plucked the cartridges out of my ears. He whispered, 'It's a miracle, Dr Watson! By Jove, he can hear.'

'Pardon?' I said.

After accepting a reviving piece of cake and a cup of tea, I asked if he could find a suitable home for my turkey, ham and case of pop. He was hosting a Christmas dinner for the poorer members of the parish on Christmas Day and the gifts were well received by him for the meal. I went to collect the box of goodies and he directed me through a connecting door into a dark garage. The Monsignor followed me in, put the light on and opened a large fridge where I deposited the food and drink. Most of the garage was occupied by a car covered with a dusty sheet. Being naturally nosy I asked him about the car, so he pulled back the cover to reveal the front of a massive Cadillac bearing Nevada number plates.

'There's a bit of a story about that,' he said. 'Would you like another piece of cake?'

I returned to his comfortable lounge to settle down in an armchair with the ceiling fan spinning gently above.

'It was a few years ago,' the Monsignor said, 'and I was on my moped when it stalled on Eastern Avenue. I overbalanced and fell over in the road. Of course all the traffic stopped and a lot of people came to help me. They picked me and the moped up and put us at the side of the road. They were all very kind, of course.

'Then eventually the traffic started moving and as I got my breath back, a huge black car with blacked-out windows pulled up beside me, the electric window went down and the driver spoke. "Are you okay, Father?" the driver said from behind rather sinister, mirrored aviator sunglasses.'

The driver and front-seat passenger were dressed in dark suits and had the look of a couple of smart but tough mafia guys. The rear of the car remained hidden behind the smoked glass. The Monsignor told them he was fine and just waiting to get his moped started again. With that the huge car set off along the road. He forgot all about it until a few days later when he answered a late-night knock on his door at the presbytery. The callers were two strongly built men who looked quite menacing in the darkness, but he recognised them from the blacked-out car.

'Can I help you gentlemen?'

'No, Father, we'd like to help you,' the driver said. 'Our boss don't like seeing you riding about on that mechanised bicycle. He don't think it's seemly for a priest to ride bikes.'

'Oh, I see, tell him I'll bear it in mind. What does he suggest I do?'

'Mr Sinatra wants you to ditch the bike and use his car as he's leaving the island tomorrow. Here's the keys. Goodnight, Father, and enjoy the car.'

The bulletproof Cadillac had remained in the garage ever since, just in case there was another farewell tour by 'Ole Blue Eyes'.

Money was very tight just before my holiday back to the UK and the adventure in Mexico, when the Jeep developed an awful rattling sound at the back of the engine. It still ran around but sounded serious enough for me to call into the Jeep mechanic to assess the problem. After the usual sucking of teeth, umming and aahing he told me the bad news: the catalytic converter had collapsed within the exhaust, needed to be replaced, and a spare would have to be flown down from Miami. That would take two weeks and the whole job would cost $400 that I did not possess.

After my chin hit the floor, the mechanic took pity on me and offered an alternative, telling me to visit a friend of his at a small workshop near the airport. I tracked this chap down and he confirmed the same issue but suggested a much cheaper option by cutting off the broken unit and replacing it with a piece of steel scaffolding pole. Now this was more like it and he was definitely speaking my language. I left him with the Jeep and after a couple of hours returned to find the Jeep outside his workshop, and he had even washed it.

'Do you want the good news or the bad news first?' he asked.

'Start with the bad news.' I had a slight trepidation in my voice.

'I had to use some stainless-steel pipe, so it will be a bit more expensive.'

'And the good news is…?'

'This exhaust pipe will never corrode, you'll get more miles per gallon, better performance and I'm only going to charge you $20.'

I could have hugged him but instead I gave him the cash plus a $5 tip and left the area smiling broadly.

Jeep sorted, the festive season was upon us, and from lunchtime on Christmas Eve, Mr Jones hosted a delightful party in his office that put the stopper on my squash game against Alec. The conversation moved on to what we were doing that evening and I hesitated before admitting that I was attending midnight mass. Instead of the expected ridicule, one of the boys asked if I could take his girlfriend and he would get there when he finished work.

It was a pleasant experience and many familiar faces were in attendance as I compared it to my previous midnight mass back in the north of England. The drunken village idiot had attended during a pang of conscience but was unable to contain the unholy spirit within him. During the sermon he rose from his pew, walked up onto the altar, lit his cigarette from a candle and blew a perfect smoke ring to the heavens above, just as the parish helpers got to him. He was gently escorted away saying, 'I've been thrown out of better places than this, you know!'

As he disappeared from view through the sacristy door he even managed to call out to the congregation, 'And a very merry Christmas to you all...'

In St Ignatius there was no such cabaret and none would have been entertained. As the lights were extinguished we held flickering, spluttering candles to welcome midnight. Then, to my surprise the Monsignor began to speak in a different tongue. It was as if there was a minor miracle happening, until slowly, and just above a whisper, different members of the congregation began singing. I knew the tune but did not know these words. I glanced around and saw a number of the Irish parishioners begin to join in with the hauntingly beautiful Gaelic rendition of 'Silent Night'. It brought tears to both eyes.

Back at Caribbean Suites I flicked the a/c to maximum as I prepared my supper of a hot whisky toddy and shortbread biscuits, before settling down to watch the film version of *A Christmas Carol* – you know, the best one, with Alastair Sim – and then allowed myself to wallow in the nostalgia of Christmas past, present and the Christmas yet to come...

Christmas morning dawned with a walk to the beach and a session snorkelling around the multi-coloured coral reef 50 feet from the shore. I recognised a large barracuda that lived there that I had named Barry, but he ignored me this morning, which was most unusual. He normally popped out of his cave to have a swim around me looking for smaller prey, but today he kept hidden just showing me a mouthful of razor-like teeth. I supposed he either had a hangover or no one had given him any presents. There was a distinct lack of the smaller fish around the reef but I thought nothing much about it as I snorkelled on. My return journey took me back past the reef then I saw something below that caught my breath. It was a huge octopus that looked as big as a bus and was glaring straight at me. No wonder the residents of the reef were keeping out of the way. I could see the two beady eyes watching me from about 15 feet away as his tentacles moved slowly and independently in time with the waves.

Everything looks bigger underwater, but this chap looked massive, menacing and out for trouble, so I took the coward's way out and quickly swam for home. However, I felt the touch of a rogue tentacle as I struck out for the safety of the beach. Of course it could have been some seaweed brushing against my leg but for the benefit of the story it was definitely a huge tentacle. I lay on the beach to dry off, keeping a wary eye out for the octopus or his dad if they scurried up the sand to catch me unawares.

I regaled the tale of my escape from certain death when I arrived at the Hyatt Hotel for the Christmas Champagne Brunch we had arranged for all the UK officers and numerous hangers-on. I made sure to enjoy a starter of deep-fried squid in golden breadcrumbs before enjoying the more seasonal fare on offer. We were all smartly dressed in keeping with the ambiance and seated outside under a cabana on the terrace of the hotel, overlooking the carefully manicured grounds, where we enjoyed a terrific meal in cheerful company.

Later in the evening I explored the ballroom which was lit up like a warehouse and spotted three tables of senior officers, wives and families, accompanied by 'Greensleeves' as a poor attempt at seasonal music. Everyone sat in stony silence looking down at the tablecloth as I walked in on the aftermath of the Commissioner finishing a drunken tirade which ended with him being grossly and inappropriately offensive to a young woman on another table. I escaped to the terrace where a few of the younger diners soon followed and we were later joined by the Jones and Timms contingents adding to the good humour and cheerful inappropriate banter far into the evening. The main topic of conversation centred on what our colleagues back home would be doing at that particular time. They might be being paid 'double overtime' for their troubles but the cold, wet and miserable UK certainly put my life in Cayman into sharp focus. The Jeep, hotel suite, swimming with octopuses, a wonderful meal on a sun-dappled terrace with a trip to Mexico planned – what was not to like?

My Caymanian travel agent had never heard of the Chiapas region in Mexico and neither had I. In the heady days before the internet she had produced a huge reference book and studied the detail of how to assist me in my quest to reach it upon my return from the UK. Mexico City from Miami was not a problem but reaching the hinterlands was more of an issue. However, these travel agents do like a challenge. Perusing a map we worked out that there was a small airstrip near a place called Tuxtla and what appeared to be a road leading up the mountains to my intended destination – San Cristóbal de las Casas.

After asking if her travel agency reference book could give me any indication of how to get from the airstrip or where to stay at my intended destination, she gave a shake of the head, shrug of the shoulders and a big smile, followed by that most unhelpful phrase, 'Search me.'

So, to recap:

1. I was heading to an unfamiliar mountainous region with poor communications.

2. To visit two young women I had met and spent a couple of hours with – six months previously – and in the meantime only exchanged a couple of letters via donkey mail.
3. I had no idea how to travel to the town from the airstrip.
4. Not a clue what accommodation there could be.
5. I would be on my own with no support.
6. There was some suggestion that the area had some local bandit/terrorist activity.
7. I could not speak a word of Spanish, with or without a lisp.

Putting it down on paper now highlights just how youth, recklessness and stupidity intertwine, but not a lot was going to stop me embarking on this once-in-a-lifetime adventure. What could possibly go right?

PART III

BUCCANEERS AND PIRATES

CHAPTER 16

UP MEXICO WAY

The bumpy landing at a rainy and windswept Manchester Airport was accurately described by the aircraft steward as the most dramatic performed by the captain since he lost half of his Lancaster's tail over Berlin. The rain was freezing and coming at me horizontally as I gathered my luggage and made my way out of the terminal. It was great to catch up with family and friends and I had a lovely, festive Christmas but I chose not to see my ex-girlfriend and reopen old wounds. Things had moved on and I wished her well. The weather soon got worse and snow and ice blanketed the northwest of England. I was missing the sunshine and warmth of the Caribbean in my bones; I could not wait to return.

My return flight from the UK landed at Miami and I rushed to get the connection to Mexico City for the next adventure. I had the address for Inga and Torhild but little else, and looking it up on a map, it seemed to be a very long way south of Mexico City. They were studying languages in the small town of San Cristóbal in the mountainous Chiapas region. Apparently the main reason the girls were studying there was the fact that the region still spoke the Spanish language in its original form. Modern Spanish speakers had had to adapt to the current way of pronunciation when one of their monarchs spoke with a pronounced lisp and therefore this style of communicating had to be accepted and used by the entire Spanish-speaking world. There was no point in embarrassing the poor man, was there? The Chiapas region held out from the rest of Mexico due to sheer bloody-mindedness and the adherence to the original language here remained strong and it was the perfect place for it to be studied by language students from around the world.

I did not know if they had replied to my letter earlier in December, but it was now mid-January and I intended to press on in any case, as I had been invited and I wanted to visit the area and would probably never get the opportunity again. Before leaving the UK, I had a bright idea of phoning the study centre, but the local receptionist could not understand my enquiry so put me through to another phone number in the village, where the lone English speaker was not available. I asked her to leave a message for them but without any conviction that it would be communicated – it must have been the Lancashire accent – mine, not hers.

The flight from Miami allocated seats on a first-come basis, so I jostled my way through and was allocated a seat in first class, which was great other than having to share my personal space. My neighbour was a fat chain-smoking Polish American of Venezuelan extraction, with rolls of body fat that flowed over into my seat. There were a few squeaks from him when my elbow rested heavily on the offending blubber until he got the message and pulled his skin out of my way. The connecting flight did not leave the now dark and hazy Mexico City until the following morning, so I got a taxi from the airport to the Ritz Hotel in the older part of the city. I presume that the four stars on the welcome sign had been painted by someone with a sense of humour, i.e. not the receptionist, as it bore no resemblance to the description or quality of the accommodation. It was pretty dingy with a number of streetwalkers hanging around the front entrance. I was shown to my little room and had to carry my own bag as the porter looked incapable and the metal cage lift in the stairwell was not working and did not appear to have ever done so. He put out his hand for a tip, which I shook vigorously and closed the door.

There was a pictorial sign over the bathroom tap indicating that it would give you diarrhoea if you drank from it. To prevent an unwelcome episode of Montezuma's Revenge, I stuck to a couple of bottles of mineral water and tried to operate the television hanging off the wall. The flimsy curtains did not meet in the middle and the bedcovers had a life of their own. I checked the hotel information sheet and read the rather unsettling advice translated into pidgin English:

SECURITY NOTISES – IT RECOMMEDNED TO USE ALL SECURITY MESURE – INCLUDING BACK OF CHAIR IF REQUIRED.

I did not need telling twice and settled down for a poor night's sleep by shoving the wardrobe against the door.

The Mexicana flight to Tuxtla was in a turbo-prop aircraft which swiftly took us out of the poisonous bowl of hills containing Mexico City into clear blue skies. I could see stunning views of the snow-capped mountains and gently steaming volcanoes over which we were to fly. Tuxtla airport was surprisingly new, clean and cheerful as I arrived in the sunshine then spoke to the tourist desk staff. They pointed me in the direction of a minibus outside the terminus with the name San Cristóbal emblazoned on the front.

The driver charged me 50,000 pesos, which quite took my breath away until one of the other passengers pointed out it was

US$17 or in real money £8.50 sterling – so I got on. The helpful passenger introduced himself as Al, and his pal as Nat, who were Americans and regular visitors to the area. Al was a writer and Nat a sculptor. We headed up to our destination at over 8,000 feet above sea level, the views from the minibus becoming more and more dramatic as we snaked around sheer drops and through luscious forests. Al and Nat were amazed that I had not made any plans or arrangements for accommodation, suggesting that there were a couple of dodgy boarding houses in the town but not much else.

'Why don't you see if they have any room at our place?' Al said. 'It's full of eccentrics, I'm sure you'll fit in just great.'

We pulled up outside a hacienda type of farm house on the outskirts of the town and saw a wooden sign with peeling paint swinging noisily in the breeze. The sign had a hand-painted picture of a jaguar together with the name 'Na Balom' beneath. The outer walls were roughly painted in a dark mustard hue with red clay roof tiles above. I followed them in through the large wooden barn doors out from the strong sunlight and saw them greeted like long lost friends by the receptionist.

'Have you got a room for our friend?' Nat asked her.

She glanced towards me. 'Only a small single is available.' I hesitated when she quoted the price.

'Take it,' said Al. 'It's a bit expensive but clean and the food is the best around. You won't regret it.'

I agreed and the receptionist showed me through the stunning courtyard propped up at the edges with stout stone pillars, to my room overlooking the countryside beyond the town. The room had a little bathroom that was sparse but serviceable. There was a small card written in Spanish propped behind the lavatory, so I asked her to translate.

'Do not use toilet paper,' she said.

'What are the alternatives?' I looked around for some fresh cut leaves.

'No, put it in that bucket with the lid on it. The plumbing is too small.'

The bedroom was beautiful, welcoming and clean with hand-woven woollen blankets of bright reds, greens and blues covering the bed. There was a little brick fireplace in the corner neatly laid with kindling and logs.

'Will I need that?'

'Oh yes,' she said. 'The day sun is warm but the night moon is freezing.'

Just before seven o'clock, I met Al and Nat in the bar before dinner where they explained the way that Na Balom operated. It was a museum, bar, hotel, restaurant and home to the elderly owner. She was called Gertrude (Trudy) Duby Blom, in her late 90s and continuing to run the hacienda as her own fiefdom. She had been born in Switzerland and in her youth had been thrown out of Nazi Germany where her first husband had been a reporter investigating reports of anti-Semitism during the 1930s. She later remarried and with her new husband moved to the Chiapas region to work with and support the local tribes in an attempt to maintain their indigenous lifestyles with a natural eco-system even before the word eco-system had been invented. Al and Nat looked forward to their stay and had always found Trudy to be strong willed, opinionated, interesting and unwilling to suffer fools gladly.

When Trudy's husband died she had to try and maintain Na Balom as a means to earn an income. The name means 'House of the Jaguar' in the local language and was also a little play on her surname. Trudy began to take in paying guests or those whose artisan skills could enhance the existence of the hacienda.

Therefore, I would have to pay. We went in for dinner where everyone sat around the huge table which could seat 26. I introduced myself to those around me as was expected by the host who sat at the far end of the ancient table and banged her walking stick on it to attract our attention. Trudy then waited for the immediate silence and said a single word, 'Grace.'

Everyone repeated the word aloud as Nat leant towards me and whispered, 'Looks like we've all said grace then.'

The waiting staff moved into the room and served the meal prepared using many excellent ingredients from the hacienda's own grounds. It was deliciously fresh, healthy and all three courses cooked to perfection. It was all a delight other than the camomile tea we finished the meal with. As the dishes were cleared away, we were shepherded into the adjacent room where there was a fine old grand piano being warmed up by Richard. He was the Pianist in Residence and lived here on a semi-permanent basis whilst composing music and providing concerts for evening entertainment. He gave a recital of 20 minutes of well-known works and his own compositions to rapturous applause from the audience. Carolyn, the manager of the hacienda, spoke at the end of the recital.

'For the benefit of those who are unfamiliar with Na Balom, whoever is last up, check all the keys have been taken off the rack and bolt the outer door. Good night and sleep well.'

I walked across the open courtyard and saw more stars in the heavens than I had ever known existed. The night was crystal clear and cold and bright despite the lack of a moon – it was not needed. Getting back to my room I found the light on by the bed and the log fire roaring away in the corner giving a burst of warmth as I entered. It had been a brilliant and interesting day and I wondered, with a little trepidation, what the following day would bring.

Breakfast was at the same huge table and I studied the menu

card stuck in a large block of polished wood. It was all in Spanish, so the writing meant absolutely nothing to me. A small waitress approached me but could not understand English, so I pointed at two items on the card. Her face showed some surprise and she repeated the order back to me. I bluffed and confirmed it. She walked off to the kitchen and returned almost immediately back through the swing doors with a couple of men dressed as chefs. She was gabbling something and pointed straight at me. The chefs shook their heads and raised their hands as they disappeared back into the kitchen.

A couple of other guests joined me at the table, so I turned the menu card to face them and pushed it across the table as my heart fluttered slightly. I was now looking at the English translation of the menu and felt myself flush – what on earth had I ordered? The waitress kicked open the kitchen door swiftly followed by five kitchen staff who gawped at me as the breakfast approached at arm's length to be dropped unceremoniously in front of me. There was an enormous bowl of steaming porridge topped off with a fried egg – sunny side up.

The lady sitting opposite me physically recoiled. 'You aren't going to eat that, are you?'

'Oh yes,' I said. 'It's a well-known Lancastrian concoction that really sticks to the ribs, you know – lovely grub!'

I set about it with gusto and finished it off with some chunks of bread, marmalade and a huge mug of Mexican coffee – it wasn't that bad actually.

I tracked down the language school but it turned out my friends were away for the day on a trip to a neighbouring village, so I left a note to say I had called and would contact them the following day. I explored the town centre and environs whilst wafting away the indigenous Indian peddlers attempting to flog me their wares.

Sitting outside a welcoming cantina, I enjoyed lunch on the Zócalo, which is the main square of Mexican towns and often framed around the church and town hall. The whitewashed walls and red clay tiled roofs were very representative of the towns I had seen on television and this one reminded me of John Wayne's version of the Alamo – but with less shooting, fewer marching bands and no racoon hats in sight. There was no pollution at this altitude, which gave the sunshine an obvious clarity that, unsurprisingly, attracted many painters and artists to this pleasant village. The sun was bright and hot, but in the shadows surprisingly cold.

I spent the afternoon roaming the sites then returned to my warm, welcoming little room to enjoy the quiet ambience until there was a light knock at my door. Carolyn the manager was there. 'Hello, there's a phone call for you.'

'But no one knows I'm here,' I said, wondering if someone, somehow was playing a practical joke on me.

'They asked for you by name, so don't keep them waiting, come on.'

I went over to the reception, lifted the receiver and identified myself.

'Hello it's Inga, how are you?'

'Great thanks, but how did you know where I'm staying?' I said, barely able to suppress my surprise.

'We hoped you might be there as we've heard it's such a nice place to stay.'

We made arrangements to meet the next day and I replaced the receiver. Carolyn then said something else that stopped me in my tracks. 'We also have an envelope with your name on it.'

'Now this is getting spooky,' I said.

'It's been here for you since last week but I did not recognise your name until just now.'

This was all getting a bit much for me as she thrust an envelope into my hand...

'Come on,' said Carolyn. 'Open it, I'm intrigued.'

I carefully peeled open the envelope and extracted a single sheet of paper and flattened it on the desk. It started with my name and explained that I had been in touch with the Language College but had spoken to the caretaker. She had been concerned that she could not clarify what I was phoning about, so put me through to Na Balom where a number of English speakers might have been able to help. The phone line from the UK went dead but the caretaker spoke to Trudy, who wrote the letter to explain the unfortunate lack of communication and hoped to welcome a fellow adventurer to her home. It was hospitality to a whole other level. Back home, I don't think anyone would go to that trouble and it was another lovely reminder of the adventure I was having.

Carolyn sat me next to Trudy for dinner that night for a thoroughly enjoyable evening during which she spoke easily in numerous languages to various visitors seated around the table. Despite the lack of TV, she was very well informed of current events especially of the ongoing issues in the Middle East and thanked me personally for providing the BBC World Service. She recommended that I should continue my adventures to a number of local villages which my Scandinavian friends may not yet have stumbled across.

The next day, fortified with a hearty full Mexican cooked breakfast (without porridge), I met with Inga and Torhild at their happy little cottage with its sunny rear garden festooned with colourful hammocks. It was wonderful to see them again and they proved to be terrific company and excellent guides. Any sense of trepidation about taking such a decision having barely known them nor the place they were going were soon swept away at the beauty of the landscape. I think the Caribbean lifestyle was rubbing off on me, and in a positive way. In the afternoon we made our way to Gravis, which was a stunning pine forest with spectacular limestone caves and waterfalls, and like a poor remake of Indiana Jones we paid $3 to ride surefooted ponies back to town.

Back at Na Balom, Nat, Al and I had become a fixture at the dinner table and each night was entertaining. This evening everyone tried to keep the news away from Trudy that the Middle East had just erupted into another armed conflict during the first Gulf War. Carolyn had even removed her longwave radio and the hearing aid batteries for the time being to stop her being upset. After the meal, I met with the girls and we went to watch the disconcerting CNN news in a convenient bar along the cobbled lane back into the town.

Friday at Na Balom was concert night and Inga and Torhild were keen to come for dinner, so I paid for their places at the packed table. I greeted them at the door. They had dressed perfectly for the evening event and I felt they really appreciated the invitation. I heard one diner arriving before I saw him. A loudmouth American in his 50s walked through the door followed by someone that could have been his son. The Yank approached the table, stood there and addressed everyone caring to listen – I had little choice.

'I've brought my friend to see this great woman. The things she's done and seen are amazing, I'm so glad that I've had the chance to come here. Say – what's she called again?'

Nat and Al glanced at me and slowly shook their heads and silently mouthed, 'Bull-shitter.' The noisy Yank tried to elbow his way to the head of the table before Carolyn escorted him to the far end just as Trudy arrived for 'Grace'. The Yank continued his pontifications from the bottom of the table. 'I'm glad I've made it before she dies, eh?'

The meal was served and enjoyed in between the never-ending opinions of the newly arrived loudmouth. 'The US of A are gonna wup the ass of those rag-heads in Arabia, hey Trudy?'

Silence descended over the table, then after a short period of contemplation she spoke in measured tones. 'If you had ever personally experienced war, you would not be so glib to speak of the loss of people's lives in such terms. I suggest you keep your ill-informed opinions to yourself whilst in my home or leave now.'!

The rest of us applauded loudly.

The feast of St Sebastian was celebrated on 20th January at a smaller village a few miles away in the sandier foothills of the Chiapas mountains. Trudy told me that the fiesta was remarkable and not often experienced by outsiders, so Inga, Torhild, Al and Nat accompanied me in a taxi to the area. The driver was somewhat reluctant to drive there but eventually dropped us on the edge of the village, promising to return later if we were still alive. I told him he would only get paid upon our safe return, which caused him to mumble unprintable oaths under his breath as he left us to our fate. I wondered what his problem was. The village was inhabited by a group of Tzotzil Mayans that live autonomously without any government interference including policing or federal influence. They deal with all matters themselves and we were told to keep a low profile and out of trouble as nobody would be coming to our assistance.

The village was living in a time warp and we could have been on the film set of *The Magnificent Seven*. The five of us walked through to the small zócalo in front of the neat white church where the fiesta was just beginning and were greeted by a sudden, huge explosion just to the front of us. With my ears ringing and eyes stinging, the white smoke cleared in the breeze and the celebrations began. It was all a little baffling, with random fireworks set off when least expected, groups of children and adults dancing in brightly coloured clothes and three different bands playing three different tunes, all at the same time.

The church was the focus of the celebration, but when I went inside noticed that there was little sign of any Christian worship. The crucifix, statues and holy pictures were missing, the benches pushed to the side and the floor covered in branches from the surrounding pine forest. There was a distinct lack of any evidence of Christianity, which was definitely at odds with the name of the festival being celebrated. The pagan ritual taking place within the church stemmed from the local beliefs which existed in the Mayan peoples prior to the arrival of the Franciscan monks over 500 years ago in an apparently failed attempt to instil Christianity among the inhabitants. I took out my camera to take an image of the unusual type of worshipping and felt a firm hand grab mine. Inga quickly pushed the camera back in my pocket, hissed in my ear, 'Put it away!' then pushed me outside.

When we emerged back into the strong sunshine the conversation continued in a whisper as she warily looked around. 'You could get us all killed,' she hissed. 'I told you not to use it before we left.'

'I know but didn't think it was that serious.' I felt rather foolish.

'Last year they stoned a tourist to death for taking a similar picture. They feel it removes their spirits and they can never enter the afterlife.'

I was more subdued as we remained to watch the confusing events proceed around the village until a group of men garishly dressed as monkeys and others wearing jaguar skins appeared dancing as if in a trance. Some women arrived with dresses made of bright pink material and joined in this group apparently as some sort of fertility ritual. Another massive firework exploded in the centre of the group, followed swiftly by a group of mounted and armed *comancheros* who rode into the group firing revolvers in the air scattering the peasants to the edges of the square. The main *bandito* had the distinct look of a young Eli Wallach about him as his gold tooth glinted menacingly in the sun. Another loud bang brought the events to a sudden halt, leaving the square almost deserted as the cloud of smoke dissipated. Nat looked around us and said, 'Wow! What the hell was that all about?'

Under a branch-covered cabana a teenage girl squatted by a fire and offered us some corn tortillas she was preparing on a large metal disc. Inga spoke to her and we agreed to pay a few pesos for the hospitality. The girl produced a couple of stoneware jars and unscrewed the cover to reveal some paste-like contents which she offered us with the snack. One of them was a lumpy green concoction which cheered me enormously as I spread it on my tortilla.

'Another Lancashire delicacy,' I announced to the group. 'It's amazing that they eat mushy peas all the way out here.'

'*No, señor,*' the girl said. '*Es guacamole.*'

She was right, and not wishing to appear a complete ignoramus, I pointed at the pot of green stuff and said to the girl, 'Avocado?'

She started to giggle, stood up and ran laughing to the back of the house. I looked to Inga for an explanation.

'It's time we were going before her father comes out with his shotgun. Avocado is Mayan for testicles.'

Safely back in the sanctuary of the courtyard bar at Na Balom, we examined what we had just experienced. It had been vibrant, colourful, exciting and we wouldn't have missed it for the world. None of us could actually understand what had been going on at the festival to St Sebastian but we were glad to have seen it, got out alive and in celebration polished off a couple of well-earned glasses of beer prior to my final dinner in the hacienda. It was a wonderful way to finish my enjoyable jaunt to San Cristóbal de las Casas.

The following day I returned to Cayman via Mexico City and Miami to be greeted by Nobby, a case of beer, my fully fuelled Jeep and life back in the less colourful but real world of drug smuggling, corruption and a ship full of pirates.

CHAPTER 17

TALES OF THE JOLLY ROGER

The presence of controlled drugs on the island bubbled beneath the surface like a hookah pipe, impacting upon the local population most of all. The expat community knew that any drug conviction would have them swiftly removed from their lucrative contracts on the island, and the luxurious lifestyle with its potential huge financial rewards would be lost forever. Caymanians would not suffer the same fate, but to them the prison sentences were a serious deterrent.

Over the previous months the Drugs Squad had seized a huge amount of illegal drugs which were due to be destroyed. The Commissioner saw the opportunity for a bit of good publicity, so he invited the reporter from the local *Caymanian Compass* newspaper to a secret location in the swamps to witness the burning of half a ton of ganga and cocaine. Expecting this to be kept confidential was a forlorn hope after they published the time and place of the conflagration on the front cover of that morning's edition. Hundreds turned up, including a number of packed tourist buses that drove there straight from the cruise ship terminal.

A recently seized wooden cabin cruiser was languishing beneath the shade of the poinciana tree, which was DCI Timms' favourite parking spot. He arranged for the drugs to be dumped inside the boat, hauled onto a trailer, then towed to the swamps. The crowd gathered downwind as Detective Sergeant Mac doused the boat liberally with a jerry can of petrol. The Governor, Commissioner and civic dignitaries preened themselves for the photo opportunities, preparing quotes destined for the newspaper. For the main event, DS Mac was given the honour of setting fire to a wooden staff wrapped in oil-soaked rags. His few strands of long, greying hair blew freely around his head as he applied his Zippo lighter to the torch. It burst into a smoky, stinking flame which he held aloft to the cheers of the crowd, then with both hands, circled it around his head and launched it into the boat like a Viking king setting forth his dead father towards Valhalla. The onlookers roared their approval as DS Mac raised his hands in salute.

There was a whoosh of fire as the plumes of coloured tongues licked around the packages, melting the plastic, spilling their contents into the bottom of the boat as the dense orange cloud spewed out towards the eager onlookers. After a few minutes the crowd became noticeably louder and some laughed inanely as they inhaled deeply, side-stepping into the fumes. Then the breeze unexpectedly altered. DS Mac's remaining flowing strands of hair abruptly changed direction as we were engulfed in a fog of pungent fumes from which the official observers starburst to escape. DCI Timms remained standing in the smog where, deep from within, I heard his crackly voice call, 'This is some bloody good shit.'

Thankfully the wind changed back towards the crowd as the official party began to move off for lunch. Then there was a sudden eye-aching flash of white, the boom of a loud explosion as a pressure wave thumped me in the chest and violently rocked the

Jeep. After a few seconds the dust cleared to show that the boat had vaporised into a mushroom cloud careering skywards. Bits of scorched planks and burning packages blew wildly about the marl revealing a small crater where it had once been. As other VIPs struggled to their feet, DCI Timms staggered out of the smoke like a resident of Pompeii coughing up dust and debris, brushing smouldering embers from his greying hair and grimy lined face. He swiftly jumped into my Jeep to dodge the wave of earth-bound shrapnel as it pinged and clanged off the bodywork like an out-of-tune steel drum. Pointlessly dusting off the knees of his trousers, he sat back in the seat and chuckled, 'Some idle bastard forgot to drain the petrol tank.'

Cocaine was the drug of choice for smugglers as there was a huge financial reward for importing it and cutting it with talcum powder to make it go further. There were many secluded coves and inlets that made the illegal importation relatively easy from Central America using large fishing boats that operated around the region. By the time these boats entered the harbour at George Town they were usually clean and empty of contraband and illegal items – but not always.

I was on the early-morning shift and drove to enjoy a light breakfast before the island woke and jobs began to pile up. I wore my favourite .357 Smith &Wesson revolver as later in the morning I was to assist with a gold bullion delivery from the airport. It was a strange experience wearing a gun in public and not a very relaxing one. Unconsciously I always seemed to be tapping or checking it, in case I dropped it or forgot it somewhere. It actually made me feel more vulnerable as I imagined someone might try and grab it at a fight or a domestic dispute, but it would be more effective than my wooden truncheon if an armed robber appeared on that warm, sunny spring day. As I was finishing my sausage and egg muffin in the café, the radio crackled into life telling me to go to the main dock in George Town harbour where a fight had broken out on a boat and someone had been stabbed. I drove through the main gates and was directed towards the harbour wall where a large rusting fishing boat with peeling black and green paint was tied up. Its radio mast fluttered with a faded, wind-ripped flag of a skull and crossbones bearing a crooked, gapped-tooth smile.

As I reached the gangplank I noted its name to be *The Jolly Roger*. The harbour master told me that a couple of the boat's crew had been fighting with knives and the injured man was in his office. Inside, wearing a greasy T-shirt and shorts, a small man in his 30s with the complexion of a conker was holding a blood-soaked towel to his forearm. I called for an ambulance and asked what had happened. He gave his name as Marco and only spoke Spanish, so the harbour master translated until Sergeant Bodden arrived to help.

Marco explained that he was the cook and had cut himself in the boat's galley peeling potatoes for breakfast, but he wanted to leave without reporting anything. He focused his eyes on the floor and spoke in short sharp bursts without looking up, then without warning another man burst in shouting at him in Spanish. It was the first mate of *The Jolly Roger*, and I turned to him, pushed him out of the office, telling him to get lost or be arrested for intimidating my witness. He walked back to the boat mumbling oaths as he went. This was giving me a bad feeling as I continued to try to get at the truth. I asked for a statement but Marco just shook his head. The ambulance crew arrived, cleaned the long, straight wound and sealed it. When they said no hospital visit was needed, his face dropped.

I encouraged him again to explain what had happened and it

began to dawn on him the enormity of his situation as very soon he would be returning to his ship. For the first time, he looked up and I saw tears welling up in his eyes; they were of fear not upset. Even within the air-conditioned office he was sweating heavily with drips saturating the desk and rough carpet. He used the corner of the blooded towel to wipe his face and arms then sat back. I told him we could go with him to recover his property but he didn't react, so it was time for us to go. As I stood to leave, Marco jumped up and grabbed my arm, gabbling uncontrollably in English.

'Don't leave me here, please I beg you…the Captain will kill me just like he's murdered other ships' crews out at sea… It's a pirate ship,' Marco said.

I did not expect that. Sgt Bodden and I looked at each other.

'They attack other ships, steal cargoes, shoot the crews then sink them.'

'We need to get you away from here to give us a statement,' I said.

'No statement, just get me away.'

'How do I know you're not just making this up?'

'There are many guns on board, hidden in the Captain's cabin,' Marco said. 'They use them to murder the other crews.'

The harbour master then spoke. 'The Captain only handed over a pump-action shotgun and ammo when he arrived yesterday. They're required to store them with me for safekeeping while in the harbour.'

'There's more than that,' Marco said. 'It's all in a locked trunk in his cabin.'

The harbour master told us the Captain had left earlier to speak to the owner of the boat, who lived on the island. I got another constable to keep an eye on Marco whilst we went to *The Jolly Roger*. The humour in the flag with its crooked smile, now had a distinctly sour taste as we walked up the gangplank to find the first mate blocking our way.

'Where's your search warrant?'

A couple of squad cars drove into the harbour yard followed by Sgt Benjamin, who got out of his red pickup with his semi-automatic M16 rifle cradled in his arms like a newborn. I pointed over to the pickup. 'He's got it.'

The first mate got the message, stepped aside, then with hunched shoulders showed us to the Captain's cabin.

Soon after, we were in the bowels of the boat standing in a dingy corridor, lit solely by a grimy bulkhead lamp with its stench of rotting fish, fuel oil and cabbage.

'I don't have no keys for the door,' he said. 'The Captain keeps 'em on his belt.'

The cabin door looked solid and a couple of preparatory kicks proved it. The movies show the hero putting his shoulder to it as it springs dramatically open – I had learnt much earlier in my career not to believe such nonsense; it only hurts your shoulder. We found a couple of bent, rust-pitted screwdrivers and began chipping away at the seasoned teak door, struggling to spring the lock, while sweat dripped from our arms and faces. For 20 minutes we broiled in the passageway of the stinking tub, skinning our hands and knuckles whilst the first mate leant against the wall puffing on a cheap cigar, smirking and passing sarcastic comments at our efforts. That, together with the awkward rolling of the sea, finally got the better of me and I cracked.

'Right,' I said as I stood up. 'I've had enough of this, get back Sarge.'

I pulled out my revolver and fired at the lock. There was a deafening bang, a crack past my ear followed by a heart-sinking tinkle of glass plunging us into darkness. The first mate ran screaming like a banshee as we were cloaked in a sickly swirling cloud of cordite. In the increasing glimmer of twilight from a distant porthole, the Sergeant spoke calmly and carefully.

'Well, Constable, that sure was the stupidest thing you've ever done.'

I had to agree, my shirt stuck to my back and my heart rate lowering, slightly. I tried to redeem myself by announcing over the radio that everything was in order on the boat then went in search of better tools. The first mate was on deck, crouching behind a locker shaking uncontrollably.

'You could a' killed me,' he said.

I shrugged my shoulders. 'You probably deserve it. I want a torch, a hammer and a crowbar, now.'

He scrabbled in a cupboard and handed them over swiftly before returning to the safety of his locker. The torch revealed that the lock was still intact but bent out of shape and would never open again, with or without a key. The good news was that the cabin door opened outwards and the sturdy hinge pins were exposed. After more hot and uncomfortable struggles we managed to force them out and lever the door open. The cleaners had not been regular visitors to the smelly and unkempt cabin where clothes and unspecified bits of detritus were strewn around; in common parlance it was a complete shithole. The first mate recovered his nerve sufficiently to follow us in, so I pushed him out again – it was becoming a habit. From beneath the bunk we pulled out a heavy steel-banded trunk secured with a formidable looking padlock. I did not waste time asking for a key.

'Why don't we just shoot it off?' I said, then watched as Sgt Bodden's eyes widened alarmingly as he shook his head slowly from side to side. 'Then again, I suppose maybe not if it's full of ammunition.'

A much more sensible option was hanging in the corridor. From the wall I took a vicious-looking fire axe and measured my swing against the low ceiling of the cabin. After many blows I was exhausted, so the Sergeant took over, and following many more muscle-aching swings the hasp and lock spun off across the floor with a metallic crash. Feeling rather like *Treasure Island*'s Jim Hawkins and his widowed mother, we knelt before the trunk and carefully raising the lid that creaked atmospherically in the cabin gloom, I eagerly pulled a greasy sheet from the top to reveal its treasures.

The chest contained a small navy's worth of weapons and boxes of bullets. There were AK 47 Kalashnikov sub-machine guns, a Browning 30.06 bolt action rifle with sniper scope, Beretta 9mm automatic pistols, snub-nose Smith & Wesson .38 pistols, and hundreds of rounds of ammunition for them all.

We arrested the first mate and all of the crew, secured the boat and all its contents after searching all the nooks and crannies. I set about the file of evidence and the CID became involved back at the station. DCI Timms walked into the interview room as I was preparing the paperwork and began to tell him about the ship, but he already knew more than I did.

'I've had loads of calls about your bloody pirate ship. Do you know it's owned by that dodgy lawyer Adamson and his mate Hollywood who's on the Legislative Assembly? They're absolutely fuming.' He walked out laughing to himself. 'Treasure bloody Island or what.'

A Barbadian circuit judge was on the island covering for His Honour Judge Rudyard and intended to make a good impression on the lawless residents. I was covering court duties when a couple of drug dealers were brought into the dock after being found guilty of committing grievous bodily harm. They had used a bicycle chain to beat a local youth for not paying a drugs debt. The Judge, resplendent in wig and purple robes, addressed them.

'I have searched the Statute Books here on the island and found a most suitable punishment for vermin like you. I have instructed the Governor of Northward Prison to obtain the means to carry out this punishment as a proportionate sentence for the disgusting cruelty you perpetrated on that child. You're each sentenced to receive six lashes from the cat o' nine tails. Officer, take them down.'

I felt really sorry for Mr Appleton General. I was covering the squad car on a busy afternoon shift when I received a call to return to Police HQ where he had asked to speak to me and only me. As I've already described, when I first arrived on Grand Cayman, I dealt with him when I was forced to issue him with a traffic ticket for riding his bicycle without a tag. He remembered my name and wished to speak to me in private. We wheeled his ancient black Raleigh bike through the foyer and into the interview room where I saw tears welling up in his bloodshot eyes. I remembered that he had served in the Royal Navy during the war, so diverted his attention chatting about the British frigate moored in George Town harbour. His weather-beaten face lit up as he reminisced about the Atlantic convoys and other adventures around the seven seas.

He then got to the point of his visit. He had cycled into town to collect his war pension from the bank and put the $200 into his wallet that he kept in his back trouser pocket. When he got home he could not find the wallet and retraced his journey asking various people along the way. In addition to the money there was a whole host of newspaper clippings and photographs he had collected from his long life travelling the world. He spoke to a young girl who said she had found it on the road near a small shop in Rockhole. She had asked at the shop but then a man in a parked car nearby said his friend had lost it, so the girl gave it to him and he drove off.

Initially I felt this was going to be a waste of my precious time but agreed to help him – he deserved to be treated better. Leaving the bike, he put his battered felt trilby back on his grizzled head and I drove him to try and recover his property. It didn't take us long to track down and speak to the young girl and she repeated finding, then handing over the wallet to the man in the car. Rockhole was a poor area comprising of a collection of shacks and concrete sheds, but the locals around the shop were appalled that the wallet had been taken. Very quickly they told me the details of the driver and precisely where he lived.

Benny drove a brand-new Chevrolet Camaro but had no visible means of support – in other words he was a drugs dealer. He lived in another salubrious area officially known as Washington Boulevard but more descriptively known as 'The Swamp'. I dropped off Mr General back at the station to collect his bike and told him to return home where I would update him with any news. I tracked the Camaro to a concrete block construction covered with corrugated irons sheets. Benny and a friend were inside lying on a filthy candy-striped mattress, unsurprised to see me, saying that they had passed the wallet on to the owner who drove a white minibus but they could not quite remember his name or where he lived. 'He was a large dark-skinned guy.'

I pointed out that most of the 50 or so minibuses on the island were driven by big dark-skinned guys. 'Yeah man,' was all he could say. He stretched out on his stinking bed knowing I had little evidence to arrest him, never mind secure a conviction. The little girl and neighbours would not give me a written statement as they did not want to bring any recriminations upon themselves by

Benny or his acquaintances. I was annoyed but could not disprove any of his lies, so searched him, his friend, his shack, the Camaro… and unsurprisingly found nothing incriminating. They were far too relaxed as it was obvious that they expected me. It was incredibly frustrating to know that this person was responsible for taking the money and lifetime souvenirs from Mr General. They probably took the cash then tossed his wallet far into the nearby mangrove swamps, never to be seen again.

Mr General took the bad news graciously, thanking me for my trouble as I apologised for not being able to help, adding my frustration. 'Don't worry, sir,' he said with a shake of his forefinger. 'The Good Lord knows who took it and he'll punish them. Have no doubt about that.'

This particular case really bothered me but I had to move on. The following days driving the squad car soon took my mind off Mr General and I knew he would receive his pension the following month after assuring me he had some savings to call upon.

I finished work late one night when it was very dark and raining heavily. I still had not got my Jeep's windscreen wipers repaired so had to use the old army way. I got my bag of potatoes, sliced one in half, before rubbing it up and down the windscreen in the forlorn hope that it might clear the screen sufficiently for the journey home. A familiar Chevrolet Camaro drove past in the direction of the airport, which I began to follow, forgetting for a moment that I was off duty. Never mind, I thought, I wanted to see where Benny was going, it could be a useful intelligence submission when I was back at work. As he was driving within the speed limit I held well back so as not to spook him, following him into Bodden Town where he pulled up at the side of Bertie's Bar – a well known house of ill repute. I drove a distance past before turning around to contemplate my next move.

Dad once told me that a bag of sugar in the fuel tank was a good way to spoil anybody's day but I did not have one to hand. The Camaro was parked, empty and in shadow, beside the bar, so I pulled off the road then walked back. The car was locked and I heard loud reggae music and chat from inside the bar, so left Benny a little memento before returning to my Jeep. The rain then stopped, allowing me a dry drive home with a smile, a clear windscreen and an even clearer conscience.

A couple of days later I drove along Eastern Avenue towards the airport and saw Benny's Camaro parked outside a motor dealer's workshop with its bonnet raised. A mechanic was looking at it scratching his head. Had he inspected it closer, he would have been very surprised to discover a couple of King Edwards stuffed up the fat exhausts. I wonder how they got there.

CHAPTER 18

THE STRANGE CASE OF DR FELIX KAMPENBOOM

Doctor Felix Sebastian Kampenboom MD was a strange and sinister person. I had noticed him at the bars and pool sides at the more expensive hotels and restaurants, ogling scantily clad females on the sun loungers. I discovered his name when he attended a garden party at Governor's House and noticed that he mingled freely with the influential residents on the island. He was a private physician to a number of these individuals. I felt a gut instinct that there was something very dodgy about him but had absolutely no reason for this concern prior to investigating an unsettling incident at his address.

I received a radio call to attend at his isolated luxurious compound on the more rugged southern coast of the island. There was a report of a phone call from a hysterical female that was abruptly cut off, which had to be investigated. I was with a sensible female officer who originated from Jamaica – Miss Major – and we quickly 'blue lighted' to the scene. This was a warm and sunny Monday morning and this was to be very different from the usual domestic dispute. As I approached the lane leading to the house, the sun was beating down through the palm trees and the sea was crashing through the iron shore blowholes providing spectacular blasts of water 15 feet into the air. The compound had a six feet wall surrounding it, with a view of the sea and palm trees beyond. This was the only house on the lane and the big clue was the gate post bearing an engraved stone plaque with the name F KAMPENBOOM MD.

The main gates were open and I drove in and parked up at the imposing and highly polished teak front doors. The white-painted concrete walls of the single-storey house framed the blue-edged windows with beautifully maintained gardens that could not be seen from the outside. I had never seen the gates open before and presumed that we were expected. We rang the bell and the door was opened by a slim middle-aged Jamaican woman dressed in a grey maid's uniform. She let us into a cool atrium with an expensively tiled floor and lit by a conical-shaped skylight. I asked if Dr Kampenboom was in. She looked down at the floor and shook her head, saying quietly, 'He be back soon time.'

'We have received a call from a female here. Have you called the police?' I asked.

'No, sir, that may be the visitor,' she said.

'Where's the visitor now?'

'Locked in that room, sir.' The maid pointed at a door across the hallway.

Miss Major and I glanced at each other then walked over. I knocked loudly and said, 'Hello, this is the police, can we come in?'

The door handle rattled from within, as a female voice spoke. 'It's locked from the outside and I can't get out.'

I noticed the maid was quietly disappearing through another door and I called her back and asked for the keys. 'The doctor has the only keys, sir.'

I gave the door an exploratory kick but it was too solid for me to break open and I was looking around for another option when the front door suddenly burst open...

'I want you to take that woman and throw her out of my house – she is mentally unstable!' said the new arrival, speaking in a deep, guttural European accent.

'Dr Kampenboom, I presume?' I said, but the humour was wasted.

He was mid-70s, tall, thin, darkly tanned with a totally bald head, lacking eyebrows or facial hair. Looking like a failed extra from *Magnum PI*, he was dressed in a bright and gaudy Hawaiian shirt, khaki shorts with thin bird-like legs dangling down to leather sandals. The large bags under his dark, hooded, piercing eyes made him a really ugly guy. He ignored Miss Major and shouted at me.

'Take her away, she has assaulted me.'

'I want you to unlock that door, I want to speak to your visitor, now.' He glared at me before producing a key ring from his shorts pocket.

As he unlocked the door, he said, 'Don't believe a word she says – she's a mad woman.'

I knocked then entered the room with Miss Major closing the door in his face, leaving him to simmer outside. It was a large, bright and welcoming bedroom with a huge bed, comfortable sofa with wicker chairs, and a glass-topped coffee table looking out of the patio windows over the rear manicured gardens. The only occupant of the room was a small, chubby woman in her 50s, with both tears and fear showing in her eyes. She visibly shook and was terrified. I sat her down on the sofa and after she'd composed herself, she began to explain what had happened.

Her name was Peggy and a Canadian citizen originally from Singapore who had become a successful business owner. A widow for 12 months, she had recently subscribed to a Lonely Hearts column for executives to correspond with like-minded men for company and, perhaps, a little romance. Over a number of months Peggy had written and received letters from Kampenboom, who appeared to her to be a charming, successful and wealthy physician. She had agreed to visit him in his tropical paradise and used it as an excuse to leave the bitter Canadian winter for a vacation.

Her grown-up children had warned her that she should be careful in meeting with an unknown individual, but she had ignored them with the comment, 'What's the worst that could happen?' She soon found out.

Kampenboom had paid for her flight to the island but had booked an open return. Peggy had been asked to bring $500 worth of ginseng, together with an 'adult' massage machine that he could not buy on the island. She was a little concerned but had been reassured that he needed them for a 'long-term condition?' Mmmm, a subtle clue perhaps, but who was I to criticise anyone for a bit of innocent fun in a holiday paradise.

She was collected at the airport but had not recognised him, as the picture he had sent was at least 30 years old. She decided this was a minor setback and was impressed with his beautiful house, but felt he was cool and aloof towards her and put it down to initial shyness. He asked her for her passport, cash and credit cards and placed them in his safe, stating that he did not want her to lose them. Peggy expected to be shown around the island and she asked if they could visit the sites and restaurants she had read about, but the doctor stated that he felt ill and did not wish to go out. She had hardly left the house for the last seven days since her arrival.

She was effectively a prisoner but had hoped that everything would improve – quickly. The only other person she had seen was Maria, the Jamaican maid who lived at the back of the house.

She felt Maria wanted to speak but was frequently scolded by Kampenboom for minor matters, so she kept out of the way. Dr Kampenboom's behaviour began to become even more erratic over the week when he began to discuss his sexual problems, impotence and techniques to deal with them. He showed her numerous photographs of naked women and asked her to pose in a similar fashion for his enjoyment to help his erectile problems. She refused to cooperate and made excuses to leave the room, fearing for her safety.

The following day Kampenboom appeared more positive and after breakfast suggested that they visit George Town for a look around. Peggy was relieved and agreed to accompany him as they drove into town. They stopped outside a bank and he informed her that she should join him inside as he had some business there. They entered an interview room and sat with a bank manager, who he obviously knew, and discussed financial matters. Kampenboom then took Peggy's passport and credit cards out of an envelope and told her to sign a pre-completed form. She was aghast to see it was an application form for a joint bank account in both his and her names.

Peggy was shocked. This was the most bizarre situation she had ever encountered. It was a bad dream that she could not escape from and found it difficult to speak. The bank manager offered her a pen and pointed at the x where she should sign. Fortunately, she found the strength to shout 'No', stood up and ran from the room. The doctor appeared a few moments later, admonishing her. They left the bank and he drove her back to his house in complete silence. She felt powerless as she knew no one on the island, had no access to her money, credit cards, passport or airline tickets and could not access the phone that was in the doctor's locked office – she was terrified.

I let her talk and gently questioned her to clarify details. She had not been subjected to any sexual attack but he had knocked the phone from her hand earlier when she had found his room unlocked. She had called the police but he slammed the phone down. I encouraged her to make a formal complaint but she was very reluctant to provide a statement and just wanted to leave as soon as possible – I did not blame her. She continually dabbed her eyes and frequently stopped to compose herself, sobbing quietly.

'Is there anything further?' I said.

'Yes, he's made me sign a form saying that I am now his common law wife, promising to respect, honour and obey him and give myself totally to him in all matters material, emotional and physical…' Peggy then produced the hand-written document on his headed writing paper confirming it. This more sinister development led me to leave Miss Major to speak privately to Peggy and explore if any physical or sexual offences had been committed. I left the room, intending to speak to Maria the maid and re-entered the atrium where the doctor was waiting.

'Well, I presume you'll arrest her for lying to police – she's mentally unstable.'

I ignored this and told him I wished to speak to the maid.

'No, I refuse. I own her…'

'I think you'll find that slavery was outlawed some time ago – I will speak to her, so don't interfere or you'll be locked up. Understand?'

I left him to consider my threat and found Maria in the kitchen. Her entire demeanour was sad and depressed. She said Peggy was just one of a series of women who had been 'guests' who usually left soon after arriving. She had not seen any violence but refused to give me a written statement as her wages paid for her four children back in Jamaica – she could not afford to leave. I asked if she had suffered at his hand but she promised me that he had never assaulted her in any form and he paid her well, and therefore she minded her own business. She felt he was capable of using violence but she had never seen it. She once overheard him say that he did not find any black woman attractive, so she felt reasonably safe.

I walked back across the atrium and re-entered Peggy's room, reviewing in my mind any potential offences if Peggy or Maria were willing to provide us with a written statement. They ranged from kidnapping, unlawful imprisonment, obtaining money with menaces, theft of money, passport, credit cards, airline tickets, to common assault and any number of other offences. Any one of them could give me the power to arrest him and take him in to languish in the cells. Miss Major confirmed no sexual incident or assault had taken place other than the slight slap to Peggy's wrist earlier in the day.

'Will you confirm in a statement what you have said to us?' I said. 'Even if it's in my pocket note book – it'll give me the evidence to arrest him.'

Peggy looked at her feet and shook her head slowly. 'No, I just want my property to get off the island and forget this nightmare forever. Will you help me leave?'

I was unsurprised that Maria and Peggy were unwilling to provide a statement. It has always been unbelievably frustrating for the police when victims and witnesses make verbal statements but feel uncomfortable to provide written evidence. This was just such a case involving a highly intelligent individual knowing how to cover his tracks and ensuring the chances of prosecution were remote. I told her to get packed and be ready to leave in a few minutes. I took a deep breath and slowly counted to 10. I did not now have the opportunity to arrest Kampenboom and without any supporting evidence had to tread more carefully. I returned to the central atrium which was now empty and saw another door was ajar and looked in. The doctor was seated behind a desk speaking on the phone and, upon seeing me, finished his call. I glanced around and saw that this was his office and also his consulting room, with the added extra of an examination bed partially hidden by curtains. An uncomfortable shiver went down my spine as I thought of less fortunate souls who may have suffered at his hands.

'Well, your guest wishes to leave and I think it's the best way to resolve this situation.'

'Take the bitch away.'

'I need to take some details for my report, could you give me your full details?'

It must have been obvious to him that I was not in a position to arrest him and presumably his phone call had reassured him.

'Certainly, officer,' he continued in his guttural tone with more confidence. 'Felix Sebastian Kampenboom, Doctor of Medicine.' He gave his date of birth in 1920 in the city of Rotterdam in the Netherlands and produced a Puerto Rican passport and a certificate of residency for the Cayman Islands. I looked around at the medical certificates in frames around the walls displaying impressive qualifications from around the world and my eyes settled on his initial qualification as a doctor. 'I see you qualified as a doctor in Germany. Did you serve in the army during the war?'

'I am not German, I am from the Netherlands.' His tone deepened with annoyance.

'I never said you were, but why do you have a Puerto Rican passport?'

'None of your business.'

Having satisfactorily touched a nerve, I returned to see how Peggy's packing had progressed. She had everything in a couple of suitcases and was standing with Miss Major ready to leave.

I grabbed one of the bags, walked out to the squad car and got Peggy to sit in the back seat.

'What about my money, credit cards and passport?' she said. In all the excitement it had slipped my mind and I returned to the house, pushed open the front door and quietly stepped towards Kampenboom's office. I saw he was away from his desk, crouching down at an open safe examining its contents. He was engrossed in his activity until I stood behind him, then he leapt like a scalded cat as he turned to me. My heart jumped as I saw the butt of a pistol inside the safe. I reached past him and grabbed the gun, moving it quickly out of his way with my heart rate racing.

'What the hell are you going to do with this?'

'I have a licence for it, give it back!'

It was a Walther P38 automatic pistol. 'Is it loaded?'

'Yes, don't point it at me.' He spoke in much quieter tones, moving slowly away from the safe back to his desk. I dropped the loaded magazine out of the handle before extracting the remaining bullet from the chamber.

'Expecting trouble, are we? Where did you get this?'

Kampenboom sat in silence behind his desk and glared at me. Eventually he said quietly, 'There were many guns around after the war.'

I was confronted with a Dutchman with a Puerto Rican passport, who studied medicine in Germany before the war, who happened to have a loaded gun in his safe. It was all highly suspicious but I knew the odds were stacked against me. 'I'm seizing the gun and will check it out back at the police station. This is all very peculiar.'

'Think what you like, I've nothing to worry about. I know all the important people on the islands and you aren't one of them. Get out before I call them and have you sent back to England in disgrace.'

It was interesting to note that he recognised me as one of the UK officers as I had not mentioned it. I knew that I could not arrest or charge him with any offences but frustration is always trumped by common sense. It was time to leave and take Peggy to the airport. As my old sergeant used to say, '*They always come again, son – sooner rather than later.*'

I got him to hand over the airline tickets, money, cards and passport from his safe and returned them to Peggy in the squad car. I started the engine and had just began to move off when Kampenboom appeared at my car window. I opened it and saw his manic eyes were raging once more as he screamed at Peggy. 'You filthy bitch, you should be arrested for larceny of airline tickets.'

I closed the window in his face and drove off, leaving him on his driveway still shouting in a cloud of wheel dust. Peggy buried her face in a handkerchief and began sobbing once more. The control freak just had to have the last word, didn't he? Or did he…?

I dropped Peggy off at the Sunset House Hotel as all the Canadian flights had left for the day. She still declined to give me any written confirmation of her evidence and I returned to the police station and called in to see Chief Superintendent Jones.

'What's been going on at Kampenboom's house?' he asked. 'I've had a couple of calls from local Big Wigs saying you've been threatening him.'

I explained the circumstances and voiced my frustration at the lack of evidence that would result in him continuing his bizarre activities. DCI Timms then breezed into Jones's office, sat down, put his feet up on the desk and repeated the query about Kampenboom. I explained again and he offered his considered opinion of the doctor.

'I hate the dirty bastard. I once caught him ogling my daughter's boobs when we were having a BBQ on Public Beach – he's a weirdo.'

The DCI offered to help with the lack of evidence and I highlighted the potential moral, ethical and legal difficulties that his suggestions would create but he continued anyway.

'I wouldn't worry about that, son. If you want, I'll give you a statement that I was driving past his house when I saw him pull the gun on you. We can go and lock up the dirty bastard and with a bit of luck he'll resist arrest and we can shoot him.'

I'm still not sure if he was joking but decided not to take him up on his kind offer as I had had a much better idea.

CHAPTER 19

THE GOVERNOR'S KNOBKERRIE

Preparing for night duty was always a bit restricting as you could not go out for a drink or a meal, but at least it meant you saved a bit of money. This particular day had started with a snorkel trip off Barry the Barracuda's reef. Just as I was showering, a detective arrived summonsing me to attend court to give evidence in the illegal guns case against the captain and first mate of *The Jolly Roger* pirate ship from a couple of weeks before.

The case was heard in front of His Honour Judge Rudyard and was presented by one of the owners, Adamson, with the other owner, Member of the Legislative Assembly of the Cayman Islands (locally elected politician) Hollywood, sitting glowering at me from the public gallery. Fortunately both the captain and the first mate were found guilty after a lengthy trial and received heavy fines.

Secondly, we had applied to seize *The Jolly Roger* with all its contents, which brought Hollywood into the dock to give all reasons under the sun why it should be returned to him and his co-owner. The Judge listened and asked relevant questions as they did their best to brand me as a liar, a racist and a corrupt British police officer. Marco had refused to give a statement so the evidence was down to me and Sgt Bodden, who gave a detailed account of the incident and allegations of piracy.

HH Rudyard dismissed their appeals and seized the $100,000 boat. Hollywood and Adamson glared across the court at me like two spoilt brats being written out of grandad's will. What a wonderful result.

I was exhausted before even getting to work at 10pm where I was the squad car driver with Duke. We had to deal with a dispute between two taxi drivers fighting for a fare. It turned out that they'd both had various complaints and grievances against each other for decades and both attended the same church. They then admitted that one of them was the pastor and the other was the usher and disagreed about everything to do with the church – but never discussed it on a Sunday as it was a day of peace. It was now early on Tuesday morning, so they had fallen out again.

The next job was far more urgent. It was 2:45 in the morning when I heard Nobby call through on the radio to control, saying that he was speaking to a rather awkward male on the beach behind Governor's House (GH). Nobby was a fit and handy footballer so would be capable of defending himself, but in reality a fight lasting more than 20 or 30 seconds is exhausting and very hard work. I began to drive quickly to GH then heard Nobby shout for urgent assistance with the sound of a fight in the background. I drove with all blues and twos blaring and was only a minute away, so drove along the wall by the beach at the side of GH. I ran behind the building and heard a struggle as I went round the corner onto the beach, where I saw Nobby being held by a huge male who was getting the better of him. Then out of the corner of my eye, someone ran from the back of Governor's House down the beach towards the fight.

As I ran at them, I saw the huge man trying to throttle Nobby with both his hands around his throat and the other person got to them just in front of me. It was the Governor who was holding something in his hand. He raised it above his head then violently brought it down on the head of the man, who loosened his grip until another vicious blow from the Governor made the male roll over onto his side and remain still. I handcuffed the male and saw Nobby was now sitting up trying to catch his breath. The Governor was standing there resplendent in his red silk kimono decorated with a large black dragon that flapped in the breeze showing his naked body beneath. He looked very pleased with himself and was holding his prized knobkerrie and bashing it repeatedly into his left hand.

'I knew it would come in handy when I heard the ruckus,' he said. 'Did you see him? He went down like a sack of potatoes.'

Duke and I dragged the unconscious male up the beach and plonked him in the back of the squad car. Nobby was recovering well with a large glass of brandy administered by the Governor's wife, who was now putting the weapon back in its display cabinet; she also tied up her husband's wayward kimono to protect his bits from catching a chill. We deposited the drunken male in the cells until he sobered up and he was later interviewed by Special Branch, which seemed appropriate given what the Governor had used to beat him senseless.

The Caribbean Police Commissioners Conference drew together all the police chiefs from around the English-speaking parts of the West Indies. This was also a way for the Foreign and Commonwealth Office to come together in a safe, secure location and discuss sensitive issues and concerns that would impact upon each country or dependency and then agree to a joint position. I arranged for a brand-new air-conditioned minibus to convey the participants to and from all of the events due to last the week, and driving the attendees was much better than the usual police work. They began to arrive over the weekend. I was the main 'meeter and greeter' and collected the first visitor and escorted him through the VIP lounge. He had forgotten his glasses, so I filled in the embarkation card for him and could have filled it in as Mr Michael Mouse had I so wished. I didn't suppose he was going to do much written work that week so his glasses would not be missed.

Rooms had been booked at the best hotel on the island and a series of functions organised to keep them and their partners / wives busy, impressed and out of trouble. Whilst the formal events were in full swing there were events at the Commissioner's house for a coffee morning, then lunch at the golf club. One attendee was the UK liaison officer based in the Jamaican Police Force. He had many tales of his experiences which were at odds with those in Cayman. He told me that he was also the independent investigator that had to review any fatal police shootings. Expecting only a couple of incidents a year, he amazed me with the fact that it was only May and he had just had the latest of the 178 fatal police shootings referred to him. After reviewing all the evidence available to him he had not found any culpability against the police officers, although one incident involving a knife and fork had come close to the limit. Over in Jamaica seemed a very dangerous place to be a police officer.

That night there was a drinks reception at GH and I made sure Duke was with me to give dramatic salutes to anyone who looked important.

The following day I took the conference's other halves on a tour of the island tourist spots and spent a full 30 seconds at Bodden Town, only due to passing a sign outside the shop proclaiming: CANNED DRINKS, SWEETS, SOUVENIRS, AND CONDOMS. I had to reverse back to prove it to one visitor. The wives of Mr Jones and DCI Timms were good friends, great company for the visitors and certainly kept the party going. I took them all up to Rum Point for a swim and back to the Light House restaurant for lunch. I could have done with a rest but the evening event was booked for a sunset cruise on a beautiful catamaran sailing boat called *Spirit of Ppalu*, which is the Polynesian god of navigation. It was due to leave from the dock at the back of the Hyatt Regency and we departed five minutes late. The captain was motoring out along the canal towards the North Sound when everyone's attention was drawn to a loudly revving engine and plumes of smoke that drew up alongside us, revealing a dirty grey car driven by DCI Timms. He was shouting incoherently, waving his fist and making rude gestures at the ship's captain, who ignored him as the car came to a shuddering halt when the dock ran out. We waved cheerfully at the DCI as the catamaran glided out into the open water. The crew raised the sails to catch a pleasantly warm zephyr that pushed us gently along.

The sun began to set and the rum punch and nibbles were distributed to the revellers as we continued out towards the west. One of the overseas visitors came over and asked me who the odd-looking chap was that kept talking to him about being shot at by the fuzzy-wuzzy in East Africa. It was our Assistant Commissioner who must have sneaked on board without me seeing him as I was under specific orders to 'lose' his invite. We had been out in the North Sound for about 10 minutes when we heard a speed boat approaching fast. The captain trimmed the sails and adjusted the helm to steer away from the boat but it continued to head straight for us.

It couldn't possibly be, could it? Of course it was. DCI Timms and his wife had commandeered the speed boat *In the Name of the Law*, and they pulled up alongside the *Spirit of Ppalu*, to the annoyance of the captain. We hauled them on board to great applause, followed by the fully considered comment by the DCI as he downed his first rum punch, 'I've never missed a free bloody piss-up yet.'

The following day involved all those who wanted to swim with the sting rays at Sting Ray City, so obviously I had to join them. It is an amazing experience to watch as they brush past your legs like friendly kittens and flick their tails away from you. They use their mouths on the white smooth underbelly to snatch scraps of fish held out for them as they elegantly dart past. We dried off in the sunshine as we headed over to Cayman Kai for a picnic under the trees. After a rest and brush-up, the final event of the conference visit was a big party back at the Commissioner's house with food provided by the excellent Crow's Nest restaurant nearby. When the festivities ended, I took the revellers back to the hotel, managing some out-of-tune pub singing along the way. It was all hugely enjoyable and it was hard to believe that I was being paid to do this.

My sister and her friend turned up to stay with me for a well-deserved holiday. They were as pale as a couple of milk bottles but quickly relaxed into life on the island. As my leave was already spoken for, I gave them the keys to the Jeep and pointed them in the appropriate directions for all the attractions. On my first evening off we went to Sunset House and were enjoying the ambience until I saw the Pale Horse screech into the car park and Duke squeaked into the bar next to us. My sister was only being polite but Duke took this as a show of affection and asked to take her home. I told him to get lost but he kept mithering on, so we sprinted to the Jeep and raced off to find a Duke-proof location.

He followed us at speed until we shook him off down a narrow alley as he shot past and we went in the opposite direction to enjoy the rest of the evening.

The following morning, I was back on duty and the Sergeant told me I had been allocated a special job. I had to interview someone that had picked up a young woman at a burger bar and offered to give them a lift home. On the way he had pulled out a pistol from the glove compartment and 'playfully' threatened her. The woman got out and reported the incident to the police and a man had been arrested and was now waiting in the room to be interviewed. I opened the door of the interview room to see the miserable face of Duke staring at the table. He was too stupid to actually have meant to threaten the poor woman and he explained it in his simple way. 'I was just showing off, man.'

'Why do you carry a loaded pistol in your truck?' I asked.

'It may be needed to sort out some bad asses – off duty. Shit man, a while back they needed some assistance at West Bay, so when I heard the call, I put my pants on, got my shooting iron and rode the Pale Horse!'

'Okay Duke, what was the urgent job then?'

'Urh… The West Bay Sergeant needed assistance to put a pedal cycle in his car… It sounds kind o' stupid now, don't it?'

'Yep, it does.' I concluded the interview, recommending we take the gun off him for a while to control his ardour as well as suggesting more bromide in his coffee.

Back on duty, Duke and I had arrested a rather unpleasant local hoodlum by the name of Kenny. He had robbed two young female tourists at a night club, but we had managed to identify him and charge him with the offences. The evidence was straight forward with written statements supporting the allegations, but Kenny denied it all. Unfortunately, Duke did not have a clue about presenting evidence even though I had taken many opportunities to explain.

The trial took place in front of His Honour Rudyard and I gave my evidence. Duke was the next witness and gave a totally different account of the whole case. I was not convinced he could remember anything even though we had discussed it 10 minutes earlier. Both prosecution and defence lawyers looked at each other, their notes, then towards the Judge, shaking their heads, for some enlightenment, but he smiled and gently nodded before eliciting more nonsensical details from Duke.

This empowered Duke, leading him to cross examine Kenny after first calling him Bob. He seemed to have got this case confused with a separate drink-driving case, which left us all very perplexed. The defence lawyer stood up and thanked Duke for his version of events, which cheered him enormously – he had never been commended before. Duke removed his very thick glasses and began to polish them on his shirt as HH Rudyard addressed the court.

'One officer has good eyesight and the other, not. One officer, a good memory and the other, not…'

Duke dropped his glasses with a clatter and scrambled about in search of them as the Judge continued to review his judgement; the public gallery found it difficult to stifle the laughter as the court reporter scribbled furiously. Luckily my witness evidence sealed the case for me, but Duke left the court with a certain misplaced satisfaction.

Money was tight, but wanting to make the most of the time we had left for our secondment, Nobby, Cocky, Alec and I discussed buying a speed boat, and foolishly we went ahead. The 19 feet 6 inches *Chaparral* had a four-litre V6 engine, and with no experience or understanding of how or where to use it, we spent good money on it. Eventually, after our first trip out into the North Sound when we struck the reef, we even managed to learn how to tie it up, back at the dock. We did not have a clue about the rules or how to navigate – but that didn't matter to us at the time.

The weather was gorgeous and the sea calm, so Nobby and Cocky moved the speed boat out in front of their condominium overlooking Seven Mile Beach and secured it to a convenient buoy. They felt that it would be a 'babe magnet' for them and could be used for practising water sports as well. They took it out for a few fast runs along Seven Mile Beach until it spluttered to a shuddering halt. As the petrol gauge did not work, we had agreed to fill a jerry can and leave it onboard but no one had checked it was done – and it was empty. They drifted for 10 minutes and waved at other craft, who all waved cheerfully back without stopping, until eventually Cocky had to take the jerry can and swim back to shore with it clamped between his teeth, walk to the service station in his trunks and flip-flops and refill it. He cadged a lift from another boat and reached ours just before it disappeared over the horizon.

The next day I called in to their apartment in good time for us to work out the best way to water-ski and interrupted them trying out a new electric shaver they had bought to save money. Nobby was sitting on a bar stool in the middle of the living room with a bed sheet tied around his neck. Cocky returned to his task and plugged the shaver back in. 'Going anywhere nice on your holidays, sir?' he asked, applying the shaver to Nobby's head with a theatrical flourish starting just above his right eye and zooming towards his crown. Cocky suddenly jumped back with a huge gasp, holding the shaver at arm's length like an unexploded grenade.

Nobby turned towards me as his tanned face drained of blood. 'What's 'appened? What's he done?'

He now sported a parting like a path mown through a luscious wildflower meadow. Unable to speak, Cocky pointed at the number 3 shaver-guard lying on the floor and began to hyperventilate. Nobby ran to the bathroom mirror where silence existed for a second before an anguished cry echoed around the apartment. 'You idiot, look what you've done.'

I left, feeling it was not the day for water-skiing.

A more suitable day dawned, and with Alec I met them on Seven Mile Beach near to where our boat was moored. Nobby had had to shave the rest of his hair off and had covered it in a baseball cap until it regrew. We swam out to the boat and examined the water-sports equipment, which consisted of a single oar, a child's life jacket, one left-footed water-ski and a long coil of blue scratchy nylon cord. That all seemed promising enough so we got the engine started and motored out a few hundred yards to where we could speed up and down parallel to the beach and not be a danger to anyone but ourselves.

Cocky took the honour of being the first volunteer to do some water-skiing and I took the helm (for a few practice runs). The engine and controls seemed fine. We tied a loop in the rope for Cocky's hands and secured the other end to the back of the boat. He put the tiny life jacket on his front, giving him the appearance of sporting a large pair of boobs, as he gingerly lowered himself over the side. After a thumbs-up from Cocky, I gradually pushed the throttle forwards and we moved off trailing the cord behind. It took a couple of attempts until we decided that we had to go faster to give him any chance of getting up on to his ski.

I felt the tap on my shoulder then pushed the throttle to the maximum and we roared off. I glanced around and saw Cocky bravely balancing precariously and gripping on for dear life. I looked back to the front and a jet ski appeared right in front of me, forcing me to pull over violently to avoid a crash. This evasive action caused Cocky to hit the wash from both us and the jet ski, which made him jump high into the air, then come crashing back down into the sea with an enormous splash. I slowed the engine and did a wide loop to find him without fouling the propeller on the ski cord, and on helping him aboard saw he was in some distress.

'Quick,' he said, 'take me back in. I need to get to the condo fast.'

'Are you hurt?'

'Just get me back in fast!'

I got close enough for him to dive overboard and we watched as he raced for the shore like a human torpedo, sprinted up the beach with both hands gripping his tightly clenched buttocks and disappeared into the condo.

'What's up with him?' I looked towards Alec who shook his head slowly as he followed Cocky's progress up the beach.

'I told him…but he wouldn't listen… He should've worn tighter trunks… For the next week or so the poor bastard will be shitting nothing but seahorses and rainbow fish.'

PART IV

MURDER AND ESCAPE

CHAPTER 20

FEELING HOT, HOT, HOT...

By now I'd been in the Cayman Islands for more than a year and, despite regularly feeling like a fish out of water, I was starting to feel really at home. Having friends visit helped me feel less far away from home, too. As a result of the extreme heat of the summer months, the cost of the flights dropped like ripe coconuts and more visitors arrived to stay with me intent on having a good time.

Barry and Babs were school chums and they needed a holiday in the tropics from his role as an officer in the military. The normal way was to let them have the use of the Jeep and socialise when work did not interfere too much. Babs did not want to do too much other than grill herself at the height of the day's sun whilst basting her skin with sun oil. Barry was very fair-skinned and tried to keep out of the sun unless he had had a few drinks. I did not begrudge them a good time and we enjoyed all the island could offer. One thing I did offer to my visitors was a bit of advice about the strength of the summer sun, which included keeping in the shade and air-conditioned areas just before and after midday.

Barry dropped me off at work, promising to collect me at tea time and we would all go out and enjoy an evening meal and a few drinkies. When I finished my shift there was no sign of him or my Jeep, so I cadged a lift to Caribbean Suites with Carlos where I found it parked up, covered in dust with the roof down. I was greeted by a very concerned-looking Babs who told me that Barry was suffering from sunstroke after driving around the island all day with the top down. He had enjoyed plenty of lunchtime beers followed by a three-mile run without his polo shirt on.

He was lying in bed with the a/c on full, beetroot-coloured skin peeling off in multiple layers, propped up on a bank of pillows with a bag of frozen peas on his head. We left him to his moans and groans as Babs and I went out to enjoy a beach BBQ at Sunset House and then on to Silvers Night Club where we danced the night away to strains of 'Feeling Hot Hot Hot' into the early morning. I mulled over why some people are just plain stupid and have to learn lessons the hard way.

My colleague Alec also learnt something the hard way – about losing an argument with a Portuguese man o' war. This rather unpleasant type of jelly fish has trailing tentacles up to 15 feet long with poisonous needles to wrap around and kill its prey. I was scuba-diving with Alec on a small shipwreck when one coiled a tentacle around his head, injecting noxious substances into his head and neck, and then stung his hand as he pulled off what he initially thought was just a strand of seaweed. As he surfaced, the pain increased dramatically and I watched as a terrible rash developed all over his head other than where the mask and goggles had protected his face. He was in terrible pain as I drove him to the A&E department of the hospital. The clinician immediately put him on morphine and told him it was going to get worse before it got better and signed him off work for a few days. Which was lucky because the morphine made him think he was gently floating above his sun lounger – until it wore off and he came down to earth with a resounding bump.

It wasn't long before I was in A&E myself. I was doing a check dive for my next diving qualification at Parrots Landing with Rafe the instructor. We were practising the emergency ascent without a tank when he said it had to be done quicker and more steadily. We went back down to 30 feet and repeated the procedure at his pace, continuing to equalise the pressure in our ears accordingly, and as we approached the surface there was a terrific bang in my head. It was like someone had hit me on the side of the head with a plank.

Rafe approached me with a look of concern etched into his face and signed to ask if I was okay. We were still about 15 feet below the surface and I now felt very dizzy. He told me to equalise my ears once more and his look of horror grew as he told me to stop. He took hold of my arm and signalled for us to go to the surface where I removed my goggles.

'We'd better get you to hospital quickly,' he said. 'There are bubbles of air coming out of your ear.'

We swam for the shore at a steady pace and my mind was whirring away about what this would mean for my hearing. I spent three long hours in the hospital A&E where the consultant said it was impossible to be breathing through the ear. I knew that as well and I hadn't studied medicine for six years either. 'Leave off the diving for a couple of weeks and you'll be as right as rain,' he said. So I did, and I was, but medical science still cannot fathom what happened. One colleague rather cruelly suggested it was my brains attempting to escape as the water pressure was decreasing in my head.

I was allocated duties as the chauffeur at GH for a few days, which included helping out at any events. There were a number of VIPs and politicians visiting the island for a British Dependent Territory conference and as I had done such a great job at the previous policing conference, my services, once more, were called upon to help make it a runaway success. Unsurprisingly it was a complete sellout and dozens of delegates were booked into the best hotels on the island, including many from the Foreign and Commonwealth Office in London and other hangers-on wanting an all-expenses-paid jolly in a safe and secure part of the Caribbean. I certainly would if I got the chance.

I made sure that Duke was on saluting duty at the main gate as the guests arrived for the formal 'Tea and Sticky Buns Party' on the front lawn at GH. The Governor's wife had bought a huge, energetic Great Dane puppy and given him the name Monty. He was not vicious but was tall, untrained and had an annoying habit of jumping up at you when you least expected.

Captain Nelson RN was a very pleasant liaison officer for the Royal Navy in the Caribbean. He arrived at the party in uniform and as he strolled across the main lawn, Monty made a beeline for him and pinned him up against a palm tree. The Governor's wife glanced across from behind her rum punch and called out, 'Just kick his balls.'

The Navy officer did as he was told and the dog collapsed with a yelp and ran off.

'No,' she shouted. 'I meant the ones on the lawn.'

The following day I took the Governor to the airport for a flight to Miami and arranged to collect him when he returned late that evening. I drove the limousine back to GH to see what other tasks were waiting for me and the butler met me outside, pointing his thumb back towards the kitchen.

'She's left a little present for you,' he said as he disappeared into his flat. I found a note attached to a plastic bag on the kitchen table that read, 'Bertie's poo for analysis.'

Bertie was the Governor's wife's horse that she rode up and down the beach even though it was illegal for anyone else to do so. She had decided that Bertie was not feeling well, so had collected a sample for the government veterinary surgeon to analyse. It was still warm, so I picked it up at arm's length and put it in pride of place on the back seat of the Daimler limousine, then drove down to their office. I imagine the vet would not take it too seriously, merely give it a cursory glance; presumably a case of just going through the motions.

The return flight from Miami was very late and the mood of the Governor was low as I collected him from the VIP lounge at the airport. I knew that his wife was out visiting friends and intended to get a taxi home when she was full of rum, ready to return in the early hours. GH was in complete darkness when I pulled up at the front entrance, with no sign of the butler or his wife to greet us. All the doors and windows were locked up as tight as a drum, so we returned to the air-conditioned car. We waited in stony silence for a few minutes, quietly hoping that they would return home and let us in. I decided to open the conversation knowing that the Governor owned a house in a beautiful part of Provence which he visited each July and August.

'I have just finished a brilliant book based in Provence. It made me hungry and thirsty just reading it,' I said.

'Which book?'

'*A Year in Provence*, by Peter Mayle.'

'Oh no, don't talk to me about that bastard,' he said. 'He *actually* lives in the next valley and now all the tourists wanting to speak to him keep banging on *my* bloody door.'

Once more an icy silence descended. I briefly considered offering him the use of my pull-out bed until he suddenly erupted into life and jumped out of the back of the Daimler. 'This is ridiculous and

I've just about had enough! Locked out of my own home! You couldn't bloody make this up!'

We walked around the back of the building and rattled all the doors and windows until I decided the best chance of breaking in was the door leading into the kitchen. We stepped back, then both of us took a flying kick that made the door spring open knocking some plates and cups across the kitchen floor.

'They can clean up the mess,' the Governor said as he kicked open an inner door. 'I'm off to bed – good bloody night.'

On many occasions in my career I have been told to 'go to hell', but this time it was for real. Harry, the Head of Special Branch, asked Alec and myself to be attached to his office for a sensitive undercover operation. It involved turning up as tourists at a specific bar in Hell and mingle with the locals and expat community. Hell was, in all likelihood, a destination both of us would eventually end up at, but in the meantime, and for the uninitiated, it was a patch of barren iron-shore rock with not much going for it. It amounted to a black limestone rock formation shaped into a burnt-out petrified forest made up of sinister-looking sponges over an area of about half a football field. It was a small hamlet in the north of the island close to West Bay with a few bars, a petrol station and a tiny post office that will frank your postcards with the postmark, 'Sent from Hell!'

Special Branch never liked to tell you too much even if your life depended upon it and Harry was no exception. Previously I had phoned him and asked if I was speaking to Special Branch and, typical of his genre, his reply was simply, 'Depends.'

We managed to extract a nugget of intelligence about our task to visit the bar. There was information that a British businessman named Noel was involved in illegal arms deals to insurgent groups around the world. 'Make friends with him and his missus,' Harry said, and handed us $100 to pay for a few drinks. 'Find out what you can and get yourselves invited to one of his parties.'

The picture he showed us was of an overweight and pasty-faced 50-year-old white man standing with his fleshy arm around the waist of a darkly tanned 20-something bimbo wearing a tiny bikini that just held back voluminous boobs. Alec suggested that the photo was from Harry's very dodgy personal photo collection, but it allowed us to identify Noel. Dressed comfortably in smart shorts and polo shirts, we rented a Jeep and began frequenting the expat bars around the area until we spotted his car outside an expensive watering hole. The hundred dollars would not last long here. Noel and friend were easily found beneath a sun-dappled cabana sipping a couple of garishly decorated 'hi-ball' glasses of rum punch. We perched ourselves at a neighbouring table and listened in as he wittered into his mobile phone about Premier League football while she soaked up the rays behind her massive, mirrored, virtual-reality sunglasses. He finished his call and called across asking which teams we supported.

'Burnley.' 'Cambridge.' Our informed answers led to a conversation that ranged from local politics to the cost of imported Cadbury's chocolate. We finished our drinks and bade them farewell, and as she removed the sunglasses, I saw Alec receive from Noel's girlfriend a flutter of eyelashes and a suggestive pursing of the lips.

'She's gorgeous,' he said as we drove off. 'She wants my babies.'

I pointed out that if Noel was an international arms dealer who suspected that someone was messing with his dame, he would probably have access to a couple of guns or gunmen happy to shoot Alec's nuts off. Alec pooh-poohed my advice and talked endlessly about how attractive she was and how much she wanted his body. We reported back to Harry who was delighted that Alec had made such a big impression on the girlfriend in spite of the potential danger of having his gonads swiftly and non-surgically removed. 'Your dependants will receive a good pension,' Harry said.

'I wouldn't worry about that' I said. 'You're not likely to have any dependants with them blown off.' We arranged to track our targets down the following day.

Over the next couple of days, we 'bumped into' Noel around the various expensive bars until we got an invite to a weekend party at their house near West Bay. We turned up at the expensive, tall-walled compound that was beautifully lit with coloured strobe lights. From afar I saw a couple of dodgy-looking security men on the front gates and then noticed that there were a disproportionate number of concealed CCTV cameras and discrete sensors attached to wires on top of the perimeter walls. Noel was a humorous and affable kind of character and I was actually looking forward to the party. We parked up outside and approached the greeters on the gate.

'You're not properly dressed, boss,' one said to me. I felt quite smart and took umbrage at his cheeky comment, so I told him so.

'No offence boss but this is a Toga Party. You's inappropriately dressed and Mr Noel want me to tell yous.'

Other guests were appearing in colourful tailored garments and robes with golden oak-leaf headdresses pinning up their hair. Some held senators' parchment rolls concealing bottles of champagne, others stage-prop daggers smeared with ketchup. In our light-coloured trousers and short-sleeved shirts we stood out like a fart at a funeral. Jumping back into the Jeep we roared off back into West Bay and drove to Harry's apartment where he was just leaving. As expected of the Head of Special Branch he thought quickly, dragged us into his house, stripped his bed and presented us with the sheets.

'There, use these. I only had them washed last week.'

We changed quickly and became Roman Emperors in an instant. The improvised costume was topped off with a couple of curtain tie-backs wrapped around our foreheads and a pair of elderly leather belts holding the fabric and our modesty together.

Sensibly, Alec asked a practical question. 'Where do we hide our warrant cards?'

'You don't,' he said. 'You're working undercover.'

When we returned, the party was in full swing to the catchy tunes of UB40 and Hot Chocolate through the hot and humid-night sky. The free food and drink were well received, and the practicalities of the togas were another Roman innovation ignored by the Monty Python team. They were cool and comfortable and I discovered just how quickly they dried after I fell in the swimming pool. Alec soon disappeared with Noel's girlfriend who was actually wearing more clothes than I had ever seen her wear, and after a while he returned all flushed and flustered, covered in leaves and grass stains.

'I nearly got caught,' he gasped. 'I had to hide in the bloody bushes.'

'Did you find out anything?'

'Yeah, she's got silicone boobs.'

I went in search of more useful information and walked in to the house where Noel was sitting in his library enjoying the a/c. I perused his display of books and chatted amicably about his collection of first editions accumulated over his lifetime. A gnawing feeling was steadily coming over me that the information that he was an arms dealer seemed out of character with what we were finding. I gently broached the subject of where he had accumulated his apparent wealth. His reply explained a lot as the penny slowly dropped.

'Prosthetic limbs. I designed and patented a unique type and sold it for mega money. I won't need to work again but I keep dabbling in my workshop. Want a look?'

Dressed in our togas we went into his converted garage, and when the fluorescent tube flickered on, it revealed a cooled and fully fitted engineering workshop with a host of false arms and feet strewn about the worktops. It had the appearance of the aftermath of an unfortunate chainsaw massacre, but it convinced me we were definitely barking up the wrong tree. The Special Branch intelligence about a suspicious 'arms dealer' finally clicked into place.

I went home to change then wandered back over to the police station and bumped into Chief Supt Jones and had a general catch-up. He mentioned one of my earlier dealings with the sinister Dr Felix Kampenboom.

'You'd better return that gun to Kampenboom, he's been mithering everyone from the Governor downwards about it. He does have a licence and we haven't charged him with anything.'

Reluctantly I agreed to sort it out and went to find Sgt Benjamin and remove it from the armoury. He couldn't help himself, he had cleaned and oiled it, and it was in better shape now than when I seized it. I asked why.

'I hadn't fired a Walther before so I took it to the range and fired off a couple of magazines – it's a neat piece of kit, boy.'

I drove out to Kampenboom's compound and parked up in front of the rather creepy palatial palace. I rapped on the door and Maria the Jamaican maid let me in.

'I'll tell the doctor you're here.' She knocked on his office door and disappeared in for a few seconds before reappearing and waving me in.

'I'm glad you've seen some sense,' he said with a strained grimace. 'I said you would not beat me.'

I really wanted to, in more ways than one.

A strange thought then occurred to me. I looked around the top of his desk and saw a clear drinking glass with half an inch of water remaining. The grubby rim bore smeared signs of his lips, and greasy finger marks showed clearly down the smooth sides, looking like it had not been cleaned for a week. I needed a distraction.

'Before I return the gun, I'll need you to sign a receipt and, er, I'd like to see your actual licence for the pistol.'

'My licence, what for? You're irritating me again. Give me the receipt and I'll sign it…'

'It's just a formality, but I need to see it.'

He scratched his scrawl across the receipt and threw it back across the desk before standing and moving over to the safe. He glanced back at me, then covered the safe combination from my view and that gave me my chance. With a paper tissue from my pocket I grabbed the glass and with a loud cough tipped the dregs into a convenient yucca plant pot. I stood and slipped the glass inside my cap.

I gave the licence a cursory glance and placed his pistol on the desk together with a well-sealed evidence bag containing its magazine and bullets. I left in silence but felt the hatred from his eyes burning into my back like lasers. I knew I was doing something rather silly but hopefully he would not miss the glass for a while and if he accused me I would totally deny it. I drove off faster than I had arrived and now, left with my ill-gotten gain, thought through what to do with it.

I took the glass to the Scenes of Crime department, made up an excuse and asked them to record the fingerprints and recover any DNA they could.

CHAPTER 21

BAT INTO HELL

My colleague, Cocky, and his new girlfriend, Ellen, had moved into a cheaper condo, overlooking the mangrove swamps at the backend of Hell. He was always careful with money and had the accurate reputation of being tight in the extreme, including the insistence that his toilet must only be flushed when absolutely brimming. He usually brought some cheap tins of beer to a BBQ or party and then ended up drinking all the good stuff before taking his cheap beer back home. We solved this annoying habit by cracking open his tins as soon as he deposited them in the ice box. One evening I went round for a meal at his new address where Ellen was setting the table out on the veranda. Noting that there was no mosquito netting on the balcony I asked if these pests were a problem out in the swamps. 'Not at all,' she said. 'They don't seem to bother us.'

She showed me her new wooden salad tongs on the edge of the matching rubberwood salad bowl in the centre of the table. She was rightly proud of her efforts in homemaking, which seemed to be totally ignored by Cocky as he slurped his beer. The sun had set beautifully behind the mangroves and the cicadas clicked and parrots screeched in the background; a silent ceiling fan whirred gently above as Ellen served the meal.

'Anyone want some mustard?' Ellen asked as she put things out.

'Good idea,' I said as I excused myself and headed to the cloakroom to wash my hands before dinner.

When I returned it had quickly become darker outside. I saw an open jar of yellowy grey mustard had appeared on the table as I resettled myself. I noticed a blob of mustard had been placed on the edge of my plate. Isn't she kind? I thought. I put a smear of the mustard on some ham and began eating. It seemed very mild and smooth but had an overpowering smell that caused my nose to wrinkle and my eyes begin to moisten. I turned the label of the mustard jar towards me to see it was some American burger relish. That's powerful, I thought without commenting to my hosts.

Around the table I noticed a number of small mustard splashes had appeared, presumably from when Ellen had opened the jar. They seemed to be increasing in number but I could see no reason why, so unconsciously blamed Cocky who was always a messy eater. I gratefully tucked in and used Ellen's new tongs to pile the salad onto my plate alongside the grilled jerk chicken, rice and peas. There was an empty Tupperware container on the table, which I presumed was there for discarded chicken bones or something. A very pleasant meal was enjoyed as the darkness crept in and Ellen lit a couple of candles as we 'put the world to rights.' We opened the bottle of wine I'd brought and Cocky put his favourite music on the CD player – it was the Meatloaf album *Bat out of Hell*. As we chatted a couple of mosquitoes fizzed themselves on the candle flame, then suddenly a loud thump happened above the table. I looked up and saw the ceiling fan had momentarily stopped and was now spinning at a drunken angle, before resuming its previous somnolent rate of rotation.

'What was that?' I said.

'It's alright,' said Ellen, 'it happens every night.'

She then took the salad tongs and used them carefully to delve into the salad bowl and remove a small bat of about four inches long, which she placed gently in the Tupperware container. The poor creature looked quite stunned and I suppose I would have if I'd been picked up with some salad tongs after ramming my head into a ceiling fan.

'It'll wake up in a bit, they usually do. More salad, anybody?'

I declined but watched enthralled as a squadron of similar bats either dodged or collided with the fan before distributing their yellow droppings all over the table. Most of the bats seemed to regain consciousness during the evening and I watched amazed as one by one they staggered drunkenly out of the box, then fluttered back into the dark twilight beyond the swamps.

I hope the actual mustard would taste better, but have never had the inclination to try.

I joined Police Squad, a plainclothes unit focused on crime and anti-social behaviour around the island. Not as grand as it sounded but it got me away from Inspector McDougal and his traffi ticki books. The idea was to use some of the experienced police officers in some vehicles to focus on the outer villages and investigate suspected drug dealing and illicit drinking shebeens. Turning up at Bodden Town police station, I was greeted by Sergeant Ness who gave me two traffic ticket books and a pad of forms to issue to motorists for them to produce their driving documents. He kindly took the traffic forms away after I asked what they were for as it became obvious we should be focusing on crime not traffic matters.

My time on Police Squad developed pleasantly and I managed to keep away from uniform patrol duties and make myself indispensable elsewhere. A team of financial investigators from a UK police force arrived on the island and needed to be collected and ushered through the usual 'jobsworths' at the immigration desk at the airport without having to answer impertinent questions. I quickly became their chauffeur/gopher and commandeered a non-police liveried minibus to carry them around the island and assist them with their various sensitive enquiries. I had just picked them up from the Hyatt Regency when a call came over the police radio asking patrols to keep an eye open for a four-door saloon in red, with five very dodgy looking males inside that had been seen acting suspiciously driving along West Bay Road. I heard a reply from DCI Timms of the Drugs Squad saying they were nearby and would have a look for it. After a few minutes, one of my passengers pointed out a car matching that description that was stuck in a traffic jam about 400 yards away in front of us.

I called up to the radio control and informed them and this was followed by DCI Timms and his team saying they would be making their way to the area. Almost immediately we watched as the suspect car pulled out of the traffic queue and raced off at high speed towards George Town. My minibus did not have any blue lights or sirens but gallantly I pulled out of the line of traffic and began to follow the red car into town. My passengers strapped themselves tightly in and looked forward to the show. One of my passengers called across. 'It's very good of you to arrange this entertainment for us.'

I threw my police radio over to her. 'Do you mind?'

I pressed on in hot pursuit of the red car as I flashed my headlights and sounded the car horn loudly through the town centre, as cruise ship tourists and old rum heads scattered left, right and centre from my path. My rookie companion maintained an excellent commentary in her clipped English accent around the unfamiliar roads.

'Just going past Burger King!'

'Left past the Bank of Canada.'

'Going 45mph back onto Eastern Avenue – just passing Wellies Cool Spot!'

DCI Timms chimed in, 'Where the hell are they? We keep missing 'em.'

The 'red mist' obscured my vision and I was cornering much too fast in the minibus to the whoops of my delighted colleagues being thrown around in the back, but I had to keep up with the red car until reinforcements arrived. Lots of other patrols were shouting up, but our chase commentary continued. 'It's pulling up in front of the Pattie Shop – opposite the harbour!'

The red car came to a shuddering halt as I pulled in front of it outside the shop. The adrenaline was pumping through my colleagues' veins as they clambered out of the minibus and ran to pull the suspects from the car. I ran around the front of the minibus where there was a bit of pushing and shoving and minor hand-to-hand combat as the UK team manhandled the occupants of the red car, then heard the dulcet tones of DCI Timms. 'Get your bloody hands off me, ye dick. I'm a DCI!!'

Oh dear. I guessed the occupants of the suspicious vehicle and shouted, 'Wait.'

Everyone turned towards me and stopped in mid-grapple. 'I think these five dodgy blokes are actually our Drugs Squad.'

'It's my new bloody squad car.' DCI Timms straightened his jacket and pulled away from the grasp of my keen female financial investigator. 'We only picked the bastard thing up this morning.'

The kerfuffle brought out Mr Brown, the friendly jeweller

I had met during my first few days on foot patrol along the streets of George Town. I had not seen him in recent weeks, but he came out of his shop and gave a cheery wave as we dusted off the crumpled clothes of the Drugs Squad. I was not to see him alive again.

CHAPTER 22

THE SECOND MURDER IN PARADISE

The following week I was engaged in financial enquiries around the island when I heard the police radio report an 'attack alarm' at Mr Brown's shop. A moment later another call reported gunfire in the middle of George Town. This was unheard of, as such incidents may have been reported over in the mangrove swamps but never in the town centre. I listened as the uniform police patrols arrived and garbled messages filled the airwaves with reports, suggestions and conjecture.

An ambulance was requested as more details were circulated to look out for a gunman who had fired two shots inside a shop before running out and leaving the scene on a pedal bike. The description of the suspect was broadcast over the radio and could have matched two hundred of the local youths, as he was described as wearing a baseball cap and had covered his face with a T-shirt. I made my way into the centre of George Town and scanned the crowds that were milling about the streets just off the main harbour road. Various youths matching the general description were being arrested as suspects for the incident.

I drove the minibus to where a couple of males had been arrested and the officers put the handcuffed youths inside for the journey back to the police station. We booked the youths into the custody office and I asked the arresting officers what had happened. My worst fears were realised as they described the circumstances of the incident and an unpleasant feeling welled up in my abdomen. Three cruise ships were anchored out in the harbour and the streets were thronged with visitors, window shopping at the expensive luxury watches and gold trinkets displayed within the small number of jewellers dotted around the town centre. A small group of tourists came out of Mr Brown's shop and politely held the door open for a young male before it clicked closed behind him. Normally, prospective visitors were visibly screened by the staff before they allowed entry and buzzing a high-security locking mechanism in the robust door frame.

The youth made his intentions known straight away, produced a revolver from his waistband and pointed it at Mr Brown. 'Open the cabinet – I want the watches – Now!'

His daughter was in the back office and pressed the silent alarm before quietly staying put. The armed robber was becoming increasingly agitated as the jeweller unlocked the display cabinet and stepped back. The robber grabbed the solid-gold timepieces and stuffed them in the pockets of his shorts and held the remainder against his chest by his left arm. A couple of them fell to the floor and as he stooped to grab them, Mr Brown unconsciously stepped forward as if to help an elderly customer, but the terrified youth panicked and fired his revolver twice into Mr Brown at point-blank range. His daughter screamed and came out of the back office as the youth stood petrified, watching as the jeweller fell to the polished marble floor. The robber dropped even more watches as he activated the door-release button and ran out across the street to his bicycle and rode away.

The Cayman Islands had never suffered such a shocking incident. The rumour mill soon started in earnest and many tall tales of machine guns, hand grenades and bazookas being used circulated wildly around the island. Other more lawless parts of the West Indies may have experienced similar events on a weekly basis but not Grand Cayman – it shouldn't happen in Paradise, should it?

The CID and Scenes of Crime officers attended the jewellers shop to do their bit whilst other officers acted on hunches/ guesswork/intuition/phone calls and arrested anyone who had had the finger pointed at them. Central Police Station had numerous handcuffed suspects sitting on chairs or floors around the building, all of whom were pleading their innocence and simultaneously naming others as being the murderer. All sorts of grudges were aired as I passed them by in the corridor and they were willing to swear their innocence on the graves of long-lost mothers, fathers, children or family pets.

Callers to the front desk of the station whispered names in the ear of the diary officer or pushed scraps of exercise books across the desk identifying the culprit as one of dozens of suspects. Sgt Benjamin issued a selection of weaponry to any officer who happened to be passing the armoury and I signed out my favourite .357 Magnum Smith & Wesson revolver with a handful of special dum-dum ammunition. 'You gotta have an edge, boy…you gotta have an edge.'

I stepped into the inner sanctum of the armoury to sign for my gun and a wonderful sight beheld my attention on a wall-rack previously hidden from my view. After a few moments of contemplation, I pointed at the rack. 'Can I have one of those instead?' I asked, more in hope than expectation.

'No man, this ain't that serious yet. Those Tommy guns are for real badass bastards. We'll wait 'til we find out who done it first…'

'And then?' I asked.

'We'll see, man, we'll see.'

The rack held eight beautiful .45 Thompson Sub-Machine guns, all oiled and gleaming metal, highly polished wooden grips and stocks with the impressive drum magazines clipped below. I had never seen one before in the flesh but had been impressed with their firepower and performance whilst watching *The Untouchables* when Kevin Costner and Sean Connery took on Al Capone and his cronies. In recent hours George Town had begun to start to resemble downtown Chicago with its gunfire, murder and mayhem.

Well-meaning but uncoordinated groups of officers scoured the island, searching homes, cars, bikes and pedestrians for any clue as to the identity of the murderer. The febrile atmosphere on the island made dusk fall with a thud as it usually did at six o'clock, and the frenetic activity began to ebb away. Alibis were checked and a few of the detainees began to be released into the darkness with parting promises to get back to us with details of the offender. The CID had put together a wall of names and started to put lines through those who *could not* have done it alongside the rapidly shrinking list of those that *could*.

Overnight the phone calls and messages from the local community had mentioned one name, more and more frequently, so much so that he swiftly became the main suspect that had not actually been traced. Strangely enough during the evening, most of the other candidates voluntarily walked into the foyer of the police station to be arrested and questioned, such was the impact on the population of the island. This senseless murder and robbery in broad daylight at the high-profile jewellers' shop of a well-respected Caymanian businessman had really touched the islanders.

Toadface was the name that continued to crop up with more and more frequency. It now looked more and more likely he had upped his game from petty theft and minor drug dealing to much more serious criminality.

It would be difficult for him to leave the island, but it was a large place to search. Throughout the day his relatives' and friends' houses were carefully searched by armed officers but we found nothing and only encountered a level of dumb insolence from the tiny minority of the islanders who could be shielding him. In the main, those criminal elements that would normally be reluctant to engage with the police now offered suggestions to track down Toadface, but without much success. I presume that he was such a nuisance to mankind even they wanted shot of him.

We spent many hours stopping and searching cars, staking out lonely coves suspected of being used to offload drugs shipments from Jamaica, but without success. Then came a breakthrough. He was caught by a couple of local officers who found him walking around Dog City trying to find a drug fix – his addiction had made him leave his foxhole in search of a snort of cocaine.

Things moved swiftly after that and he was positively identified by numerous eye witnesses as being responsible for the murder. He was matched to CCTV footage recorded around the area and his identify proven beyond all reasonable doubt even though the gun had not been found, but that was unsurprising as miles of land and swamps enclosed the island. The big question remained, why had he committed the robbery and shot Mr Brown? He would not have made much money selling the watches as they were obviously stolen and no one on the islands would have touched them. During the interviews with the CID he refused to comment on all questions asked, as advised by his lawyer, the dodgy Adamson.

The prosecution case was prepared and a number of weeks

passed until the day of the court was convened. Toadface was a sad and pathetic figure as he was placed in the rear of the van inside Northward Prison. Sgt Benjamin had picked a number of us to provide an armed escort for the journey to the court where we arrived to be greeted by the stares of a small gathering of onlookers. At this time the Cayman Islands Penal Code still retained the ultimate sentence of the death penalty for murder. It had not been carried out in living memory after successful appeals to the Privy Council in London, but there was no guarantee that these would succeed, especially in such a violent case as this.

Bristling with firearms we took the prisoner into the dock within No 1 Court where His Honour Judge Rudyard presided with a couple of High Court judges from Jamaica. Toadface wore handcuffs held fast by a short chain to leg irons tied to his ankles and they were looped through a metal ring concreted deep into the floor of the dock. The Prison Service were not taking any chances. We had been told to expect an attempt to release him and this would be the most likely time and place to try it. I stood to the side of the dock as the court proceedings went through the necessary levels, but his defence barrister was clutching at straws. The evidence was overwhelming that he had cold-bloodedly murdered Mr Brown during the botched robbery of a few gold watches.

His representative pleaded for clemency on the basis that the robbery was to pay off a drug debt, that he was a 'good Christian' who went to church on Sunday and that his girlfriend was now expecting his baby. That didn't do his case much good. HHJ Rudyard listened intently, made notes copiously, before telling all to rise as he and his colleagues left to consider their decision. After an almost indecently fast period they returned – I thought they could at least have had a cup of coffee. Rudyard read out the charges and pronounced him guilty of committing the robbery and then the murder of Mr Brown. Toadface slipped down to his hard wooden seat before being hauled back to his feet for the sentencing.

HHJ Rudyard placed the black silk square of material on top of his wig and spoke directly to Toadface, who was now quivering uncontrollably and having to be held upright and still by two warders.

'You will be taken to Northward Prison and held there until the Governor can arrange for and carry out your lawful execution when you will hang by the neck until dead. May God have mercy on your soul.'

There was an audible gasp from the public gallery where some wept openly.

The action of the past few days had rocked me and I decided I needed a change for a time. Transferring to the Drugs Squad was just the ticket. It took me away from the shift work and gave me the opportunity to use my experience from the UK. One of the first things I showed my new colleagues was that if you drive through puddles very fast at night with your full headlights you can produce beautiful rainbow effects.

DCI Timms put me with Detective Sergeant Mac who had a rich vein of stories having worked on ships travelling the globe prior to returning to the islands and joining the police. He was an eccentric-looking character, tall and strongly built with a sunburnt bald head and a few precious strands of hair going from temple to temple and tied into a ponytail. He often wore a flowing kaftan and always mirrored sunglasses, but knew his stuff and didn't suffer fools gladly. The commando dagger carried in his cowboy boot pointed to this assertion.

We got an early call out to the *Regal Princess* cruise ship anchored out in the harbour regarding four US passengers who had bought some ganga in Jamaica. They were arrested and we decided to conduct a full search around the ship and requested more resources to help. Sgt Benjamin joined me and we crawled through vents and air-conditioning pipes down in the bowels of the enormous craft. We found a packet of what looked like drugs measuring as big as a thumbnail. We radioed for DCI Timms to give his opinion. Fifteen sweaty and uncomfortable minutes had elapsed in the humid and hot conditions as we waited with our find until Benjamin said, 'Where the hell is he?'

'He's here.' The DCI was carefully climbing the metal ladder, wheezing loudly. 'You've taken me away from my lunch with the ship's captain, it'd better be worth it.'

I proudly showed the DCI our find, which he picked up, glanced at and threw on the floor in disgust.

'That it? What a load of rubbish,' he said between laboured breaths. 'We've already found four suitcases containing 140 kilos of the stuff destined for the States. Now go to the restaurant, have some lunch and keep out of my way.'

We found half the occupants of the police station already enjoying a free meal, with the mechanic, car washer and uniform tailor tucking into the buffet with gusto. The motorcycle sergeant stomped past us still wearing his leather boots and motorbike helmet.

'I'd try those chicken-wing things,' he said through his visor, pointing at a tray warming on the hotplate. 'They're really good.'

I noted a definite spring in his step after I looked more closely at the menu card, which listed '*des cuisses de grenouille*' (frogs legs). We filled our plates, grabbed a drink and found a sheltered spot on the veranda deck where the other half of the police station staff were already stuffing their faces with dessert.

CHAPTER 23

GUNFIGHT AT THE OLD HAUNTED PLANTATION HOUSE

Northward Prison was built near to the swamps just off the road to Cayman Kai. It housed all the offenders on the island and I had transported them to and from there on many occasions. It had an impressive-looking front entrance built in concrete, and steel gates secured the administration part of the complex. Looking around the back and sides you could see it was surrounded by a layer of barbed and razor wire compounds with wooden huts within. Think of it as similar to Stalag Luft III in *The Great Escape*.

Carlos and I had been tasked to go and visit a drug dealer to see if he was willing to admit who his drug supplier was, with the possibility of a more lenient charge being offered. We were booked into the site and a prison governor escorted us as we walked past a concrete blockhouse in the middle of the yard behind the main entrance. As we approached, we heard a lot of hammering, banging and wood being sawn, then walking around the corner we stopped in our tracks. In front of us a group of cheerful, jokey men were building a wooden scaffold. It was like walking into a cowboy movie set and the prison governor read our minds.

'Yes, boys, we're planning to hang that badass Toadface if we get the chance. The only things we waiting for is the proper rope and trapdoor coming in from Birmingham.'

'Alabama?' I asked.

'No man, England. Nothing but the best for my boys. We wants it quick and painless. Great British engineering you know.'

'I thought there was an appeal to the Privy Council.'

'No guarantees boy... Ain't that right, Toadface?'

He shouted towards a window in the concrete blockhouse and Toadface appeared, holding onto the bars. His cell looked directly onto the scaffold.

'Do you pay extra for the view?' Carlos asked, but this was met by a foul-mouthed tirade from the prisoner, ending with a more coherent rant. 'No prison is going to hold Toadface – you boys see – I won't be swinging from dat gibbet...'

We left the less photogenic 'Cooler King' to his own devices, allowing him to reflect on his own cold-blooded killing.

Visitors always forgot that I wasn't just on an all-paid holiday, indeed I often forgot it as well. My brother had arrived for a holiday and we headed for Silvers Night club to round off the evening. I was quite sober when we arrived back at my hotel but my brother was enjoying the holiday and threatening to stay for a long time. He was quite merry and was really enjoying his time on the island, finding it all intoxicating, especially the Red Stripe. He said he would soon start looking for a job and stay for a while in any case.

I was sleeping soundly when I heard a distant shout. It was a cry for help and the hairs on the nape of my neck stood up. Somebody was in real trouble. It was still dark and the clock showed 4am. I looked out the front windows but the subdued lighting around the pool area and cabana bar showed it to be deserted. I didn't want to worry my brother, so quickly and quietly went through the lounge and opened the door before stepping out into the still, humid night air where the sounds of the cicadas seemed louder than normal. I walked the circuit around the hotel but saw and heard nothing suspicious and returned to my room.

I was replenishing my glass of water in the kitchen when I again heard a strange, strained, hollow voice saying, 'Help me.' It chilled me to the bone. In the twilight I went over to the pull-out bed to rouse my brother but it was empty. Where the hell was he?

'Help me.' The voice resonated once more around the rooms like an echo chamber. I plucked up courage, grabbed my truncheon, pushed open the bathroom door and snapped the light switch on.

'Help… I'm paralysed.' My brother was kneeling on the floor in front of the toilet where he had been speaking to God on the great white telephone. He had been sick and was unable to move as the toilet seat had dropped over his neck preventing him from standing up. I took a photo for historical purposes, then went to help. I lifted the seat, miraculously cured his paralysis and conducted him back to his bed to sleep it off.

I didn't get much more sleep as at seven o'clock the phone woke me.

'Get your arse down here to the nick. Toadface has escaped from prison.' DCI Timms rang off.

The police station was buzzing as we went into a briefing with Mr Timms. The scaffold at the prison had been completed with the noose and British-engineered trapdoor successfully installed. The first appeal to the Privy Council had been unsuccessful, so Toadface had somehow got out of his 'high security' cell, crawled through the layers of wire and disappeared.

Blitz, the long-haired police dog, had attended and searched the area to a distance of 10 feet before collapsing into a breathless pile of fur and crawling back into the air-conditioned Jeep. Uniformed officers were searching the swamps for any signs and we and the CID were trawling the island for his girlfriend and other likely helpers. The trail had gone cold, so we asked for some assistance from Miami.

The following day I drove the police minibus to the airport to collect four Miami Police dog handlers with their very well-trained short-haired German shepherd dogs. The handlers' attention was drawn to the Cayman Airways aircraft that had overshot the runway a few days earlier and was now languishing in 3 feet of water in the North Sound. Nobby had been on duty and been involved in rowing out in a rescue boat to help the stranded passengers. A number of complaints were made when he asked if they were enjoying the scenic cruise around the island after experiencing Cayman Airways' recently purchased flying boat.

I booked the dog handlers and their dogs in at the Hyatt hotel and took them up to Northward where they conducted a sensible area search to track down Toadface. It was hot, sweaty, uncomfortable work, but the handlers and dogs did not complain or flinch at the awful conditions. I accompanied them as they carried out a steady methodical search through the bush without any success. One of the dog handlers was wearing two shoulder holsters, one on the left and the other on the right, with meaty-looking revolvers. During a break for some water, I asked why.

'Firstly, I prefers revolvers 'cos they don't jam in crap conditions,' he replied, pointing around at the dense vegetation. 'You keep squeezing the trigger and the bullets keep coming. Next, my .44 Magnums will knock the bad guys over even if I just wing 'em. And lastly, I can reach one of 'em no matter which hand is holding the lead.'

We called it a day when dusk arrived and the mosquitoes began attacking. I dropped them at the hotel and returned to Police HQ ready to drop off the vehicle keys and go home. Unfortunately, DCI Timms had other ideas.

'We've had a call saying that Toadface may be hiding out at a clapped-out house just beyond Bodden Town. Go and have a look and if it's looking likely I'll bring the bloody 7th Cavalry, but it's probably just a load of bollocks. Take Duke with you, he's a much bigger target.'

'You'll have to give us a clue whereabouts it is.'

His face cracked into his version of a smile of crooked, tobacco-stained teeth, and his smoker's cough crackled into a laugh as he cleared his throat. 'You're going 'cos the local cops won't go near the place – they're shit scared. They reckon it's used for obeah and a lorry load of zombies live there... It's called the Old Haunted Plantation House.'

He continued his bronchial-induced laughing as I went in search of Duke, who I discovered hanging about the armoury boring everyone who passed by with one of his tall tales of manhunts he had carried out back in the swamps of the Mississippi. It seemed sensible to take a gun with me, if only to shoot Duke.

'Not got much left, boys,' Sergeant Benjamin said. 'All the good stuff's gone off with the CID on wild goose chases around the island.'

I told him and Duke where we were going and both stopped in their tracks. Duke started to visibly sweat, extra droplets rolling down his face. 'Shit, man, do we have to?'

'It'd be a good place to hide out,' Benjamin agreed. 'People don't like going there, strange things happen.'

'Thanks for the pep talk, Sergeant. What guns have you got left?' He went rummaging in a drawer and brought out a couple of elderly revolvers that looked left over from the Zulu wars. They were cleaned and oiled and he handed over a bucket of his 'Special Ammunition' specifically created by him for shooting bad bastards. I counted out 12 dum-dum bullets for each pistol and checked that they fitted, then asked about a holster. The Sergeant sucked his teeth and thought for a moment.

'These'll have to do.' He went to another filing cabinet and lay a box carefully on the wooden counter before me. He opened the lid and folded away a crisp sheet of white tissue paper.

'You're joking,' I said but knew he wasn't, his big toothy grin said so. I gently picked up the pair of beautifully engraved tan leather holsters. There was a lovely warm smell of fresh unused leather that creaked evocatively as I held them. They were a work of art and totally impractical.

'Strap 'em on boy.' It was a boyhood dream come true and brought visions back of Dean Martin strapping on his gun belt before the final shoot-out in John Wayne's classic western *Rio Bravo* – I was totally enthralled. I tied the big silver buckle around my waist and the leather thong on my calf. I put my – unloaded – revolver in the holster, which fitted like a glove. I tried the quick draw, I just couldn't help myself.

'What about the left-hand holster?' I asked.

'I've no guns left, stick a banana in it.'

'Have you got a holster for me?' said Duke.

'You're bloody joking, aren't ye,' said the Sergeant. 'We'd have to tie two together to fit round your belly.' Eventually he produced a right-handed shoulder holster of the type made popular by Eliot Ness of *The Untouchables*. Duke struggled to work out how to attach it and managed to have it upside down and back to front, looking more like lingerie.

'Before you go,' he said, 'I've heard that Toadface has a gun and promised to take some cops with him if he gets cornered. Do you want a bulletproof vest, I found a couple in the cupboard?'

That sounded like a good idea to me. He returned from his inner sanctum and threw one at Duke, who held it in front of his massive chest. I laughed out loud as it was no bigger than a baby's bib.

'You'd have to be a bloody good shot to hit that,' I said.

Scarily, Benjamin laughed even louder as he threw me the next one. I held it up to my front and saw it was marked 38 DD. It had two massive bosoms sticking out like Dolly Parton's blouse.

At that moment DCI Timms walked past the armoury, stopped, retraced his steps and did a theatrical double-take. 'Haven't you two gone yet? There's no time to be hanging around here waiting to be invited to some weird fancy dress party.'

Duke and I took the hint and drove my Jeep towards Bodden Town along roads that were much quieter than normal – perhaps the locals could feel the sinister vibes of the escaped murderer in their midst. Radio Cayman must have known that we were on a scary mission, as 'Ghost Town' by the Specials blared out from the Jeep's speakers. This did nothing for Duke's frayed nerves and little for mine.

The Old Haunted Plantation House was along a marl track off the road beyond Bodden Town on the way towards Northward Prison. It would be an ideal hiding place for an escaped murderer with nothing to lose. In daylight it looked quite presentable from a distance. It was a white clapperboard building with a steep shingle-covered roof and wooden steps up to a veranda that went around the entire house. The paint was peeling and the bush was encroaching on its land but there was little damage – presumably the local youths kept their distance because of the rumours of strange goings-on.

It was just before midnight when I pulled the Jeep off the road at the end of the lane and could just see the house a couple of hundred yards away. The engine pinged as it cooled, mixing in with the sounds from the still, humid air which magnified the cicadas playing loudly, accompanied by myriad unseen creatures singing in the backing group. Duke rechecked his revolver for the hundredth time. 'Shit, man, why don't we just drive up there with all the lights on an' shoot it out with him. The Jeep'll protect us.'

'Oh no, Duke, I want to show this lot there's nothing to be scared of.'

I nearly managed to convince myself I wasn't worried, but I really wanted to catch Toadface and if necessary shoot him, instead of seeing him high tailing it back into the swamps. A full moon lit the way as we approached the house that glowed eerily phosphorescent against the grey background shadows of the swamps beyond and the surrounding bushes nearby. There was some movement in the humid air as we walked quietly along the edge of the track. We stopped about 20 yards away and listened carefully for any sign of life – or the afterlife – but all I could hear was my heart beating in my ear, at 20 to the dozen. The house was in darkness and I could see the lower section of each sash window was covered by wooden-framed mosquito netting in various stages of disrepair. The front door had a similar frame hanging on drunkenly by one hinge, moving to and fro in the gentle breeze.

'Shit man,' Duke said in a strained hollow whisper. 'I'm spooked out, this ain't one of your practical jokes, is it?'

I pointed him towards the front steps leading to the main door and told him to wait until I went around to the back. The stone marl crunched beneath my boots like deafening eggshells as I circled around the edge of the shrubs and gingerly approached the back veranda facing the swamps. By the back door an ancient swing chair rocked like a hypnotist's pendulum. I concentrated all my senses on the back of the house that was dark and foreboding in the shadow cast by the moon. Aiming my revolver towards the house, I ignored the back steps and lifted myself onto the worn wooden floor boards of the veranda and peered through the filthy window into the kitchen. It all looked undisturbed and the back door and windows were closed. I put my hand on the door handle then felt the breeze stiffen around me like something was going to happen; goosebumps appeared on my arms.

Suddenly there was a loud bang from the front of the house followed by a shout from Duke as two gunshots rang out and cracked past my head as I ducked down. The glass in the kitchen window beside me smashed over the veranda floor as I aimed my gun inside and fired twice. I dropped down once again as more shots came from within and thudded into the walls somewhere around me. I aimed inside then fired a third time until I heard the empty click as I pulled the trigger. My ears buzzed with the noise as the cloud of cordite caught the back of my throat; my heart raced as I glanced in but couldn't see anyone.

I heard, 'Shit man, shit, shit, shit,' which was followed by a further couple of gunshots that thudded somewhere inside. I reloaded my pistol, lying low beneath the window, scattering the used cartridges.

'Where are you, Duke?' I called out. I could hear him saying something, over and over again, but wasn't sure if it was 'I'm hit,' so I gingerly crawled on all fours around towards the front, keeping away from the windows. Duke was lying on the front steps pointing his gun at the front door.

'Are you alright?' I asked quietly.

'Shit, man, I thought he was coming out the door – I heard

a bang. I saw the guy, he shot at me... Honest, man, he kept shooting back.'

Just then the breeze caught the outer mosquito net frame and slammed dramatically into the front door. The rusted hinge had finally had enough and fell with a clatter to the veranda floor. Slowly the truth began to dawn on us.

'You fool, you nearly killed me. I think you'll find it was me you were shooting at, it's a bloody good job you're such a shit shot.' I knew I was as scared as he was, but you can't admit it, can you?

Still keeping a close eye on the front of the house he reloaded his gun and we went inside through the bullet-ridden front door that was unlocked. Sgt Benjamin's 'special ammunition' had done a huge amount of damage to the front door, walls and windows inside and I was eternally grateful that one did not connect with me during the melee. A careful search of the house revealed no signs of life or the afterlife to suggest the presence of Toadface. We quickly made our way back to the Jeep after collecting the spent cartridge cases for a counsel of war. Our gun battle would have woken all the zombies in Bodden Town and we had not bothered telling the uniform officers of our quest – we wanted to catch him ourselves.

We took off the joke bulletproof bib, bra and holsters and threw them in the back of the Jeep. We would have had a lot of questions to answer if we were found out, so in the best traditions of British Policing we planned to cover our tracks and deny everything.

'We can go to my place, clean up the guns and I have a couple of boxes of ammo we can drop back in the Sergeant's bucket.' Duke smiled as he had actually had a sensible idea for a change.

I turned the Jeep around and began driving back towards Bodden Town just as I spied flashing blue lights in the distance, coming our way at speed. They slowed down and the headlights flashed at me before slowing and pulling up alongside.

'What's 'appening boys?' The Bodden Town Sergeant looked in at us. 'We've had reports of gunfire.'

'We heard some as well,' I said truthfully. 'We've been looking for Toadface and we've got some info for DCI Timms.'

That seemed to do the trick and we moved off with huge sighs of relief as he continued on his wild goose chase.

A colourful dawn broke on a hot and sticky morning and things were becoming fractious between the Drugs Squad team as Toadface had been on the run for seven days without a trace. Some took it as a personal insult that none of the usual 'snouts' or informers were telling us where he was hiding – if indeed he was still on the island. Then came the breakthrough and his girlfriend was the key. She was regularly followed and her phone was tapped but she was careful, usually. She phoned in an order for a hot chilli beef and rice meal to be picked up from the street café in Bodden Town. I remembered she had insisted on a vegetarian meal when she had been arrested – a one-off or was it for Toadface?

DCI Timms and his fine band of police brigands made their way towards Bodden Town and I went to pick up the Miami dog handlers from the hotel. We rendezvoused at the police station and were briefed that a young child on a bike had collected the meal then taken it to a small cul-de-sac of bungalows on the edge of town. A local constable named Smythe said the house with the blue door was currently empty and he had seen some suspicious activity in recent days. We parked away from the area and walked quietly to the edge of the lane where we could clearly see the blue door on the left side.

Mr Timms drew all his troops around him.

'Listen up everybody' – and for some unknown reason he pointed his thumb at me – 'Tricky Dicky here reckons we need to professionalise our briefings so here goes. You six climb over the back wall and wait in the garden. The rest of you go up the front path, kick the front door in and don't bother knocking. If you get the chance boys, just shoot him.'

I stayed with the dog handlers sheltering behind a convenient truck away from any stray bullets as we watched eight of the team stomp up the front path. One of the group launched themselves through the blue front door, splintering and cracking as it disappeared inside in a cloud of rising dust. There was a moment of complete silence followed by a female scream then a torrent of abuse. Faster than they entered they returned outside into the blinding sunshine, hotly pursued by an ancient lady wearing a voluminous flowery dress and wielding a damp fish fillet in one hand and a very sharp-looking knife in the other.

As she was cursing all present, everyone looked viciously towards Smythe. He immediately pointed towards the house opposite. 'Thinking about it boss, it might've been the red door.'

The dog handlers and I ran towards this house where I saw a figure disappear quietly back inside from the shady veranda. The DCI ran across the lane and I heard the sound of a loud slap and a resounding 'Ow' from Smythe. Glancing back I saw him vigorously rubbing his right ear. The police dog sprinted around to the backyard where I heard the rear door slam shut. Whoever it was, was still inside. The German shepherd dog was barking and pawing at the door and as I looked through the window I saw Toadface inside the kitchen leaning on the front door with one hand and trying to drag furniture behind it with the other. Muffled shouts from Mr Timms' band of brigands resonated with the kicking at the front door as the dog handler politely asked me to move away from the window. He picked up a sun lounger and used it like a medieval battering ram to hammer the window and frame straight through. In one movement he scooped up his dog and gently dropped it inside. This was immediately followed by a short bark, a growl and a series of screams.

It didn't take too long before Toadface was returned to his grandstand window overlooking the now-completed scaffold.

I didn't have much time to reflect on the action of the last few days and weeks. I was still so sad about Mr Brown the jeweller but resolved to keep Toadface in prison for as long as possible. Within a few short weeks the Privy Council overturned the death penalty imposed on Toadface and converted the sentence to life imprisonment. This was the last time that anyone was sentenced to death on the islands and this sanction was removed from the Cayman Islands Penal Code a couple of months later.

I soon cheered up when I received a message from the Governor that he had a 'top secret' job for me. Go to the airport, the Governor's secretary said, and hold up the cardboard sign emblazoned with the name and crest of Government House. 'The person concerned will come and speak to you, so you don't need to know his name. He's from the Foreign Office,' she added, with a knowing tap to the side of her nose, then mouthed silently, 'M-I-6'.

CHAPTER 24

NO MR PYLES, I EXPECT YOU TO DIE

As I waited for the Miami flight to disembark I thought, what a load of old cloak and dagger nonsense. At the entrance to the VIP lounge a tall, healthy-looking chap in his 30s came towards me. He had blond tousled hair, Ray-Ban sunglasses, and wore well his expensive chinos and crisp pastel coloured short sleeve shirt. With a winning smile he indicated to an equally attractive strawberry blonde female to head in my direction. She wore a blue-banded, wide-brimmed straw hat and a beautiful floral summer dress that blew gently in the breeze as she stepped confidently to the airport terminal. They were a stunning couple and looked better than film stars; there was an effortless charisma to them.

'I wasn't expecting two of you but that's fine. We need to go through the VIP lounge where I can sort the paperwork out for you.'

'That's very kind,' she said in a slight Canadian accent. 'I didn't expect such a warm welcome.'

They followed me through the sliding doors out of the heat and presented a couple of Canadian passports. What a great idea I thought, using overseas documents, clever these MI6 bods.

'When we've sorted out the formalities I'll take you to see the Governor.'

Her companion looked sideways to her, then back at me. 'Sounds great, we can't wait.'

I went through to the passport control and got the documents stamped and returned. At the entrance from the aircraft apron a perspiring rather rotund male in a creased linen jacket was waving through the glass doors. I ignored him and told my visitors we were ready to go. Annoyingly the sweaty man started tapping his keys on the outer sliding-glass doors. He was mid-40, about 5 foot 10 with slicked-back black hair and a bit too small for his clothes. I waved him away and pointed towards the main arrivals hall. He shook his head vigorously then energetically pointed inside the lounge at a nearby coffee table where I had discarded my GH sign.

I pressed the door release button to speak to him and they glided open silently.

'I'm sorry but you'll have to use the arrivals hall next door.'

He ignored this and briskly side-stepped past me into the air-conditioned lounge.

'No,' he said loudly, 'I'm expected at the government building this afternoon.' Glancing furtively towards my guests he pointed once more at my sign.

'What's your name?' I said, as if it made any difference at all.

'That depends,' he said quietly in a younger, more gravelly voiced version of Sir Alec Guinness.

Oh dear, I thought, we've got a right one here. I sent my Canadian visitors to retrieve their belongings and remove any potential witnesses before dealing with my amnesiac visitor.

'I presume you are here to collect me, the Governor's expecting me when we're finished here. I expect you'll need one of these.'

He placed his shiny, black leather attaché case on the coffee table and flicked the lustrous brass clasps open. He moved a manila folder aside, then like a magician with a pack of cards, held up four British passports.

'Ah, I like using this one best,' he said, and selected one for me.

It opened with a newish creak revealing a recent photo of him alongside the name of Jeremy Pyles. I compared the photo with my new visitor who now wore a wide, cheerful grin. A single, chilling bead of sweat ran down my back.

'Who are they?' He pointed his thumb towards the baggage reclaim.

I pathetically shook my head. 'I don't actually know – but they're lovely people – from Canada…'

'Some of my best friends are Canadian, shall we give them a lift?'

'I told them they were going to see the Governor…'

'No problems, I'll explain your youthful enthusiasm, you all make mistakes.'

We dropped them off at their hotel – Governor's Harbour – after Jeremy had explained my little faux pas and even arranged to meet up with them for a drink later that evening. He was a fast worker was Jeremy.

I stepped into the Governor's office with Jeremy where his secretary was busy on the phone. She covered the speaker, smiled at us, then pressed an intercom button.

'They've arrived, sir.'

'Send them right in.'

I waved Jeremy in front of me and followed him into the mahogany-lined office that smelt of beeswax. The Governor was behind his executive desk, sitting with his back to us in his high-backed tan-leather swivel chair. He was looking out towards the sea, then his chair slowly creaked around to face us. He wore a monocle and was gently caressing a toy pussy cat.

'Good afternoon. I've been expecting you Mr Bond...'

Jeremy erupted into a huge belly laugh that wobbled up and down until he found it difficult to breathe. It was impossible not to join in. Eventually the mirth subsided enough for the Governor to give me a thumbs-up and waved me off. As I closed the door the Governor asked, 'What name are you using this time?'

'Pyles, Jeremy's Pyles.'

This was instantly followed by a loud guffaw and the suppressed laughter of a couple of naughty schoolboys passing wind behind the teacher's back.

Mr Pyles needed some trustworthy and willing assistants able to keep their mouths shut and be flexible enough to help with a number of unusual enquiries around the island. Mr Timms chose Nobby and myself and we were happy to keep busy by helping. A secure office away from prying ears was found next to Mr Timms' office. Jeremy was an affable, cheerful raconteur who regularly dropped names and regaled us with tall tales and adventures from his time at Oxford, as a barrister at the Inns of Court and as a Lt Commander in the Royal Navy.

'I take it you went to Eton?' I asked.

'Good god, no. I was at Winchester. I'm not gay and I wanted a proper job away from politics. Anyway, Eton's a complete dump.'

On one of our trips to the Pattie Shop for a leisurely lunch, Nobby shared one of his concerns. 'I think he's a complete Walter Mitty, you know. I mean James Bond was a Lt Commander, Ian Fleming was as well. I reckon Jeremy's just a fantasist – but a pleasant one.'

He did seem a bit too young for all his stories, which were entertaining but a little farfetched with a possible grain of truth mixed in. Nevertheless, we were asked to help him out and his stories helped to pass the day. We returned to our office from lunch and as we entered I whispered that David Niven once said, 'The truth is a poor storyteller.'

'Oh yes, I agree,' said Jeremy, 'I was at one of Niven's parties in Switzerland – it was bloody marvellous. Wine, women and song but not necessarily in that order…he asked me to sing "Nessun Dorma"…'

Nobby's eyes went up to heaven.

We were approaching our final six months of the contract and were given the opportunity to remain for a further two years, should we want to. I made an appointment to see the Commissioner in the early morning to ensure the greatest potential of a sober reception. Mr Jones accompanied me and we chatted through the options as we approached the Government building.

'What would you do in my situation, sir?'

'You've passed your exams back in the UK, so life is on hold for you here and I can't guarantee keeping you with Mr Timms and his team. Some of the locals see it as preferential treatment for the UK boys. And I've had a few grumbles from some senior officers as well. Personally, I'd be delighted if you stayed.'

The Commissioner had been authorised to recruit from the UK once more but to keep the overall numbers the same. It was a six-month recruitment process, so we were given a couple of days to decide, after which we could not change our minds. There were many ifs, buts and maybes, which we chattered through together over the following days with loads of opinions and differing perspectives. My brother still remained with me and his tainted approach was for me to stay.

'Oh yeah, I think you should stay. I might get a job sometime and I like driving your Jeep.'

That, unsurprisingly, didn't help much as I pondered my future.

I submitted my report to the Commissioner confirming that I would return to the UK. But things were never going to be that simple, were they?

There was plenty to look forward to in the coming months, including the weather cooling down a little, a skiing holiday to Colorado and a much-anticipated long weekend to Cuba. Meanwhile, I continued to really look after my beautiful black Jeep. As well as servicing it myself, I washed and waxed it regularly to maintain the luscious deep glow protecting the bodywork from the harsh rigours of the Caribbean sand, sea and sunshine. It had become my pride and joy. My brother was covering many miles around the island looking for jobs at the furthest corners possible, then returning to Caribbean Suites, emptying the fridge for lunch and resuming his odyssey of visiting everyone he had ever met on the island, at least once a day. I asked how he would travel to a job on the island without relying on my Jeep. He dismissed my question with a nonchalant wave of the TV handset. 'Transport,' he said.

You can tell it was beginning to annoy me, can't you? One morning he dropped me off at work and said he was going out to East End where a hotel was advertising for bar staff. There was no public transport to speak of, so the Jeep was the only option; I made a note of the mileage. Later that evening he collected me and I read the odometer. I could not quite comprehend the increase. He had driven 160 miles in eight hours on an island that is only 22 miles long. When I calmly pointed out this fact, he explained that:

1. He had gone to East End, had a brief interview, and returned home for lunch.

2. He then drove back to East End, for a further practical interview on how to 'Shake a Cocktail' after having watched a video of Tom Cruise in *Cocktail*.
3. He returned home for his passport and work permits and dropped them off.
4. The petrol tank was now empty.

To get my blood pressure and heart rate down a bit I went for a very long run...

Things always look better the next morning, don't they? He dropped me off at the office and I suggested that he wash the Jeep and clean out the inside. Nobby and I were given a sensitive enquiry in the West Bay area and it was a particularly hot afternoon. Money was pretty tight for us, so I suggested raiding my fridge for a cooling drink before returning to the office. We pulled up outside and saw the Jeep parked up, looking a bit more presentable. The ground around it was bone dry, so I assumed my brother had taken it to the car wash instead of using the nearby hosepipe. We went inside to the cold air-conditioned sanctuary and stopped dead in the entrance hall at the open door into the bathroom. My brother was sitting on the toilet, stark naked and reading a classic car magazine. I saved his blushes as he tried to reach the door and closed it myself.

'You know what,' he shouted through the closing door, 'the E-Type Jags in Florida are really good value.'

'I'll take your word for it. I assume the magazine is very absorbing?'

He then appeared wearing a pair of pants and handed me the reading material, which I declined. Nobby was examining the empty, echoing fridge. 'Have you been burgled?'

'I've been too busy cleaning the Jeep to go shopping.'

'Which car wash did you use?' I said.

'I did it outside.'

'But there's no water on the ground.'

'No. I wiped it.'

Once more I felt my heart rate and blood pressure beginning to increase. Nobby stepped in to try and assist. 'You mean you wiped off the water with a sponge, of course.'

'No, I used that old towel in the back to wipe the mud off. Looks great, don't it?'

I ran outside to examine my lovely Jeep. The gouges in the paintwork could not have been deeper had he danced a jig on the bonnet wearing hobnail boots. I flew back in to grab his throat, only to be held in a bear hug by Nobby who shouted in my ear.

'It's not worth it – if you kill him, they're sure to hang you.'

He dragged me away from the crime scene as I continued to shout obscenities at my brother, who remained perplexed. Standing in his underpants in the doorway his only reply amounted to, 'What? What? What's happened?'

Mr Pyles briefed us on a couple of tourists who were due to arrive on a cruise ship.

'I want you to find them, follow them and photograph them, wherever they go and whoever they see before they reboard the ship. Okay?'

'What do they look like?'

He went to his magic laptop and printed off a photo. Mr Timms leant over for a look. 'Bloody hell, it's the Man from Del Monte, from the ad, and Morticia from the Addams Family.'

The photo had been taken on board a cruise ship of a swarthy-looking male in his 50s with an impressive black Mexican styled moustache, dressed in a white linen suit and a wide brimmed fedora hat. He was walking along the promenade deck with a shapely woman in her 30s, dressed in an expensive-looking black dress down to the ground. She had long, straight black hair framing sharp, pale features and was smiling widely at her companion as she linked his arm. Jeremy told us the name of the ship and the time it was due to start transferring passengers to shore. We went and dressed accordingly, like tourists, with shorts and polo shirts, and took the office camera. Luckily the Pattie Shop was directly opposite the cruise ship terminal, so we set up our observation point in the window table while munching on an early lunch of our favourite spicy chicken patties and tuna sandwiches. They tasted even nicer after Jeremy said we could claim any expenses. Life was good.

Like bees around a hibiscus bush, taxis and minibuses waited eagerly outside the harbour gates for the cash-rich passengers. Just as I was wiping the remaining crumbs of a cinnamon and apple pastry from my lips, Nobby spoke. 'It's them, look.'

Del Monte and Morticia appeared through the harbour gate and stepped onto the footpath, waving away the taxi manager. They were dressed exactly in the same clothes as in the photo. They either possessed a very limited wardrobe or the photo must have been taken that morning. Very efficient, I thought. They strolled off together, arm in arm without a care in the world, and reviewed the historic site of Fort George. This took about 10 seconds in total before they set off with a bit more of a spring in their steps. Nobby took a couple of tourist snaps of them before we tailed them around the town centre, doing our best to keep out of the way. They were stopping and glancing in myriad jewellers' shops around the town with expensive watches, and expensive celebrity endorsees floodlit in the windows.

Suddenly they turned down a quiet lane and climbed an external wooden staircase leading to a jewellery shop on the first floor of a wooden clapperboard building, brightly painted in blue and white.

I had never actually noticed these premises before, it was out of the way, a distance from the usual hub. There was no way of seeing what was happening inside without giving us away, so we found a spot in the shade and waited. Half an hour later our two targets came out of the door at the top of the stairs. Del Monte carried a paper gift bag, similar to the type offered to you by a friendly local bookshop owner, who smiles and then charges you a fortune for the privilege. He held the base and folded the handles in his hand as he descended. From the top of the stairs an elderly man waved goodbye. He had a look of satisfaction across his tanned face as he turned back into his shop.

We were very curious and followed the couple, who walked to an expensive restaurant a little further up Seven Mile Beach. I didn't think Jeremy's expense account would run to this establishment, so we found a spot to watch them from the bar next door. They ordered drinks and scanned the menu card, then were joined by two males who sat with their backs towards us. Nobby set off to the other side of the building with his camera as I watched the four diners animatedly choose the food, followed by cheerful chatter punctured by the hubbub of quiet conversation.

'You won't believe this,' said Nobby as he returned out of breath. 'I've got the photos of them. The two blokes are Adamson, our favourite dodgy lawyer, and Hollywood, his equally dodgy mate on the Legislative Assembly.' I gave a low whistle as I settled back into my bar stool. Adamson and Hollywood left first followed by the two visitors who walked back towards George Town, then made straight for another of the smaller jewellery shops, which they entered without hesitation. We could see little of what they were looking at and as I was familiar to the shop staff, I was reluctant to go in. I saw that the owner did invite them into his secure office at the back of the shop away from prying eyes.

A quarter of an hour later they reappeared with a wrapped gift box about the size of a paperback book. Morticia held it with both hands close to her bosoms. They did not show any interest in the tourist tat displayed in other venues around the town and walked leisurely back to the harbour in answer to the cruise ship klaxons giving notice of the pending departure. Nobby took a final snap as they disappeared in the queue for the tenders ready for the return voyage to the ship. We needed to know what was in the packages, so ignoring the protocols walked down the side lane and climbed the steps to the first-floor shop. I buzzed the bell and the elderly shopkeeper appeared at the door.

'What do you want?' he asked, rather rudely I thought. I showed him my warrant card and he reluctantly opened up; we stepped inside.

'We are making some enquiries and we need your help.'

'If I can, of course.'

'What did you sell to the couple earlier today? He was wearing the white suit and fedora.' The man's eyes narrowed as he considered his answer.

'Don't mess us about now,' said Nobby. 'We saw them come in and buy something. Just tell us or I'll think of something to lock you up for.'

The shop owner waited for a long quiet minute, considering his options and the truth of his possible answers. 'I've never seen them before and they asked to see what gold sovereigns I had.'

'Go on.'

'We agreed a price and he paid in cash, US dollars as it happens. One hundred thousand US dollars.'

'Wow,' said Nobby.

'Right, but don't tell anyone we've been in. Especially if they come back. Here's my details if you need to contact me.'

We walked out into the sunshine and back down the lane to the other shop. We didn't need the 'Bad Cop' routine here as the owner was up front with the information immediately.

'Yes, they were a very pleasant couple. They bought a proof gold ingot for just over a hundred thousand dollars. They didn't even haggle and it was paid in cash!'

We dropped the film off at the Scenes of Crime office for them to process and went back to our office where Jeremy and Mr Timms were in deep conversation.

'How did you get on?' Jeremy asked.

We explained the activities of the day with Adamson and Hollywood and kept the details of the sales until last.

'Bloody hell,' added Mr Timms with a low whistle. 'I'm in the wrong game.'

'That's cleared up a few queries for me,' said Mr Pyles as he rocked back in his chair. 'We were wondering what they were up to here and it now makes perfect sense. It's all hush, hush of course, but he's a major drug exporter from Colombia and needs to clean up his dirty cash. Nobody ever gets checked or searched on a cruise ship, do they? They're probably doing it in every port of call around the Caribbean. He can now sell the sovereigns and gold ingot anywhere in the world, no questions asked. Great job gents, I'll stand you lunch tomorrow.'

The following morning, we collected the photos from Scenes of Crime and after removing the inappropriate images of scantily clad tourists Nobby had taken with a massive telephoto lens, we presented Jeremy with the remainder. Lunchtime beckoned and I drove to the Wharf restaurant which, unsurprisingly was on the best plot on the west coast, overlooking the nicer part of the harbour with stunning views along Seven Mile Beach. Neither Nobby nor I had ever dared to visit this very expensive haunt of the rich and famous, but Mr Timms joined us and he had no such qualms. 'You know me, boys, I never miss an opportunity for a good time.'

A smiling waiter presented the menu card and offered the chef's recommendation. 'Surf and Turf, gentlemen, with 28-day aged fillet steak accompanied by the tail of a lobster – who is not yet dead.'

I must have paled under my tan when I glanced at the price. Jeremy leant forward. 'As I mentioned gentlemen, this is courtesy of Her Majesty the Queen – do enjoy.'

So we did, starting with fragrant turtle soup, followed by the most tender conch fritters. I thoroughly enjoyed the chef's recommended main course – it was succulent and almost fell apart as the knife touched it. I felt obliged to offer to pay for the drinks, which was waved away by Jeremy. He mentioned a couple of his adventures in the Royal Navy, Winchester and Oxford, then as a barrister before joining MI6. Over the last couple of weeks, we had certainly warmed to him even though some of the stories were still a little hard to take. He was such a pleasant character we actually wanted to believe it all.

Having finished the main course, we were basking in the semi shade beneath a well-placed umbrella when Jeremy placed his elbows on the pristine linen tablecloth and covered his mouth with his hands.

'Who's the bald Bond villain?' His eyes flicked towards a table over my shoulder. I dropped my napkin to the floor and glanced back as I picked it up. My nemesis was staring intently at the back of my head. He was at a table with three local bigwigs, including Lawyer Adamson and his pal Hollywood.

'Oh dear,' I said with a sigh. 'That's the infamous Dr Felix Kampenboom. He's a complete bastard and I suspect him of being a Nazi war criminal... I didn't know he was chummy with those two.'

Jeremy's eyes widened as he leant back in his chair, nursed his glass of chilled white wine and listened to my tirade. I went on to explain what had happened several months earlier when I dealt with the doctor and the unfortunate Canadian lady he held in his compound against her will. I also mentioned the unsupported evidence I had obtained from his drinking glass, including his fingerprints and DNA samples. I waxed lyrically about Kampenboom, his loaded Walther pistol, and his influential friends on the islands.

Mr Timms carefully wiped the remains of his lunch from his lips with a crisp linen napkin. 'I said we should've gone back an' shot him for resisting arrest but you wouldn't listen, would you?'

'He doesn't look particularly well either,' said Jeremy as he glanced over to the other table.

I turned and stared. His once tanned features were now liverish yellow and his cheeks had hollowed.

'Well, Jeremy,' I said, 'any chance of getting him bumped off for me?'

'If only…' he said with a smile. 'When we get back to the office, let me have his details. You never know.'

DCI Timms' fingers twisted his linen napkin tightly one way, then the other. 'I'm pissed off gents. Recently we've had a number of tip-offs and drug jobs that have been compromised and it's been topped off today. Over the weekend some bastard's removed the bag of evidence from the safe at the police station. It was absolutely crucial for the case in court today. We're having to offer no evidence in that conspiracy-to-supply-cocaine job that Mac was dealing with. I'm beginning to suspect everyone and that's not healthy, it's becoming invidious.' We all glanced at him. 'I know what it means – I looked it up. *Likely to cause ill will.* It bloody is doing.'

The other table were ignoring us, laughing and joking among

themselves, so I finished off the meal with an apple strudel and double cream that was so light I practically held it on the plate. We returned to the office, replete and contented.

After a couple of weeks of setting intriguing enquiries for Nobby and myself without any explanations, Jeremy Pyles was due to leave the island. 'It's a need-to-know basis,' he explained, and we didn't need to know. We joined him for a few farewell drinks at Sunset House.

'You really must meet Olivia,' he said and nodded towards the car park. 'She's a delightful creature and has just pulled up in her car. I'll introduce you.'

He greeted her like a long-lost friend and we swapped names. She was really nice, if you can say that sort of thing. Tall, slim, bobbed dark-brown hair, a natural complexion of freckles with a slightly turned-up nose above a ready smile. Originally from Canada she worked as a lawyer in one of the many international banks on the island. With a bit of sarcastic humour, she was fun to chat to and we exchanged phone numbers and agreed to go to the next performance at the amateur-run Prospect Theatre, where intended or unintended laughs were guaranteed. Reluctantly I had to leave the bar early to pack for a trip. We were heading off on a long weekend to Havana, Cuba.

CHAPTER 25

A CLEAN PAIR OF CUBAN HEELS

It would have seemed impossible to comprehend for anyone back home, considering the political isolation of Cuba at the time, but the Remembrance Day bank holiday weekend in November provided the ideal opportunity to visit Cuba. It was a huge draw for all of us Europeans and proved so popular that an additional aircraft had to be chartered from Cuban Airlines to carry us all. We stepped out of the airport terminal into the bright sunshine that was not reflected off any part of the Cuban aircraft. I think they call the colour 'marine grey' and it is designed to blend military boats and ships into the background. It was an ancient Antonov warplane, a cast-off from Russia with four engines sporting massive propellers and no distinguishing markings. We were waved over to the steps at the rear of the aircraft and I watched as my baggage was firmly stuffed into the bomb bay. I felt a firm prod in my back from an unsmiling uniformed attendant who pointed me towards a row of seats made of grey 'wipe-clean' plastic seats of the type I had last seen in a clapped-out Moskvich car my dad bought for £50.

Alec and Sgt Mac's wife, Mary, were on my row and immediately behind me sat Carlos. I looked around for the seatbelt and found only one side of the strap. I motioned to a stern-looking stewardess and used sign language to point out my problem. It was obviously no surprise to her as she gripped her muscly hands together and bellowed, 'Links arms.' Even those with seatbelts immediately linked arms like a command performance of Jools Holland's *Hootenanny* and altogether we loudly began to sing the first verse of 'Auld Lang Syne'. The perplexed faces of the cabin crew looking at each other caused four heavily built men in bulging, ill-fitting suits to stand up and survey the passengers from their strategic and presumably armoured seats by the cockpit door. I bet they had seatbelts. The oldest and ugliest of them looked at us for a small lifetime from beneath his monobrow, before a wave of his furry paw diffused the situation and they sat back down with a collective grunt.

A stewardess handed a metal platter of quarter-sized sandwiches to Alec, then slapped his hand as he tried to take two. 'One,' she shouted in his face. We passed the plate along the row under her dutiful gaze and each extracted a single quarter to show her before eating it. Next, a human chain passed tins of mango juice and Crystal beer along the line before handing the spares to those behind us. The engines started up one by one and the ensuing Richter scale vibrations shook my beer to a froth as I attempted to place it to my lips. I gulped it down to save spilling it on my clean polo shirt and it hit my tummy in a bubbly lump to join the nondescript sandwich.

The engines began to pop and roar as we felt the brakes release and move the mighty airplane forward along the taxiway. There was a tremendous metallic clunk beneath us as the bomb bay doors sealed our luggage in. I prayed that the pilot didn't press the wrong button as he left the airport and flatten part of the island with diverse bags of toiletries, spare undies and other essentials for the wild weekend ahead. We got to the beginning of the runway and I linked arms with Alec and Mary Mac whilst others mumbled prayers. The pilots must have pushed the throttles through the emergency 'gate' and the plane leapt violently forward, causing my seat back to collapse into Carlos's lap like a poleaxed drunk. He screamed, 'Aghh. Get off me family jewels, you're crushin' 'em.'

'You've got a lot of nasal hair,' I said as the aircraft raced along the runway, pinning me to the seat. It was quite relaxing in this prone position, but after a while his aftershave became distinctly overpowering and I was relieved when the cabin crew returned my seat to the more conventional position.

Now all profoundly deaf but very relieved, we arrived at a brand new and swish-looking airport terminal where we had to pay $10 in US currency to obtain a tourist card for the officials to stamp instead of your passport. It was still forbidden for US citizens to visit Cuba, and other nationalities would be given a long, uncomfortable and protracted interrogation by US immigration authorities if a Cuban visa was discovered in your passport. We were loaded onto surprisingly modern air-conditioned coaches for the eye-opening journey to the hotel in Old Havana. We were taken through quite beautiful countryside with lush fields and woods, cheek by jowl with the blonde sandy beaches washed by the turquoise sea. The sun shone brightly and when we stopped it was warm with refreshingly clean breezes.

The guide subjected us to a list of mealtimes, which she repeated several dozen times during the half-hour journey to the 25-storey Havana Libre Hotel. In a previous life this was the Havana Hilton and it had not been updated since the Americans were chased out of the country by the Castro brothers and their mates. We were booked in and I was sharing with Alec. We took in the panoramic stunning views of the city from the room, which was clean but basic, and we did not intend to stay there much. Remembering the mealtimes, we wandered into the restaurant that reminded me of my primary-school canteen, as did the food on offer, so we excused ourselves and went out into the setting sun, framed seductively along the narrow alleyways pointing towards the sea.

We came across a first-floor ice cream parlour/bar with spectacular views towards the National Monument where beneath the enormous copula roof there is reputedly a massive diamond embedded into the marble floor. The staff must have overheard us plotting the best way to steal the jewel, so unsurprisingly they threw us back down the rickety wooden stairs after we asked for some more beers. A couple of smartly uniformed off-duty soldiers were seated under the shade of a cabana by the neighbouring café. They noticed the kerfuffle and gallantly came to help. After confirming we had US dollars, they led us down a series of progressively dark and dingy lanes into the oldest and crumbliest part of Old Havana. One of our squaddie guides had taken an obvious shine to Mary Mac, therefore due to her basic command of conversational Spanish, warm Killarney charm and the possibility of drinks purchased using US dollars, we were entertained to a guided tour well off the beaten track. By six o'clock, darkness had dropped like a shroud as we navigated the ancient parts of the city.

The most intriguing part of our nocturnal journey was when we suddenly came across a lonely, very plain stone chapel of an unknown age standing in the centre of an empty, poorly lit plaza. There was not a breath of wind, nor a sound to puncture the silence. It had become quite unsettling, without a sign of any living creature nearby. Of other humans there was neither hide nor hair, other than mine that was standing to attention on the nape of my neck.

On a closer inspection of the flaking and barely legible wooden chapel sign, its name provided us with the definitive oxymoron. It was simply called the Atheist Church.

I had an increasingly bad feeling in my tummy as we walked deeper into the labyrinth lined with shuttered, peeling windows and doors along pitch-black, deserted lanes.

Eventually our guides motioned towards a darkened doorway. One of them tapped a short tattoo on the door panel and a small hatch quickly opened, revealing a face that shocked me so much I made a strange squeaking noise and unconsciously stepped back. It would have been better suited to the downspout hanging onto a medieval cathedral but I heard it say a single word in the form of a low grunt: 'Dollars?'

We nodded vigorously then the speakeasy hatch slammed and caused a circular neon sign to flicker into life like a crimson halo just above my head. I glanced up and wondered what Simon Templar would have done to get us out of this self-inflicted predicament. I imagined our trip was soon to end horribly, down in the bowels of a dodgy, vermin-infested and damp cellar where we would be tied up, robbed and subjected to untold calumny. Glancing around I sought an escape route, seriously considering running away, and the others would have to take their chance. Then the rest of the neon sign burst into life revealing we had arrived at The Karachi Café.

Numerous bolts slid back before the ancient door creaked open. 'Tiny' the doorman was massive and would have had to exit hunched over and on his knees. He secured the door behind us to prevent my hare-brained ideas of escape and beckoned his frankfurter-sized forefinger at me. He led us along a small dingy corridor, up a few steps and through a green baize door into a brightly lit room where we were greeted by the comforting sound of an elderly tinkling piano. I relaxed a bit, as no one has ever been robbed to the sounds of Scott Joplin's 'Maple Leaf Rag', have they?

As my eyes got used to the glare, I blinked to see we were in a large bright room with open shutters overlooking a wide piazza facing the fading sunset. The high-vaulted whitewashed ceiling was hung with three slow-spinning fans gently moving the air above a long, wooden bar edged with a highly polished brass grab rail. John Wayne would have been proud to lean on it, had it not been in communist Cuba. The elderly barman wore a vibrant waistcoat decorated with myriad coloured butterflies, so we christened him Joseph. He raised his hand and smiled in greeting as we followed Tiny towards a circular mahogany table placed in pride of place within the open bay window, overlooking the busy square.

Tiny barked an order at the two elderly incumbents who reluctantly grabbed their tumblers and swiftly vacated our table, giving Tiny a few black looks whilst keeping out of his arms' way. As Tiny returned to his lair with his knuckles dragging beside him, I looked around the bar with its raised dais at the far end occupied by an assortment of musical instruments leaning against ancient bentwood chairs. The pianist continued to play jazz favourites without sheet music. His skin was as cracked, black and as shiny as the well-used upright piano that I imagined he had mastered long ago. The other clients were an array of courting couples quietly smooching in the corners, singletons nursing a glass, and larger, louder groups of friends enjoying life together. I felt safe.

As the room lights darkened, members of the band returned to their instruments and tuned up. Joseph limped across with a clean folded linen tea towel over his arm and numerous glass ash trays filled with the sweetest sultanas and freshest nuts I have ever tasted, like food from the gods. We ordered beers and a wide grin appeared across Joseph's face. 'No beer. Rum!'

Rum it was then as he removed the cork with a satisfying plop from an unlabelled black bottle and poured generous glasses for us all. It was delicious, like a thick, viscous navy rum it stuck tenaciously to the side of the glass and I felt like asking for a spoon. The musicians didn't need amplification and they were good, in fact they were very good, and it took my mind back to my favourite jazz club in a basement in Manchester – Ganders Goes South. The Karachi Café was hot, sultry and infused with happiness as the black rum seeped into my veins; like a rejuvenating medical drip it made my fingertips tingle.

It was an eye-achingly bright breakfast at a smart street café in Old Havana that consisted of a black coffee and a sweet pastry to reinvigorate a body unused to such energetic dancing of the night before. Sensibly we decided to ignore the mid-morning, semi-compulsory lecture and film show back at the hotel. We were expected to attend, as the words of the tour guide rang out over the loudspeakers, calling us to prayer. 'Capitalists must understand why communism is the future for the world.'

We left the propaganda machine behind and set off on foot, under crystal-clear blue skies, around the ancient parts of Havana, past the parked, neglected wrecks of 1960s American cars. Many of these were now convertibles and I saw the rough evidence of where hacksaws had been used to convert them from saloons eons ago. Stretched steel wire and pieces of metal tins seemed to hold them together like a First World War biplane; both deadly and dangerous in more ways than one. Most were pushed behind old buildings away from the tourist spots, and a precious pampered few cruised slowly along the main streets providing photo opportunities for the tourists. The majority, I discovered, were on concrete blocks, lacking wheels and tyres, and their once-gleaming headlights and chrome radiators looked thoroughly miserable like a down-in-the-mouth clown, rusting in pieces.

We caught a taxi to enjoy a 'Day with Hemingway' and the first chapter was a visit to Hemingway Marina. This great pillar of the literary world is venerated in Cuba, even though he was American, as he used to fish from here and reputedly wrote numerous books based on the area and fellow game fishermen whose descendants still eke out a meagre living. After a delightful meal of fresh red snapper 'Caught Today!' we sat back and absorbed the sunshine and pleasant ambiance before reluctantly stirring for the next instalment. We kept the same taxi and driver, who motored off at a speed about double his level of proficiency as we eagerly headed for Hemingway's Farm.

It was closed. And as tight as a drum. The gardener was scraping away with a hoe and lifted his head just enough to indicate that we could look in the windows if we wanted. Mary asked him in Spanish when it would be open, after lunch perhaps. He stopped for a moment, leant on the well-worn wooden shaft and shrugged one shoulder. Balancing on tippy toes and fingertips I looked inside. It appeared to have been preserved in dust. There was no apparent sign of human activity since Hemingway left in 1960, with discarded pens and papers strewn on the oilcloth table covering. Cobwebs caked the windows with a melancholy hue. We could not quite work out why they maintained the garden but ignored the inside of the house when they could capitalise on the marketing potential of this internationally renowned writer.

Moving on to our final part of the day our taxi driver hurtled back to Havana until he had to brake viciously throwing us off balance. An old 'rum head' had leisurely crossed the dusty road through a sleepy village and he made a rude sign in answer to the taxi horn blaring.

'You want play chicken,' the taxi driver bellowed. 'I play chicken.'

He swung the steering wheel and drove after the drunk over a footpath then up a narrow dried-up riverbed raising plumes of dust behind. The drunk produced an excellent and unexpected turn of speed and launched himself over a wall, disappearing into the safety of a convenient ditch. This cheered the driver up enormously and he continued to roar with laughter all the way back to our final part of the Day with Hemingway.

Still giggling to himself the taxi driver dropped us off at the Floridita Bar in Havana. We were welcomed by Sergio the manager into a beautiful haven of crystal chandeliers, gleaming mirrors and beaming waiters adorned with scarlet blazers. After being shown to our table I began to take in the bar and the obviously wealthy clientele. Everything about it was clean and smart and polished. Sergio placed the drinks menu before us and in hushed tones spoke in perfect English. 'I hope you will enjoy your time with us today. I will ask a favour that you must not tip anyone. My communist manager is here this evening and will be most distressed if you do.'

His eyes briefly flicked towards a man sitting alone, close to the main entrance door, nursing a coffee cup. We nodded in agreement and examined the drinks menu. 'The Cradle of the Daiquiri' was printed at the top, so in line with our themed day we ordered Hemingway's little tipple. In itself it was indeed a masterpiece, a true work of art. The long-stemmed cocktail glass was placed before me with all the reverence worthy of a holy relic. Its rim was encrusted with sparkling, crystallised demerara sugar with a twist of lime attached. Clear white Havana Club rum had been poured over large cubes of ice that cracked as two spoons of cane sugar helped the juice of a lime dissolve with an imperceptible hiss. I sipped it slowly whilst contemplating the previous occupants of the bar who enjoyed its atmosphere, history and joie de vivre. After his happy times here, Graham Greene wrote *Our Man in Havana*, and as I contemplated my good fortune, the daiquiri warmed my heart and fired my imagination. What a wonderful way to prevent scurvy.

We moved on to the restaurant where I devoured a sea food platter that was so fresh it seemed to crawl, swim and slither across my plate. The resident pianist ended as the five-piece mariachi band formed and played the 'Mexican Army' theme from *The Alamo*. I'm still not sure whether it was some sort of anthem to remind any Americans present that they were not invincible. They soon cheered up and began playing tunes more in keeping with the warm and welcoming ambience of this beautiful establishment. As it was my birthday, I asked for the wine menu to toast the occasion with my chums. The sommelier almost ran across the room with the wine list, removing the dust with a blow that caused a rainbow in the remaining shaft of fading sunlight. I must have gone pale as I read that each bottle was to cost more than our entire meal. I sobered up quickly, swallowed my remaining pride and told everyone I would pay for beer instead.

As it was to be our final night in Cuba we discussed where we should go. My eager suggestion of a revisit to the Karachi Café was shot down in flames.

'We all want some fun this time,' said Alec.

Others wanted to head to the widely advertised song and dance extravaganza show at the Tropicana, but to me the cost seemed the most extravagant part. I could have bought an entire bottle of house red with the money.

BANG! I thought the piano had collapsed and nearly jumped out of my skin. The band had moved immediately behind me and played a surprisingly loud chord. A line of the blazered waiters walked with gusto towards us and stopped in a semicircle around our table before parting to allow Sergio to pass through their ranks. He carried a plate with a wedge of Key Lime pie skewered by a single red lighted candle and placed it before me. As one, the band burst into life and the waiters took full voice and sang 'Happy Birthday' in Spanish. As they finished, the diners joined in with a ripple of light applause to add to the wonderfully moving moment, one which I have never forgotten.

In the morning, I threw open the threadbare curtains letting in brilliant sunshine reminiscent of the South of France. It was bright and clear and enhanced the colours of the Old Town beyond; it was a beautiful start to the day. There was a light tap on my door and Mary stepped in. We'd both left Alec in the arms of some Cuban señorita the night before as we went home to bed and to pack before heading to the airport for our flight back to the Cayman Islands.

'No sign of him?'

I shook my head, pointed at his empty bed. 'We'd better get going for breakfast, I'm sure he'll return.'

'I hope so,' she said.

We walked out to our favoured street café for pastries and coffee and sat at the table that was bathed in warming early-morning rays and absorbed the views and sounds of the locals beginning the day. Shutters creaked and banged open as residents spoke across from building to building, and they could have been discussing football scores for all I knew.

We took a stroll around the Old Town and walked past a queue of people, probably 70 or 80, lined up along a pavement. We followed it around the corner where a uniformed attendant held a roped barrier closed. The front of the store was decorated with ornately carved statues of Greek gods, male and female, with cloths carefully placed to maintain their modesty. In its day it would have been a high-class store for the rich and infamous but inevitably had suffered the neglect of the weather and lack of maintenance seen so often on our travels. There were the remains of a covered canopy over the footpath that presumably had disappeared in some distant hurricane. Now there was nothing to shelter the steadily increasing number of females queueing in the baking sunshine.

I was curious. There was nothing visible in the shop windows, just empty, dusty glass partitions obscuring the inside. I indicated to Mary and approached the Camp Commandant. Presumably he recognised us as tourists; I suppose my khaki 'Eric Morecambe' shorts gave that away. 'Dollar,' he said.

'Dollar,' I replied and the rope barrier was removed with a theatrical flourish and a smart salute.

It was dark and dank within and smelt musty. As my eyes became accustomed, I saw we were inside what had been a high-class clothing emporium with many glass display cabinets. They were wooden-framed types with sliding drawers historically accessed from the rear by overeager sales assistants. Except here all the cabinets were bare. As we followed in line, I passed the time by drawing 'Kilroy Wuz Here' on the dusty panes as the snake of potential customers shuffled slowly along towards a bare electric lightbulb dangling above a display case. Looking about I noticed the females were contented to queue with no hint of urgency and chattered with their companions as if in line for a theme park ride in Orlando. Mary suggested that the clothes looked homemade and looked all the better for that.

From the front of the queue, I heard a couple of gasps, oohs and ahhs of delight as we anticipated the approaching wonder. No one seemed to be buying anything but they glanced for a moment, then were firmly moved along as if staring for too long at the Crown

Jewels inside the Tower of London. The successful viewers were steered towards the exit, where they fanned themselves to recover from all the excitement. It was soon our turn and what I saw was humbling. The contents of the glass cabinet were unattainable for these poor people – it was a simple plastic cooking spatula.

I got back to my room at the Havana Hilton to grab my bag and get ready for the flight back to Cayman – without Alec. A glance around the room made me stop as a finger was holding the wardrobe door closed.

'Hello,' I said to the finger.

'Have they gone?'

'Has who gone?'

'The secret police.' Alec peeked through the gap. 'They've been after me all night.'

As he stepped out there was a distinct smell of burning and his shirt was buttoned up wrongly. He was missing a sock and his eyes looked like they were supported by sandbags. He dumped his belongings in his bag, put on his sunglasses and pulled his baseball cap low over his face. He crossed the hotel foyer with a pronounced limp as he launched himself into the waiting coach before hiding behind the curtain, scanning for the posse of secret police.

'Well, I hope it was worth it and I hope you took precautions?' Mary said as the coach gathered speed towards the airport.

Alec kept glancing behind. 'It was great fun, other than being chased around Havana. We got the "Bum's Rush" at a couple of hotels until Jessica (with a G) said we'd have to use her flat. It was a bit poky but ye know, needs must. Anyway, when we was in the throes of passion she kept saying "Casa el Fuego, Casa el Fuego." Man of Fire!'

Mary's eyes rolled to heaven. 'I think you'll find that meant the house was on fire.'

Alec was silent for a couple of moments chewing his bottom lip. 'Oh, I thought the sirens were the secret police… And I really hurt my ankle when I jumped out the bloody window. Ah, well.' He winked at me then sat back. 'It's been a great trip though, I've thoroughly enjoyed it…' He folded his arms and his laughter lines gradually drew his eyes closed as he caught up on his long lost slumbers. But would he have slept so well had he known then, that Jessica (with a G) was destined to appear once more, and not just in his dreams.

PART V

SAILING CLOSE TO THE WIND

CHAPTER 26

EDUCATING ARCHIE

Back in Cayman, I called Olivia. The phone was answered by a female with a heavy Jamaican accent. 'Yes boss, I'll just go get 'er.'

When Olivia came on the line, I reintroduced myself after the meeting at Sunset House and was happy to hear she remembered. After a bit of chunter about Cuba I noticed that there was a lot of noise in the background. 'Do you live near the mangrove swamps?'

'No, why do you ask?' she said.

'I can hear a parrot squawking in the background, it must be really annoying.' The noise became more intrusive.

'That's Winston,' said Olivia through the din.

'What's that? You've got a parrot called Winston.'

'No, I haven't got any parrots, my son's called Winston.'

'Oh… I see…that's nice…' My face went crimson. 'He's very good at imitating parrots, isn't he?'

In spite of this inauspicious initial conversation, we met and many pleasant occasions followed. One included a wonderful beach BBQ at Public Beach where Mr Timms came up with a nickname for Olivia's little one.

'How's YW then?' he said.

'Who?

'Young Winston of course!'

At last, things were all clicking into place, some would say the stars were aligned as I settled into a bit of domestic bliss. I was seeing a lot of Olivia and therefore YW and enjoying the fruits of a steadying relationship. Work had reached that nadir of working with Mr Timms' Drugs Squad, whilst Mr Jeremy Pyles was away from the island.

Detective Sergeant Mac found me in the office and indicated towards me with his stumpy index finger in a curly sort of way. 'We've got a druggie in the gaol who needs interviewing. He's not letting us know who's supplying him, so we'll have to have a little chat.'

We brought him over to the Drugs Squad office, together with his sealed bag of assorted drug paraphernalia. Gander was about 45, 5 feet 6 tall and dressed in shorts and a ripped dirty vest top. His skin was baked to a burnt crisp from too much lounging about on the ground when either drunk, drugged or sleeping either off into oblivion. His eyes were permanently bloodshot without a trace of white and his torso and cheeks were stretched over his bones so much they looked like they had been sucked in by a very powerful vacuum cleaner.

Mac started the interview casually. 'See anything of the wife and kids?'

'Nothing since they moved up to Miami, they reckon I'm a failure.'

'Well, you are. You shouldn't have been importing coke into the States, should you? Surprised they ever let you out.'

I was intrigued. 'How long did you get?'

Gander's burst capillaries glared at me. 'I was important once, I shouldn't have taken the rap. They hung me out to dry. Can I have a fix…please…boss?'

'No fix,' said Mac. 'Just tell us who's supplying and we'll get you back to the cells in time for food.'

Gander looked intently at the large evidence bag on the table. 'Let me see if there's anything in there – I needs a fix, real bad…'

Mac turned to me and pointed his thumb at the druggie. 'How the mighty have fallen, eh? He was a real big shot once, an' had it all going for him, big house, pool, beautiful wife, kids, the lot. Then he wants easy money and starts importing loads of white powder into the States – and gets caught.'

Gander was still looking longingly at the bag while Mac continued his character assassination.

'As if being a Captain for Delta Airways didn't pay enough, greedy bastard.'

He had not heard a word, he was visibly sweating with drips pooling on the table, staring at the bag of evidence, without seeing.

'All we want to know is the name of the main supplier round Dog City? Couldn't be easier, could it? Just tell us, they'll never need to know,' I said.

He ignored us for a while, then stirred into life slowly shaking his head. 'No man, he'll put a bullet in my head…not worth it…'

Mac stood up and began to collect the evidence bag.

'Wait now, I might remember a bit if I has a fix – maybe…' Gander's eyes were like misused pool balls, ready to pop out of their sockets. 'Let me try an' get a suck outa me tings…'

I looked at Mac, who shrugged his shoulders. I broke open the evidence seal and poured the contents of the bag onto the table. Gander picked up the stone pestle and held it aloft like the Holy Grail before gently placing it on the desk. He sniffed it and smiled, revealing brown stubs where teeth had once been, then in spite of the freezing a/c he broke out into a spontaneous oozing sweat. He began to scratch the inside of the bowl with his cracked and misshapen fingernails. For a couple of minutes he scraped it down until he had a tiny pile of brown dirt in the bottom of the pestle.

He looked up. 'I needs a drinks can.'

I found a discarded can in a bin and presented it to him. He crushed and flattened the sides together then took an ancient screwdriver and began to drill a hole in the middle. He spat into the pestle, then with his grubby fingertips melded the contents into an ugly mess and scraped it out onto the hole in the drinks can. Mac threw a packet of matches onto the desk. Gander struck one and held it under the can where I watched the brown deposit evaporate, leaving a pat of dust a couple of millimetres wide. I saw a vein in his neck racing and a quick check with my watch showed it was pumping at 150 per minute. The perspiration tumbled down his face like a tropical waterfall.

It was ready. Gander placed his lips around the top of the can and lit the brown smudge that fizzed brightly. He inhaled heavily and tightly held his breath. The vein slowed to a crawl and the sweat evaporated from his forehead. His eyes closed. He breathed out as the can dropped from his mouth to his lap, to the floor with a dull clang.

'Archie' – his voice squeaked like a cartoon character. 'Scottish digger driver at the hotel building site, up West Bay Road. And here's something for nothin', he's just the middleman, the main boss man is higher up the chain.' Gander opened his eyes. 'Try looking very close to home.'

We relayed the news about the drug supplier and the cryptic clue to DCI Timms. 'Great, we'll wait 'til Friday morning.'

'Why not today?' I asked.

'You'll see on Friday afternoon after we've locked him up.'

My social life continued to fizz along like a cartoon fuse, zipping towards the keg brimming with gunpowder. Parties, trips away, visits to the unintentionally hilarious performances by the Prospect Playhouse Players et al. The job in the Drugs Squad was equally fun and fulfilling, with Nobby and I officially now part of the team. It was all too good to be true when the two of us were enjoying lunch at the Bakery, where the Phil Collins song 'Another Day in Paradise' was playing in the background. Nobby eventually mentioned the elephant in the room. 'What's Duke doing over there?'

I turned and saw he was having lunch with a female and they were hiding at the back of the shop. Both points were equally surprising. We went over and said hello and I recognised her as a Customs Officer. She seemed a pleasant companion for him and she was Caymanian to boot. As we left the shop Nobby pointed his thumb back at the diners. 'He's set up for life now.'

'How do you mean?'

'If he marries her, he gets to stay on the island and becomes a resident, simple…'

We walked on in the silence of our thoughts. I was having a great time, socially and workwise, so was Nobby. He was going out with one of the Irish girls working at a hotel for the winter season but she had accepted a job on the island for the next couple of years. We were halfway back to the police station when my thoughts surprised me and my innermost feelings blurted out from deep within. 'I don't want to go back home, I'm having too much fun.'

'Me too, but we've said we are.'

'Let's go and have a word with Jonesy.'

We knocked on Chief Supt Jones' office door. 'Afternoon gents, what can I do for you?'

'I don't know how to put this, but we want to cancel going back to the UK—' I said.

He put up his hand to interrupt. 'Sorry gentlemen, but it's too late. Everything has been signed up, costs arranged, interview dates, flights, the lot, all sorted.'

'What if we spoke to the Commissioner?' I said.

Mr Jones's eyes widened alarmingly. 'Not a good move, I suggest. He's as likely to chase you out at the point of his ceremonial sword, if he doesn't skewer you first, like a couple of kebabs. Personally, wouldn't take the chance myself, why poke the bear, eh? We can't rescind the decision and to be honest you're better off returning – you two will get promoted when you get back – staying here will only delay the inevitable. You can't be happy all your life, you know.'

I did know, but it didn't help. He called after us down the corridor, 'For your info, every single one of you that said he would be returning, has been in to see me and been given the same answer. Enjoy what's left of your time here…' We kept on walking.

Building sites on the island tended to start work at daybreak to make the most of the less ferocious heat of the day. Nobby and I had tracked Archie down to his poky condominium and identified his tiny clapped-out car. There was no outward sign of any unearned income from his unlawful supplying of illicit narcotics – perhaps he was just clever. We saw his car was parked close to the site office and pulled up behind it. A digger was working over on the back of the site near to the North Sound as we approached the foreman and asked to speak to Archie. He showed neither surprise nor emotion as he called Archie over the walky-talky to tell him that someone wanted to speak.

Archie was strongly built with an abundance of tattoos showing around his torso, face and arms that were partially hidden by his Scottish football shirt. We didn't offer to shake hands but I noticed his knuckles had self-inflicted tattoos with an unpleasant word on one side and ACAB (All Coppers Are Bastards) on the other. I just knew we would get on famously.

'What do you wankers want?' His strong Glaswegian accent shone through beautifully.

'Right, Archie, you're being locked up for supplying drugs. I've just cautioned you – okay?' I said.

His eyes were weighing us up against the glare of the sun. He was quickly deciding if he could take us on or at least inflict a bit of pain; thankfully he thought better of it. We handcuffed him, drove him down to the police station and booked him in.

'I've been in better bridewells than this shithole,' he said looking around. 'I'll be out in no time – you've got nothin' on me…'

We put him in the holding area and went to his condo to see what treasures we could find. It was all quite disappointing really but we did seize his passport, bank statements and other useful documents. On the small dining table was a compact set of weighing scales, plastic snap bags and a roll of US dollars containing $1,500, but little actual direct evidence. It was all pretty circumstantial with no quantities of drugs or the consequential drug profits.

We took the items to the Scenes of Crime office for a more in-depth examination. An hour or so later, I got a call from them. 'Can confirm traces of cocaine in the weighing scales and on some of the banknotes, but insufficient to charge supply…just possession…'

This was like the Curate's egg – good in parts. I went to see DCI Timms and outlined the investigation so far. 'Go and interview him anyway,' he said, 'and make sure it lasts 'til after one o'clock.'

I glanced at my watch – it was midday. He continued his

explanation. 'Cos then the courts will have closed. He can languish in the gaol all weekend and think about all the lives he's ruined…'

I understood.

Nobby and I went back to the holding room to collect Archie for his interview. The Custody Sergeant beckoned us into his office.

'One of the "hot-shot" lawyers is at the front desk – he wants to be present when you interview Archie.'

The jungle drums had been beating loudly to summon Mr Adamson. There was no legal aid on the island and we knew he was a dodgy character who charged a fortune for his services. Archie's meagre bank account would not suffice, so we presumed he was being provided by one of the island 'Big Shots'. It was unsurprising but disconcerting. We collected Archie and took him into the interview room to put our long series of questions to him. 'No comment' was his response to each and every one of them.

There was a sharp knock at the door and the Custody Sergeant popped his head round. 'DCI Timms wants to speak to you both. He has some interesting developments in this case.'

'Just a moment,' Adamson said. 'I want my client bailed…'

'Not yet,' said Nobby, 'we're still investigating this case and there may be some significant developments. See you later.'

They both looked at each other with matching furrowed brows as we locked them in the room together and headed over to see Mr Timms.

'Oh hello, it's Holmes and bloody Watson. Did you get him to cough the job, then?'

'No, sir, it was all no comment.'

'I'll tell you, you two couldn't get a cough in a TB ward. Anyway, I've been doing some real detective work – stick around – some of it may rub off on you. I've been onto the police in Scotland and they confirm that Archie is a right nasty bastard. He's got more form than Red Rum and last time he was locked up for supplying drugs he broke the detective's arm, then laughed.'

We mentioned his lawyer and Mr Timms sucked his teeth and rocked back in his chair. 'No problem, I've also found he falsified his immigration form by not declaring all his offences. Plenty to keep him in over the weekend and interview him on Monday. Sounds like a plan. Oh dear, by my watch it's one fifteen, what a shame, we can't bail him.'

We went back to re-interview Archie with his lawyer, who was not happy.

'I know your game, officers, you're deliberately delaying the investigation. I'm going to make a formal complaint to Inspector Rowe. That'll stop you smirking.'

I shrugged and started my questions. They ranged from a rerun of the possession and/or supply of cocaine, to the false declarations on the immigration forms, and I even threw one in about the lack of a windscreen wiper on his car. The lawyer launched his papers up in the air at the mention of that one. Eventually after we had all had enough, we charged him with all of the offences we could find. The Custody Sergeant informed him that he would go to court on Monday morning.

Nobby and I walked him across the rear yard to the gaol. Archie was not quite as cocky now. 'I've been in worst places than this shithole. My brief's gonna get me out – you see – and I'll sue your arses.'

The uniformed officer opened the outer steel gate and we went through, booking Archie's name in the sweat-stained ledger. The smell of unwashed bodies, poo and piss brought it all back to me of my earlier times as the gaoler.

'It's a bit full boss,' said the Constable, 'but you can put him in with George.'

It was like my Christmases coming together. I looked across the open-air courtyard and standing at his steel-barred cell door was George the Gentle Giant. He must have had a further mental health episode and the family had asked for him to be held here until the full moon went away. He recognised me.

'Officer, officer. Has you come from the Queen?'

'I certainly have, George. She hopes you'll be better soon. We've brought a friend for you – he's called Archie.'

'Hello Archie, do ye like Bob Marley, I loves Bob Marley.' George turned on his ghetto blaster at full pelt.

For the first time in our short acquaintance, the Scottish drugs dealer looked worried as the Constable opened the cell door where George was standing with his music machine on his shoulder. He was stark naked.

'Ye…ye can't put me in there,' said Archie.

'Just you watch,' I said as the door slammed with a satisfying clang.

'Now George,' I said, 'Archie doesn't like Bob Marley played quiet – he prefers it loud, very loud. Also he once called the Queen a nasty name and do you know what the letters on his knuckles mean?'

'No, officer, I don't.'

'ACAB is rather rude and stands for All Caymanians Are Bastards. Now you two have a nice time and we'll see you on Monday.'

I had a lovely weekend starting on Friday evening at Sunset House for drinkies with Olivia and anyone else that turned up, before heading for a meal at the Cracked Conch. There was far too much to enjoy here instead of dwelling on returning to the UK – that was months away.

*

Monday morning dawned with a bright, pleasantly warm autumnal feel and there was a definite buzz in the air, which was probably coming from the insect-infested gaol. We walked across the police station yard, up wind to delay the inevitable stench, where we were let into the courtyard and saw Archie with his arms reaching out towards us, through the cell bars.

'Let me out boss, I'll admit everything…please…'

He spoke in a croaky whisper and glanced back at George who was lying on his bed, slowly blowing smoke rings. Archie's face, arms and body were now pockmarked with bug bites and oozing sores. Other than wearing a ripped pair of Y fronts, his clothes were scattered around the floor in torn-up piles.

'How you doing, George?' I said.

He stood up and approached the gate as Archie recoiled into the corner. 'Archie ain't a nice man, boss. He tried to break my music box and I'd ta teach him some manners.'

'Quite right too, George. We're going to take him to court now, but he might be back if he doesn't behave.'

I thanked George for all his help in supporting the Queen and Her Commonwealth and all the people of the Cayman Islands as we removed Archie to the Courts.

I was very happy to see HH Judge Rudyard QC, in the chair as the Presiding Magistrate. The Clerk to the Court outlined the charges against Archie, who stood in the dock looking thoroughly sorry for himself, staring at the floor. His lawyer was nowhere to be seen – Archie was no longer of use to him or his backer, whoever that could be; he was a busted flush. He visibly shook as the Judge spoke quietly from beneath his half-moon spectacles.

'How do you plead to these charges? Guilty or not guilty?'

A low mumble was heard.

'Speak clearly, man! I must be able to hear.'

'Guilty, sir.'

'Good, we can proceed without delaying justice anymore.' He glanced in my direction and nodded. 'Officer, to the dock if you please.'

I stepped into the dock and the Clerk approached me with the Bible and laminated oath card.

'Oh don't bother with that,' said the Judge and waved him away. 'I'm sure the officer will be telling the truth, won't you?'

'Absolutely, your Honour.' He sat back and listened intently as I outlined the case in all its gory detail.

'You in the dock. Have you any comment to make regarding the officer's version of the facts?'

He merely slowly shook his head.

'I presume the accused has a financial bond to pay for his flight from the island?'

I answered in the affirmative as Archie perked up and took notice.

'Good, we don't need to pay for that then,' the Judge said. 'Unfortunately, the police cannot prove that you were responsible for the abhorrent supply of cocaine on this beautiful island, but you obviously were. However, they can prove you were in possession of the drugs and assorted paraphernalia. You also completed the immigration forms with false information – of that you are also guilty. What assets does he possess officer?'

'Three thousand dollars in a bank and fifteen hundred in cash.'

'Does he have a car?'

'It's rather clapped out but worth about a thousand, your Honour.'

'Oh yes, I see, you're also fined $50 for no windscreen wiper. Great, we'll seize the car as well. Therefore, I will fine you your car, all your cash and the entire contents of your bank account.

I'm sentencing you to six months in Northward Prison after which you will be deported from the island. Officer, please ensure that when he leaves Grand Cayman that the authorities in Miami are informed that he is a convicted drug dealer and that they may wish to detain him. Take him down.'

All in all, it was a very satisfying result – it gave me a lovely warm feeling of justice being seen to be done. I followed him down to the cells to await the prison transport and spoke to him in the cell corridor. 'You've been hung out to dry Archie. If you tell me who supplied you, I might forget to inform Miami when you get released.'

He beckoned me nearer, then glancing up then down the empty corridor, whispered, 'Your flies are undone.'

That was a shame but worth trying nevertheless. Having crossed swords with Adamson the dodgy lawyer, Hollywood and Dr Kampenboom, I was convinced that they were key, but Gander's cryptic comment still rang in my head. Try looking closer to home…

CHAPTER 27

A COMPLETE OVERACHIEVER

The run-up to Christmas was hectic when Jeremy Pyles paid a flying visit. 'If any of you chaps are in London over the festive season, my wife and I are arranging a bit of a charity do. You're all very welcome if you can make it.'

Mr Timms accepted with his usual repost to social invitations. 'Excellent, excellent. I shall let you have the details, it'll be a wonderful event.'

I was leaving the island for the two weeks over Christmas and New Year, when my hotel room would again be re-hired at the height of the tourist season. But a boring charity event in London would still not be my first choice of event. So I returned home to chilly Lancashire to enjoy a proper festive Christmas, preparing myself for my eventual return in just a few short weeks.

I returned to the warm welcoming winter weather on Grand Cayman after a hectic visit home that was damp and chilly. Cocky was waiting to collect me at the airport with my Jeep that he had cleaned, filled with petrol and in which he had left a case of beer in the back. I was walking out of the terminal when I saw a female that I recognised but couldn't immediately remember. She nodded then glanced away. I looked again and saw she was in the queue for the Jamaican flight and that her luggage amounted to two large suitcases, each tightly strapped to a white plastic picnic chair.

I went up to her and said hello.

'Hello boss, I'm going back home to Jamaica now, to look after my babies, for keeps.'

I then remembered. 'Hello Maria, have you had enough of Doctor Kampenboom?'

'He a bad man but he gone now. I bin paid off for six months work and the house bin closed up.'

'Where's he gone, when?'

'Couple o' week ago some men come and see him. One say they take him out for dinner – he never come back.'

'Tell me more,' I said.

'I never sees 'em before, they were three of them who came in a big rental car, but were real nice with me. Few days later I gets a letter signed by the doctor saying to close up the house and money be paid to my bank. Said he'd contact when he'd return. I won't come back – he bad man.'

She was smartly dressed and relaxed and looked me straight in the eye. 'Thank you, officer, you helped that lady, god bless.'

With a smile she turned and dragged her heavily laden luggage through to the departure lounge without a backwards glance. This was all very intriguing and I had to satisfy my curiosity, so after dropping Cocky off at his place, I drove over to check out the Doctor's house. The outer gates were closed and chained up, dried-up weeds appearing in previously immaculately maintained borders.

Jeremy Pyles had returned to the island, so we collected him from the airport and dropped him off to see the Governor.

'Did you see Mr Timms back in London?' I asked.

'Oh yes, I think he thoroughly enjoyed himself. In fact he's flying back later today.'

A Royal Navy frigate had docked at the harbour and we had received invitations to attend a 'Bangers and Mash' Party, so we invited Jeremy along. We parked on the harbour beside the ship which was festooned with bunting and sparkly lights strung along the deck. The light breeze was warm and gentle and the night sky filled with hundreds of constellations beyond the sea. A canopy covered the rear of the deck and wonderful smells of frying onions and sausages greeted us as we reached the gangplank. Our invitations got us past a couple of machine-gun-toting ratings until we went aboard where we were welcomed by the Captain with a warm handshake and a point over towards the chefs and the small band playing maritime ditties.

'Good Lord, it's you, sir!'

I stopped and turned to see Jeremy's hand being shaken vigorously by the Captain.

'I've not seen you since you sprung me from the cells in Hong Kong. What on earth are you doing here?'

'Just helping out the FCO, you know – not much.' Jeremy was being far too modest, but the queue was forming behind him and with a promise to catch-up shortly, the Captain had to let his hand go.

'Hong Kong?' Nobby said with raised eyebrows.

'Yes,' said Jeremy. 'He got himself into a frightful pickle during a fight with another officer. I smoothed it all over and got him out. It's nice to be remembered…'

We were enjoying the wonderful ambience on board, with the plentiful, delicious food and drink as the band played on, until we heard a disturbance coming up from the gangplank. I looked over to see where the raised voices were coming from.

'Now listen, sonny, don't bother pointing that gun at me or you'll end up with it hanging out your arse.'

I waved towards Mr Timms and his wife who were on the harbour and the cause of the rumpus.

He pointed up at me and shouted, 'See, he'll bloody vouch for me – he's got my invitation – haven't ye'?'

I produced mine from my pocket and waved it at the armed guard. He reluctantly removed his gun from Mr Timms' pot belly and let them pass, grumbling oaths at each other.

After downing a very large drink Mr Timms eventually calmed down as we watched Jeremy chatting away to the great and good of the island. I pointed my thumb towards Jeremy. 'How did his charity event go?'

'It were bloody marvellous. Jeremy was the compere at the Tower of London. There were more celebs and politicians than you could shake a stick at. We all had to cough up a bit of dosh for his charity but it were worth every penny. He sang a couple of classics then played the piano for his wife's choir, who sang like a flock of angels.'

'What's his wife like?' I asked.

'She's gorgeous, a senior consultant at some children's hospital and really nice.'

Jeremy then appeared at my elbow. 'I believe your do went well,' I said.

'Indeed, we raised thousands for the charity and everyone seemed to enjoy it. It gave the girls the chance to sing "Pie Jesu" by John Brunning – a wonderful arrangement.' He looked towards Mr Timms. 'Did you enjoy it?'

'I did, it was the best piss-up in ages.'

Nobby and I dropped Jeremy off at his hotel and headed for home. Nobby was in a contemplative mood as I approached his condo and pulled up in my Jeep outside.

'You know what?' he said. 'It's all true about Jeremy, isn't it? All the stories he tells, all the adventures he's had. Being a barrister, Royal Navy officer, an MI6 spy. Pianist, singing at David Niven's Swiss chalet, charity worker, married to a gorgeous, high-achieving doctor. It's not bloody fair, is it? And he's such a pleasant bloke, it makes me feel like a complete underachiever.'

The following morning it was just Jeremy and I in the office catching up on work, so I took the opportunity to speak confidentially. 'The other day I spoke to Maria – the maid of Dr Kampenboom – remember he's my suspected Nazi war criminal.'

'Oh yes, how is he?'

'Good question. He appears to have left the island with three unknown men who took him out to dinner. His house has been closed up, Maria was paid off and has returned home to Jamaica. Have you got anything to do with it?'

A wry smile passed across his face as he pushed his laptop away and relaxed into his chair with his fingertips joined as if in prayer. 'You might think that but I couldn't possibly comment.'

There was the occasional pang of conscience when I contemplated my return to the UK, but in the main – the Spanish Main – I concentrated on having a great time. Parties, BBQs, a work trip with Olivia to Texas, a liaison visit to Miami to assist the US Drug Enforcement Administration. Everything was racing away at a thousand miles an hour – which is usually when things begin to get out of control. The difficult conversations were creaking into place. I was returning to the UK, she wasn't, so when do we accept the inevitable? It was history beginning to repeat itself, yet this time it was going to be me on the receiving end and perhaps I deserved it?

We tidied up the speed boat and polished the wood, eventually selling it back to the original owner – with a loss of a thousand dollars – but that was our second good day of boat ownership as the money syphoned back into the bank. As often in life, something unexpected happened to lift the mood – well, my mood anyway. I was strolling across the rear car park at Central Police Station when all hell let loose. Uniformed officers were running to various squad cars carrying revolvers and shotguns. Sgt Benjamin – the armourer – called across as he loaded boxes of armaments into the back of his truck.

'Come on, boy, we're being invaded by the Cubans.'

I was deep in thought, wasn't particularly bothered, and quite hungry, so I waved cheerfully and just kept walking. Lunch at the Bakery would not eat itself. They all roared out of the car park surrounded in plumes of dust towards Bodden Town. I stopped – what did he just say?

I went in and spoke to the desk officer who confirmed that hundreds of Cubans had landed on the north coast in huge warships, attack helicopters and everything. There was a pitched battle going on and we had called in the Royal Navy, US Navy and the US Marines. The invaders would be here within hours. So I went for lunch.

The warm sun kept shining, the breezes remained temperate and the Jamaican patties flavoursome. Life was pleasant. I strolled back into work and called into Mr Jones's office to ask about the invasion. He pulled his face and shook his head. 'There's a rubber boat of Cuban refugees arrived on the northern coast, a few women and kiddies included. One of the ladies is expecting, so she's been taken to hospital. Let's call it another Operation Damp Squib. Harry from Special Branch is dealing with it.'

The following day I was with Alec when he got a phone call from Detective Inspector Harry of Special Branch. 'You're in the shit, Alec, better come and see me.'

'Why, why, what's happened. I deny it…' The phone had been put down so we went to see him.

'You know these Cuban boat people, well the pregnant one is claiming asylum here because the father is a British police officer on the island called Alec. Narrows it down a bit doesn't it, eh?'

'Well, well, it's nothing to do with me… Could be anyone…'

'She's called Jessica but spells it with a G and describes you to a T. Also she keeps mentioning something about "Man of Fire" or some such bollocks.'

Alec remained silent and looked at the floor.

Harry continued to explain. 'Anyway, your problem now is that under Cayman Law you become responsible for her and have to support her and the twins…'

'Twins…twins…what do you mean twins…?'

'Two babies,' said Harry. 'Are you thick or something? The Governor and Commissioner have been informed and we need to try and deal with it to stop this becoming an international incident.'

'What happens now?' Alec said.

'If I were you I'd work out how much money you can put your hands on and be ready to fly out, possibly change your name and maybe go back to Rhodesia or somewhere…disappear like Lord Lucan or Shergar.'

Harry told us to leave, then called after us. 'Might mean marrying her, I suppose…'

Out in the car park, Alec's brain was spinning. 'Where are they keeping the ones from the boat?' he asked.

'The women and children are up at the hospital, I think. What are you going to do?'

'I'll call up and have a nosy round, see if I can see her.' I left him to it.

I met with Alec that evening at the Lone Star Bar on West Bay

Road, where he held his beer bottle tightly and hardly glanced up. 'Everybody on the island knows… I was driving the Governor to his golf lesson and he asked me all about it.'

I nodded sympathetically as he drowned his sorrows. 'I went up to the hospital and started calling out Jessica's name outside the windows of the maternity ward until some snotty Matron appeared and told me to bugger off. She called me a pervert…'

Cocky, Nobby and Carlos joined us as the night wore on and Alec's situation became more desperate with each successive bottle. He hung his head down on his arm on the edge of the bar. 'I knew I should've used a condom… Hang on… I did. She give me one…'

'Shouldn't it be the other way round?' said Nobby.

Alec looked straight at me and the understanding began showing in his eyes. 'Hang on a minute… I've been thinking about this… This's your doing, isn't it?'

It certainly was, and as there was little point in denying it, I ran and crashed out through the rear fire door into the mangrove swamps where a cry of 'YOU BASTARD' followed my flight.

CHAPTER 28

NEMESIS

I was certainly winding down as departure day approached, but prior to that, fate had a little surprise waiting in the wings. Nobby and I had walked out to get lunch at the Bakery and were sitting watching the world go by from the wide picture window overlooking the harbour when a vaguely familiar youth walked by glancing in at me. He stopped, then indicated at me with his finger for me to go outside. I remembered his name, it was Rob who I had saved from the clutches of Professor Marmaduke, the obeah witchdoctor, many months earlier.

I followed him down a narrow lane beside the Bakery and he hid beside a refuse bin. He was gaunt, burnt to a frazzle and sweating heavily enough to smell from a yard away.

'How's things?' I asked.

'I owes you one, officer. All I'm going to say is that there's a real bad bastard running the drugs in George Town. I think you should check out the laundry down that lane. He banks the cash every Monday morning.' With that he walked off with his eyes already glazing over seeking his next fix. I regaled the tale to Nobby and when back in the office ran it by Mr Timms. He sat back in his chair, then phoned the Commissioner.

'Right, Cagney and Lacey come with me. The Commissioner wants my two best men, but you two will have to do and I think this is all connected.'

We were ushered into the Commissioner's office where Mr Jones was already seated; he greeted us with a tired smile and a wave as we sat down alongside Mr Timms. It was early and the Commissioner seemed, more or less, in control of his faculties. 'Right, gents. This info stays within this office and no one else – understand? From what Mr Timms said a little earlier, your informant backs up what MI6 has disclosed to us.' Everyone nodded and he looked directly at Nobby and I.

'First thing on Monday morning both of you will dress up as tourists, sunglasses caps etc. Do not use the radio, do not tell anyone what you are doing or where you are going and do not start off from Police HQ. Start from home at eight, meet up and stakeout this address, take any photos you deem necessary, follow anyone of interest, but don't get seen or found out.'

The Commissioner glanced towards Mr Jones, who then spoke in a quiet, measured tone. 'All I would say gents, is that if you happen to recognise anyone, don't be surprised but see what they do and where they go.'

He pushed a piece of paper across the desk with the same address mentioned by Rob, a quiet backstreet in the centre of George Town.

Monday morning couldn't come quick enough. I picked up Nobby in the Jeep and we headed into town. It was a clear, hot day with more to come, so we parked up at the burger bar to enjoy a breakfast muffin with a thick black coffee that we hoped we could claim back on expenses. Fat chance. We left the Jeep and waited for a few tourists to promenade around the town and headed the short distance to our target location. Nobby strolled along the street and reported back that there were a few small-scale businesses that were beginning to show signs of life including the one of interest – a launderette and dry-cleaning shop. The sign on the door showed it to be closed from 12 noon on Saturday until 9am Monday morning – anytime now, and we did not have long to wait.

Keeping out of sight Nobby found an ideal observation point and began to take a couple of photos, then waved at me to move along the street parallel towards the centre of the town away from the harbour. A tall, slim male emerged from the street, striding out, carrying a dark brown attaché case. Nobby gave me a thumbs-up and pointed towards the male who I followed at a distance, and from the back, I thought I recognised his gait.

After a few minutes he stopped outside a bank and formed the head of a queue, waiting for it to open. We let plenty of others join before Nobby and I felt at our most inconspicuous but did not acknowledge each other, looking instead inside the branch. The shake and rattle from the front doors stirred us as we trooped in. I joined one queue three people behind our target while Nobby put himself in an adjacent queue for the cashiers. There was only a low glass screen separating the female cashier from our man and we clearly heard her greeting above the hub-hub of the bank.

'Morning Mr Rowe, paying in again, you was only in on Friday.'

'Yes, yes, it's been a busy weekend in the shop…'

'I'll count it for you now…' A couple of minutes passed. 'I'll just make out the receipt for the cash…that's 10 thousand in US, okay?'

I could not believe what I was hearing but made sure the peak of my cap remained well down over my face as Inspector Rowe turned from the teller and began to walk out. We both left our places in the queues and strolled towards the exit.

Nobby shook his head and mouthed, 'Ten grand in cash…' I nodded in agreement.

We followed Rowe at a distance as he went through the town centre until he walked across the car park and disappeared inside the police station, then we went back for the Jeep.

DCI Timms was waiting as we returned to the Drugs Squad and ushered us into his office. 'Well?'

We gave him the blow-by-blow account of what we had just witnessed. His hands were clasped across his ample tummy as he blew a low whistle. 'Bloody hell…bent bastard. He's got to be the one tipping off our drugs jobs, he records each search warrant and he's got access to the evidence safe.'

Mr Jones invited us over to his office in the main Police HQ where we had to walk past Rowe's door, which thankfully was closed. Once more we outlined exactly what we had seen and as the detail sank in, he remained his normal calm self but sat heavily in his chair, visibly deflated. 'I'll go and see the Commissioner and see what he wants to do, and I'll let you know. Well done, gents, you've done a good job even though it's not what we wanted to hear.'

Later that afternoon Chief Superintendent Jones arrived at the Drugs Squad office and we were ushered into Mr Timms' smouldering opium den of an office and his door was closed and locked. The eagerness of youth was pent up in me and I was preparing for the chance to arrest Rowe, search him and his office, house and business that was run – in name only – by his wife.

Mr Jones spoke clearly. 'The Commissioner and the Governor have agreed that this information remains confidential. They are going to present it to him and suggest he resigns on ill-health, immediately.'

I felt my frustration rise, especially as Rowe had treated me so appalling many months previously. He was a corrupt copper and had now been outed as a potential money launderer and drug dealer. No legitimate shop could make so much money, so quickly, even in Grand Cayman. Mr Jones continued with his explanation.

'If he refuses to cooperate, we'll then start the ball rolling with searches, warrants to access bank accounts and arresting him. As you're all aware he's very friendly with many local politicians and lawyers, so this is very political and we will have to deal with any fallout carefully, sensitively. Leave it with us, gents. I know you're disappointed but it'll get rid of him, one way or another. Trust me, it's for the best.'

Mr Timms vocalised our thoughts as he rocked back in his chair. 'We should lock up the bent bastard – it's corrupt – plain and simple. We shouldn't let him get away with it, he's been tipping off his mates. Loads of jobs have been compromised and he had access to all the info… It stinks.'

'I understand and sympathise with you and I'd feel the same in your situation but there are other considerations at stake here – and the decision has been made.' Mr Jones drew the conversation to a close.

Within the week Inspector Rowe had retired on a police sick pension with not a stain on his record.

CHAPTER 29

SMITH'S COVE

The final flurry of social activities spun past in a tropical heat haze as the weather began to warm up. I was settled on returning to the UK then back to the real world. The last two years had been the most enormous fun and a totally unique experience of policing in the West Indies and travelling around the region, enjoying or reluctantly accepting everything that was thrown at me.

There were no regrets. I felt that my colleagues and I had made a real difference to those we were serving on the island, using sensible discretion, being independent, not needing to curry favour with anyone; keeping residents and visitors just that little bit safer than if we had never arrived. I thought of individuals like Mr Appleton General who although I had not managed to recover his wallet or cash had attempted some sort of noble cause retribution. I subsequently arranged for him to visit the next Royal Navy ship that docked, where they entertained him regally, and well he deserved it.

I felt I had helped Peggy the Canadian lady held against her will by the dearly departed Dr Kampenboom. Her dream had been shattered but I'd managed to prevent it deteriorating further and she left paradise with memories that would ultimately fade.

Then there was Duke, who we had trained and guided to be an effective member of the police, who was later to marry and remain on the island looking fitter and happier than I had ever seen him.

I had been a thorn in the sides of Adamson, Hollywood, Archie and Marmaduke, managed to remove Inspector Rowe from his position of power, and all very satisfying it was, too.

I took the Wrangler Jeep for my last drive around the island, with the canvas roof stowed away and my sunglasses in position, to revisit all my adventures. Parking up at stunning Smith's Cove allowed me to watch the sunrise appear in a gentle glow burning through the whispers of mist on the horizon. Right at the beginning of my time in Grand Cayman, a publicity shot of me in my new uniform had been taken at Smith's Cove for the article in the *Police Review* magazine, now the sea gently splashed up this tiny sandy beach protected by robust iron-shore borders. It remained a little haven of calm to which I often retreated away from the frenetic life beyond.

Some weeks earlier, Olivia and I reluctantly agreed that it had been a wonderful – but temporary – time in our lives and (the phrase which continued to haunt me) we promised to stay friends, whatever that meant. She was to remain on the island to continue with her career and look after Young Winston. I was going back to the UK after an unbelievable two years in the tropics with a huge feeling of contentment and accomplishment. On the way back home, I was going to stay in Florida with my sister who had been bitten by the overseas bug and was working as a nurse in Sarasota.

I discovered a long-forgotten cassette inside the Jeep radio, so turned it on at full volume, and across this special part of my own desert island felt the deep throbbing boom from the speakers as I sang along to the Electric Light Orchestra anthem – 'Mr Blue Sky'. It was time to leave paradise and return to reality.

EPILOGUE

I arrived at Manchester Airport with a heck of a bump, and I mean that in more ways than one. It was a complete shock to my system leaving the warmth of the tropics, my luxury hotel, my Jeep, the close circle of friends, and was a surprisingly emotional wrench for me. It was cold and damp and miserable when I arrived back in the UK and that included the terraced house I had rented in Oldham upon my return. The culture shock of being back home was a huge surprise, but as I am not one to dwell on misfortune, I counted my blessings and soon got on with it.

It did not take me too long to appreciate the positive aspects of living and working back in the UK. The presence of all four seasons is a pleasurable phenomenon. I had become accustomed to the summer climate on Grand Cayman being hot, very hot or hot as hell unless I was in an air-conditioned car, shop or living room. Such extremes of heat did not affect me back in the Pennines where once again I was working on uniform shift duties, scraping ice from the windscreen of the police Land Rover in July… After the initial shock to the system had dissipated, I jogged along the rocky career path and was soon promoted to the rank of Sergeant and posted to the challenging areas of north Manchester. A few years later I was promoted to Inspector in the similarly demanding city of Salford.

You may well ask if my two-year secondment in the Caribbean was anything other than a jolly, or merely an easy number away from the stresses and reality of inner-city policing. Well, it was certainly a unique opportunity and a hugely enjoyable one that I do not regret for a single moment. As with any job there were frustrations, irritations or feelings of being overlooked or ignored, but this must be the same for any career. Especially one like policing which, when done well, is tantamount to a vocation.

Of course incompetence and corruption is not limited to any single job or organisation and is not restricted to the Cayman Islands. A lot is asked of our police officers in the UK where any mistakes are quickly highlighted, publicised and subjected to the ill-informed opinions of keyboard warriors. They are willing to criticise actions carried out by officers in the heat of the moment, who have to take snap decisions based on the minimal amount of information available to them. There are, of course, a small number of bad apples that should be thrown out of the barrel and charged or sacked if their actions warrant it. I despise bent coppers more than anything in the world and they give the other 99.99 per cent of hard-working, dedicated officers a bad name. There is often no easy way to explain the whole situation during an unfolding incident, but I admire chief constables who are willing to face the cameras and give a balanced explanation while the reports are still fresh.

A lot is expected of police officers, who are not superhuman and are subject to the usual gamut of vulnerabilities and frailties others may hope to conceal. Overworked officers often deal with horrific incidents that members of the public would run away from. When most folk are safely behind their front doors or tucked up in bed, the police and the other emergency services are dealing with awful situations that you are better off not even thinking about. There are several horrible incidents that continue to revisit me when I least expect them.

Professionally, I feel that Greater Manchester Police benefited by my time overseas. On my return from secondment, the new experiences and insights I gained having worked in a diverse culture and community were used to good effect throughout my subsequent careers. Elements of these experiences were especially important during my time working within the shadowy smoke-and-mirrors world of Counter Terrorism Policing in the north-west of England.

Personally, my time overseas provided a wonderful illustration of self-reliance and character building. It enabled me to grow up a bit, be more understanding, accept differences, and showed me that if you put the effort in, you will reap the rewards. Stepping out of my comfort zone and grasping the opportunities offered to me provided a clear example that the harder you work, the luckier you become.

At the start of this adventure, and as I contemplated the job application to join the Royal Cayman Islands Police, one of my old sergeants peered over my shoulder and said, 'Go for it, son, life is not a dress rehearsal.'

I could not have put it better myself.